POSTCARD HISTORY SERIES

Monmouth County, New Jersey

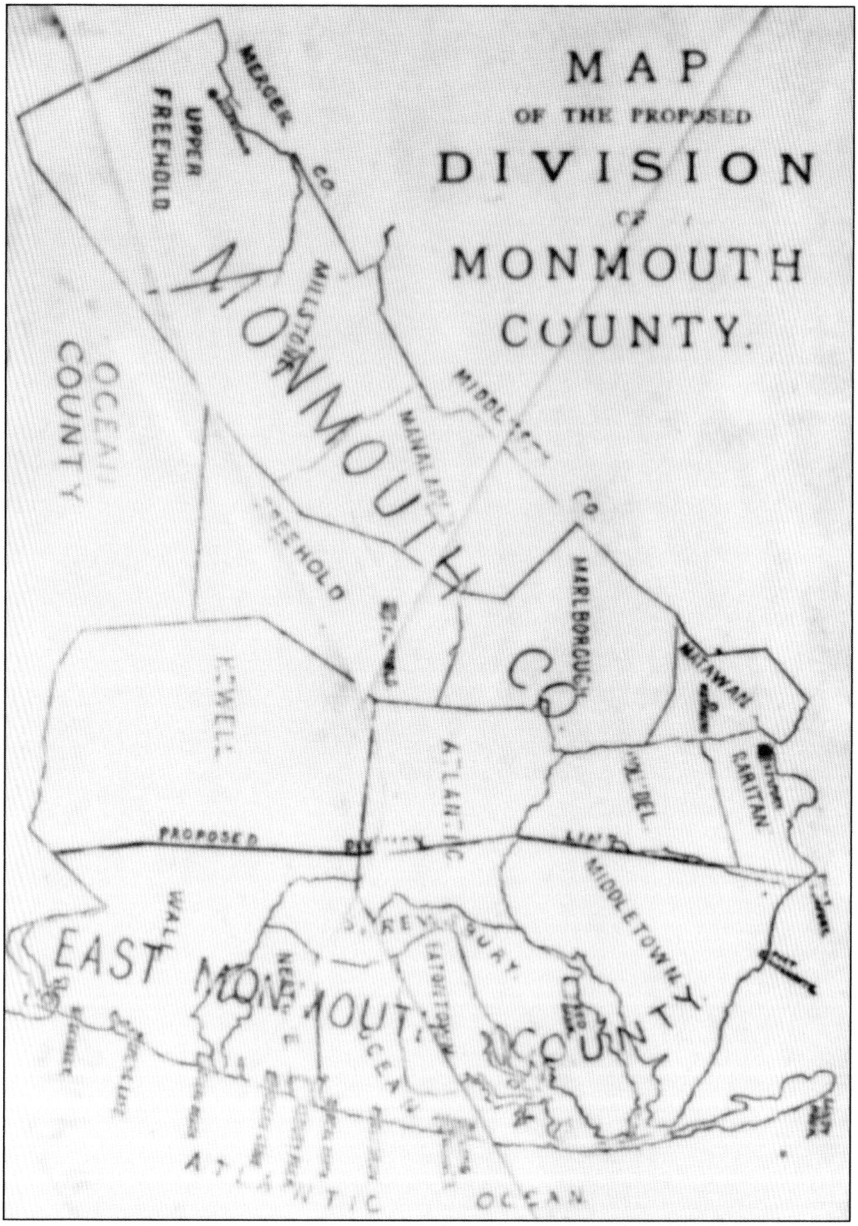

There was a serious campaign in 1883 to split Monmouth County, its advocates using a map on the back of envelopes as part of their publicity campaign. The issue was simple: taxes, combined with political control. The shore was more developed than the rural interior, and eastern Monmouth adherents expected a reduction of their tax obligations. At the time, the county government was comprised of one freeholder from each township, giving disproportionate representation to the rural west. The underlying issues were addressed, at least in part, by equalized valuation and the "one man-one vote" principal. The usage pre-dates postcards, but the image is probably the county's most significant example of a mailed illustration.

Cover Photographs: Please see p. 64.

POSTCARD HISTORY SERIES

Monmouth County, New Jersey

Randall Gabrielan

ARCADIA
PUBLISHING

ISBN 978-0-7385-6620-9

Published by Arcadia Publishing
Charleston, South Carolina

Printed in the United States of America

Library of Congress Catalog Card Number: 2008935732

For all general information contact Arcadia Publishing at:
Telephone 843-853-2070
Fax 843-853-0044
E-mail sales@arcadiapublishing.com
For customer service and orders:
Toll-Free 1-888-313-2665

Visit us on the Internet at www.arcadiapublishing.com

This book is dedicated to John Rhody, an enthusiastic collector whose extensive holdings are matched by a willingness to help writers and share his pictorial gems with the public. He is the county's foremost practitioner of the tradition of collector munificence that has long enriched American cultural life. A devoted family man, John is pictured a couple of years ago with his wife, Leslie, and children: John (left), Matt (center), and Kathryn.

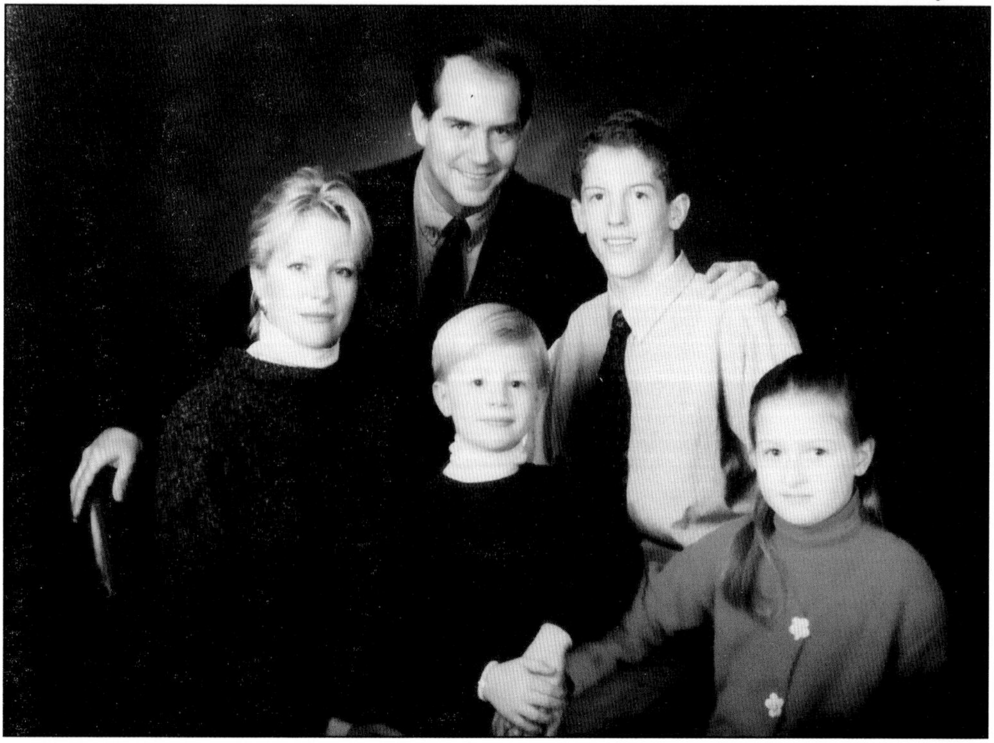

Contents

Introduction

This book depicts the development and use of postcards in Monmouth County over their entire 20th-century history as seen and described through historical places and events. Thus, it is both a postcard and history book. The limited opportunity for text focuses on the history, but the card is also treated as a communications medium.

The book is organized by postcard periods, grouping illustrations with contemporary examples, even when separating sites depicted in different eras. Half of the pictures are from the postcard era of 1905–15, the so-called "golden age" of postcards when most of its finest examples were produced. However, the "golden age" is better appreciated in the context of what preceded and followed it. The opportunity to fill the book exclusively with examples from the height of the postcard era was rejected in order to present a broader examination of the entire history of postcards.

This volume is the author's 14th book for Arcadia. No card used in any of his prior books appears in this one. However, similar views of compelling places frequently pictured on postcards were selected; indeed, many are sites the reader would expect to find in this work. On the other hand, several novelty images were included because they are fascinating as postcards, although finer views may have appeared in the previous Images of America books. A guide to the book's organization follows.

The Private Mailing Card Era—Postal illustration preceded postcards as depicted by two fine illustrated envelopes. The Columbian Exposition of 1893 is usually accepted as the beginning of postcard use in America, but for practical purposes in Monmouth County, postcards originated following the Private Mailing Card Act of 1898, a law that effectively standardized the appearance of postcards. Their backs (the address side) are inscribed with the slogan "Private Mailing Card—Authorized by Act of congress, May 19, 1898." Monmouth County examples tend to be few in number, and are often dull, marginally printed examples of mundane scenes. Examples used prior to 1903 are rare. Few exist after 1905.

The Postcard Era—The capture of public imagination by mailable pictorial souvenirs created an international collecting mania, a period of extensive publication and intensive use roughly timed between 1905 and 1915. The era is sub-divided into "undivided back" and "divided back" periods. Early regulations reserved the back of the card exclusively for the address, requiring messages to be written in margins on the picture side, a structure that ruined more cards than any collector would like to imagine. Legislation effective March 1, 1907, authorized placement of written messages on the address side. Postcard publishers accommodated the change with a printed vertical line that "divided" the back into address (right) and message (left) halves.

Kodak's 1902 introduction of photographic paper facilitating the printing of pictures in postcard format paved the way for production of the finest cards of the era, the photographic card, or "real photo," the redundancy by which they are popularly known. (If it is not a photo, then it is not "real.") Monmouth's photographic cards are among its most eagerly sought examples. Many were produced by three skilled photographers: Charles R.D. Foxwell of Red Bank, A. Merriman of Howell, and Frank Yarnall of Belford, Middletown Township. Their careers strike interesting contrasts, but are beyond the scope of this brief introduction.

Most high-quality cards were printed overseas, typically by German lithography. Outstanding English producers included Valentine & Company and Raphael Tuck & Sons. American products of quality were produced by The Albertype Company and the Detroit Publishing Company.

Dating cards is a challenge for any period, perhaps more-so for the postcard era in view of their numbers and the changes in the landscapes. The author has followed a few guidelines. Any undivided back is nearly always prior to March 1, 1907. Used examples prove a card is no later than its postmark. Some dates are estimated based on known publication of other cards in a series. Others are dated based on known construction or demolition dates of buildings in streetscapes. Most dates have the qualifier of circa (c.).

Several cards more recent than 1915 slipped into the postcard-era chapter, perhaps unconsciously following the collector's instinctive eye response to old views of quality. Fewer, but still outstanding, photo cards were produced in the 1920s, while a reduced output of quality printed cards continued. The age of one better American publisher's output, The Albertype Company, can often be best judged by careful study of content.

The close of the postcard era stems from at least two conditions: lower quality product and waning interest following the excesses of any mania. A protective tariff in 1909 placed high duties on overseas cards, effectively eliminating the quality imports from the American market. Any collecting mania will in time see its overheated market deflate, and so it happened with postcards.The onset of World War I is cited internationally as a cause of the era's close, but postcards had already waned by the time of America's involvement.

Sub-chapters were chosen to provide a geographic divide for the chapter's 60 pages. Their organization was arbitrary with the author, and inclusion of a section under any geographic heading does not imply public acceptance.

The White Border Era—The dismal, often poorly printed cards of the white border era represent the low point of postcards. Inferior graphics can turn-away even the untrained eye. The period is generally defined as 1915–30, although overlaps exist. Perhaps the only redeeming virtue of white borders is the realization that the oldest cards of places built in that span are white borders. Particularly disappointing are American-printed white border images that replicate earlier imports.

The Linen Era—The period spans the years 1930–50 or so. Linens were widely shunned until c. 1980, with their renaissance attributed to at least two inherent qualities and one fiscal factor—they were inexpensive while prices of older cards soared. Their artist-chosen colors are often outrageous, while their content embraced popular roadside subject matter as the linen era coincides with a boom period in American automobile travel. Indeed, the diner is conspicuous by its absence from this book. Linens, too, at times represent the earliest card available for projects built with their era.

Mid-Century Miscellaneous—The term is of the author's coinage, one needed to categorize the diverse product in smaller numbers that was produced between the postcard and chrome eras. This output includes later work of The Albertype Company, photo cards, monochromes issued by Art Vue, Collotype, and Mayrose, and a variety of often better, not otherwise classified cards.

Chromes and the Modern Era—The chrome era began nationwide c. 1940, but Monmouth County saw few chromes issued in that decade, perhaps excepting Asbury Park and Ocean Grove, making it lack a classic chrome era comparable to the well-known Fred Harvey productions in the west. A period lasting at least half a century should be sub-divided; two come to mind.

The first is the size of the card. Most of the cards in Chapter 6 are the standard size, approximately 3.5-by-5.5 inches, with six continental-size exceptions. Those cards measuring 4 1/8-by-5 7/8 inches are both examples on pp. 116 and 117, plus the bottom of pp. 120 and 124

Frequency of publication may better demark sub-periods. Cards fell into decline *c.* late 1960s. Now only Twin Lights and Sandy Hook appear to have new cards in any noteworthy numbers. However, in the 1950s and early 1960s, new attractions, such as Storyland and Wild West City (see p. 128) issued many cards to obtain inexpensive publicity. Cards also appeared in significant numbers later in such popular attractions as Allaire, Asbury Park, and Ocean Grove. Some towns, such as Red Bank, had numerous *c.* 1950s chromes, which are often harder to find than their postcard-era counterparts.

Higher printing costs and postage increases contributed to the decline of the postcard. One little tapped means for greater publication could be offset printing. The medium works best with artist sketches and is inexpensive to produce. A single example is on the top of p. 119.

Editing the pictures was a challenge, as Monmouth County has an extensive stock of fine postcards deserving publication. The author expects to publish them in a second volume and invites correspondence with those with material they would share through copying. He can be reached at 71 Fish Hawk Drive, Middletown New Jersey 07748, or (732) 671-2645.

Acknowledgments

The assistance and images provided by John Rhody over the past five years have been broad, deep, and of the highest quality. I am truly blessed by his generous support and offer my deepest gratitude and appreciation. Thank you, John, for making the four most repeated words in this book be "Collection of John Rhody."

Michael Steinhorn appreciates the enhancement of his cards' interest by their being shared and placed within the body of historic knowledge. Thank you, Michael, for being willing to help each project.

Glenn Vogel shares his images with a boundless enthusiasm and generosity. Keith Wells appreciates that sharing enhances the collecting process and has expressed his pleasure with the readers seeing his images. Gary Dubnik cheerfully leads two postcard clubs. His first assistance to the author is one outstanding image herein and his ongoing help has been offered with a maximum of interest and with images of rarity and beauty. Harold "Boots" Solomon is one of Monmouth's most avid collectors. It is a pleasure to publish his first postcard contribution to the author. Wesley Crozier offered the two oldest images, including the most interesting, the envelope on p. 2. Neither is a postcard, but Wesley, a distinguished postal historian, provided vital links between illustrated postal history and the postcard. Thank you Glenn, Keith, Gary, Harold, and Wes.

Thanks, too, to all contributors, including the following: Albert Benoist, Michael F. Bremer, Joseph Carney, Michael Cassone, Mo Cuocci, Gail Gannon, Margaret "Peg" Jordan, Kathleen McGrath, Joan Parent, Robert Pelligrini, Special Collections & Archives, Rutgers University Libraries, Karen Schnitzspahn, Robert W. Speck of Deal, and Marilyn Willis.

A thank you to the many others who shared memories and/or historic information. I will mention several by name: Wesley Banse, Florence Buchman, Patricia Colrick, James Lindemuth, and Marie Sylvester.

One

The Private Mailing Card Era

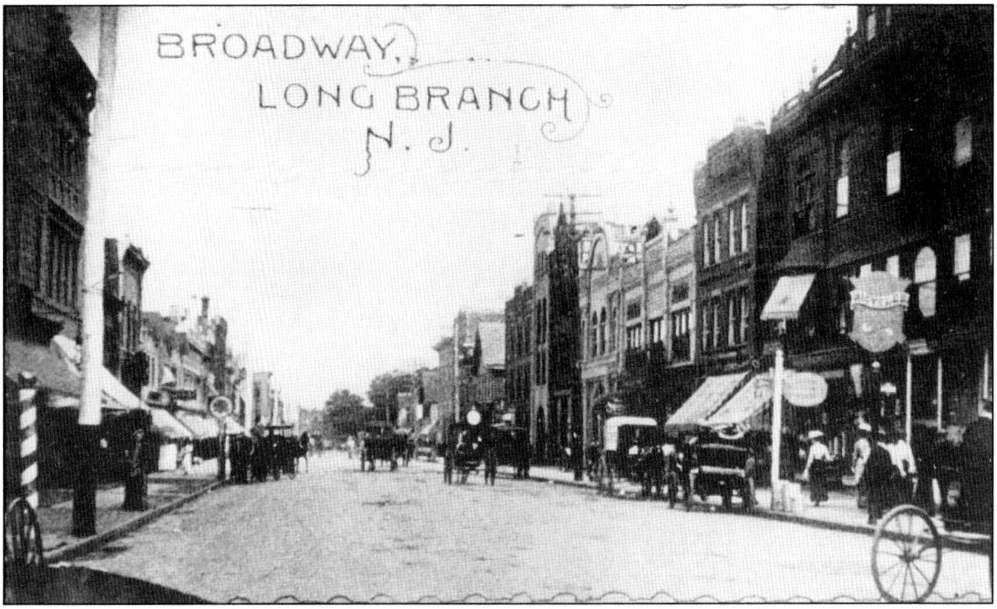

Monmouth County had relatively few private mailing cards. Our examples tend to be common scenes of marginal print quality, from populous or well-traveled towns, such as this Broadway, Long Branch example. (Collection of John Rhody.)

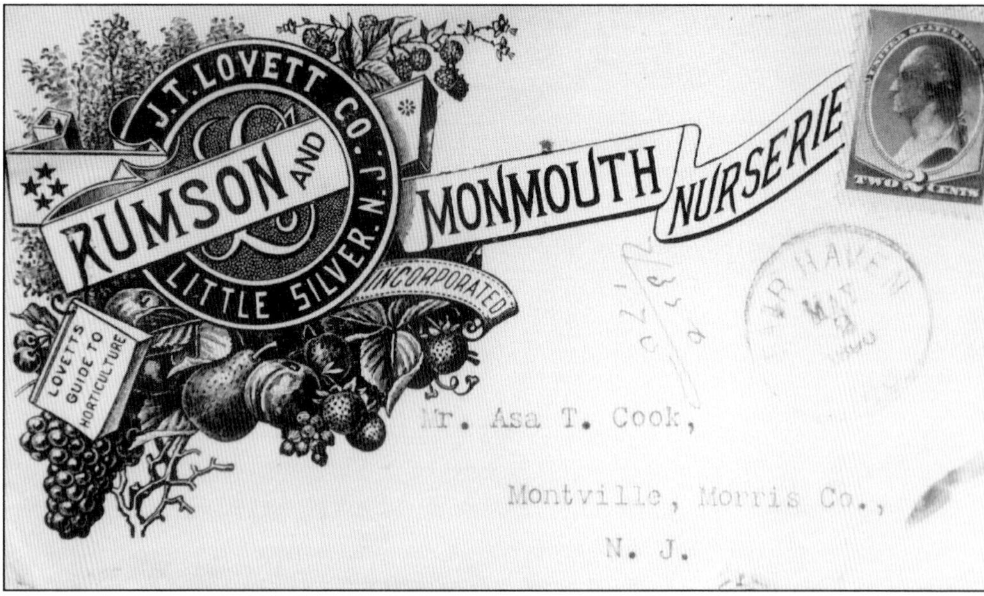

John T. Lovett opened the Monmouth Nursery in Little Silver in 1878 and used the mail extensively to attain a nationwide customer base. He advertised in many popular magazines and used attractively illustrated envelopes to draw attention to his operation. The first Lovett horticulture guide was issued *c.* 1883. One suspects his embracing "Rumson" in his nursery's name stemmed from the adjacent town's famed stature as a country home location.

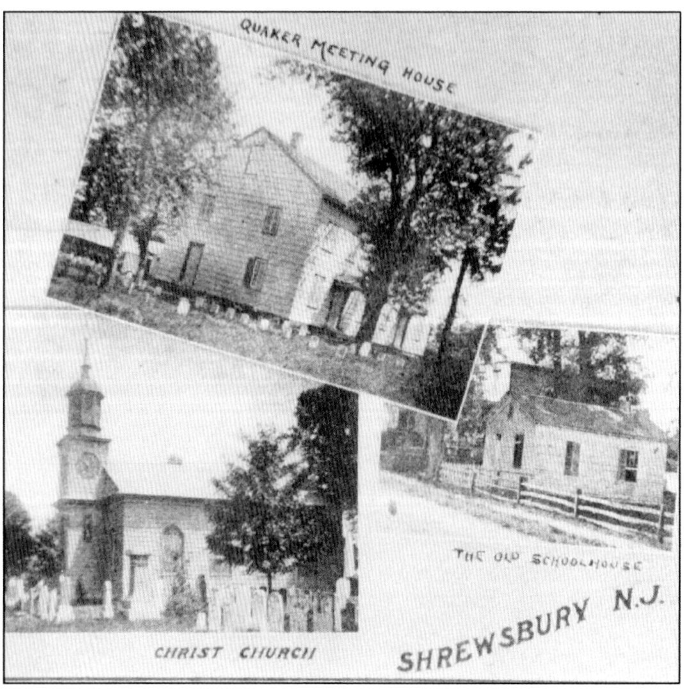

This private mailing card illustrates two surviving Shrewsbury landmarks and a by-then obsolescent one-room school, replaced in 1909. Christ Church is described on p. 32. This Quaker meetinghouse, built in 1816 on the northeast corner of Broad Street and Sycamore Avenue, is the site's third. The Religious Society of Friends was present from the 1665 settlement of Shrewsbury; its first meetinghouse and cemetery existed by 1701. It and a replacement brick house were destroyed by fire. (Collection of John Rhody.)

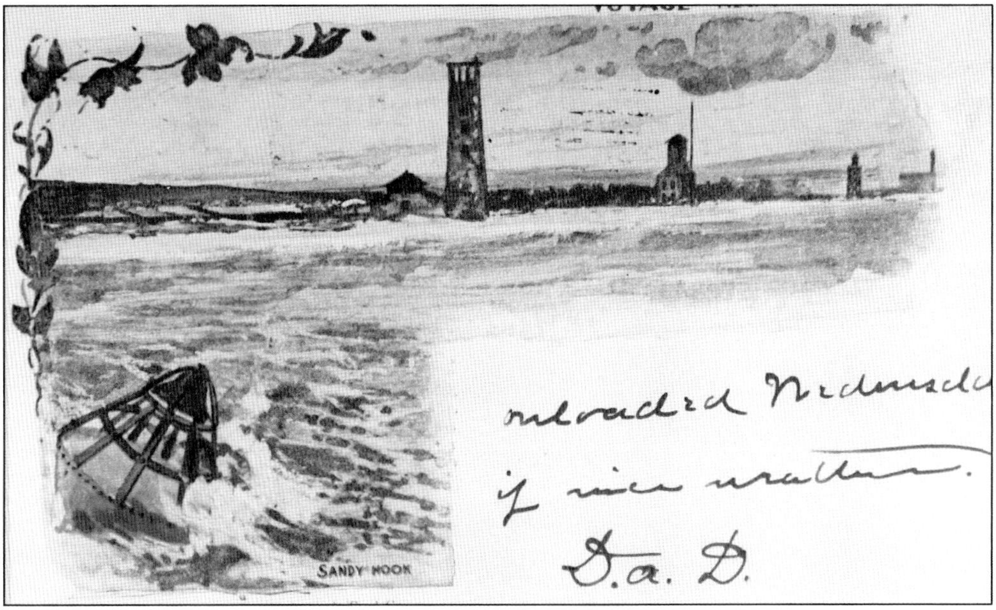

This Sandy Hook example from a travel series added color of marginal quality, but its layout suggests it was more a message card for travelers than a pictorial souvenir. (Collection of John Rhody.)

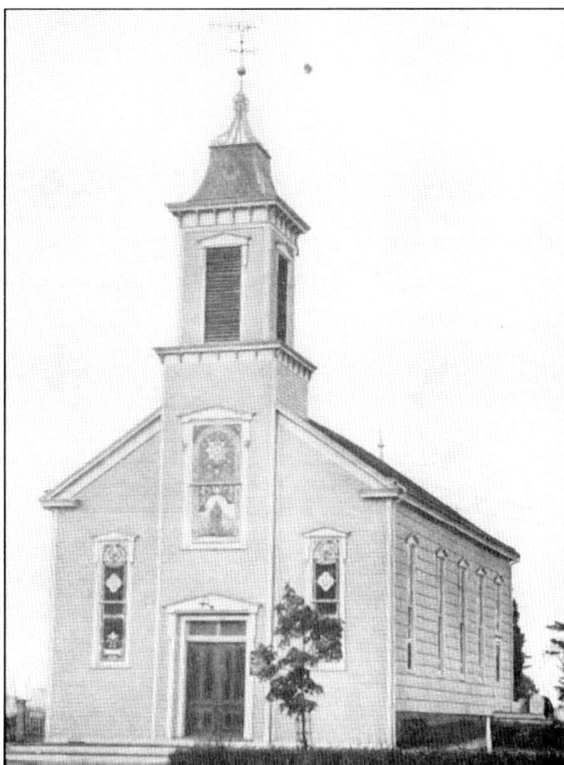

Methodism in the Long Branch area is traced to the 1780s; early organized worship began c. 1790 with an early church on William Brinley-donated land. The Methodist Episcopal Church at Long Branch was incorporated in 1809. This edifice, at the southeast corner of Locust Avenue and Wall Street in today's West Long Branch, was completed in 1819. The church was reorganized after merger in 1939. The well-preserved building still stands. This image is c. 1903.

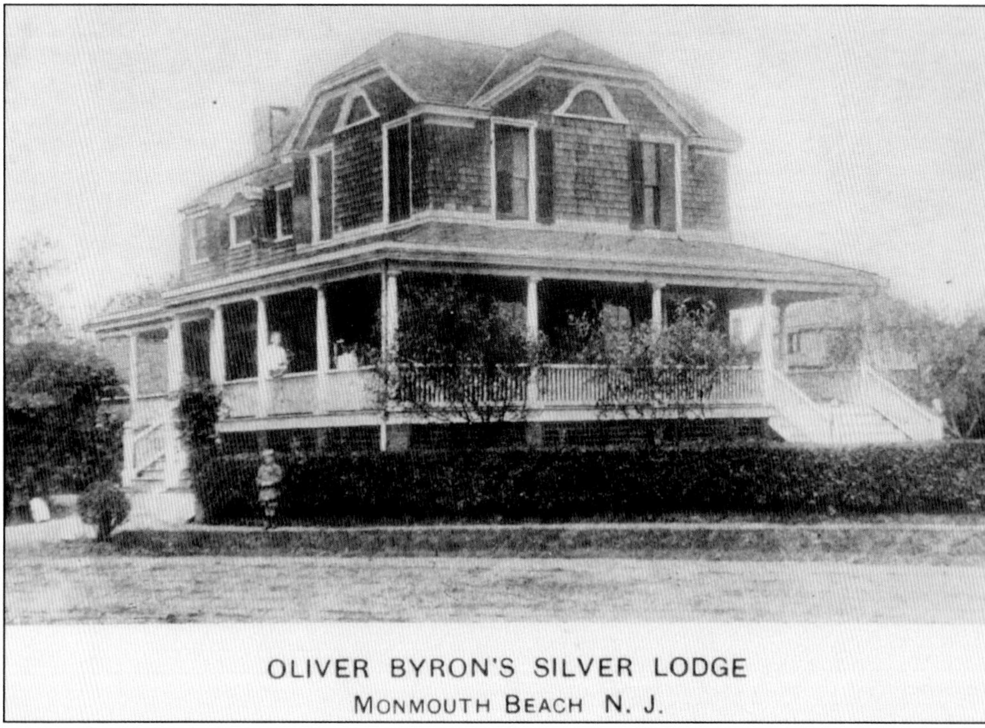

Oliver Byron's Silver Lodge was one of about six properties the dramatic stage actor and his wife, Mary, owned. This one, located at the foot of the east side of Ocean Avenue, Monmouth Beach, was demolished in 1982. Note its interesting jerkinhead gables. This private mailing card example was not mailed until 1917.

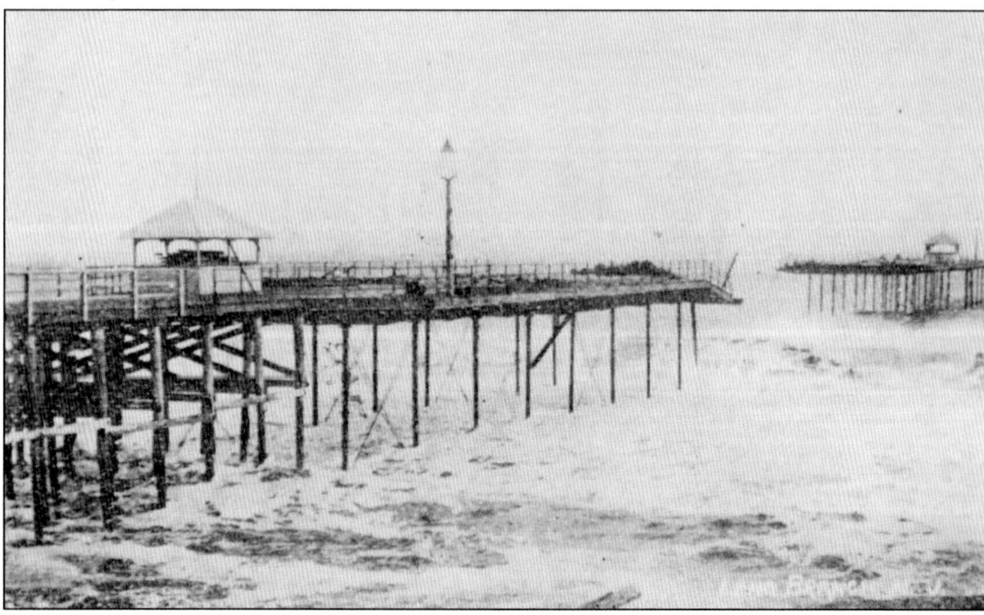

This card of Long Branch printer J.N. Van Horn's series on his town depicts the partial wrecking of the Long Branch pier. The pier was damaged several times. The card dates *c.* 1903; the date of the damage is not clear.

Two

The Postcard Era

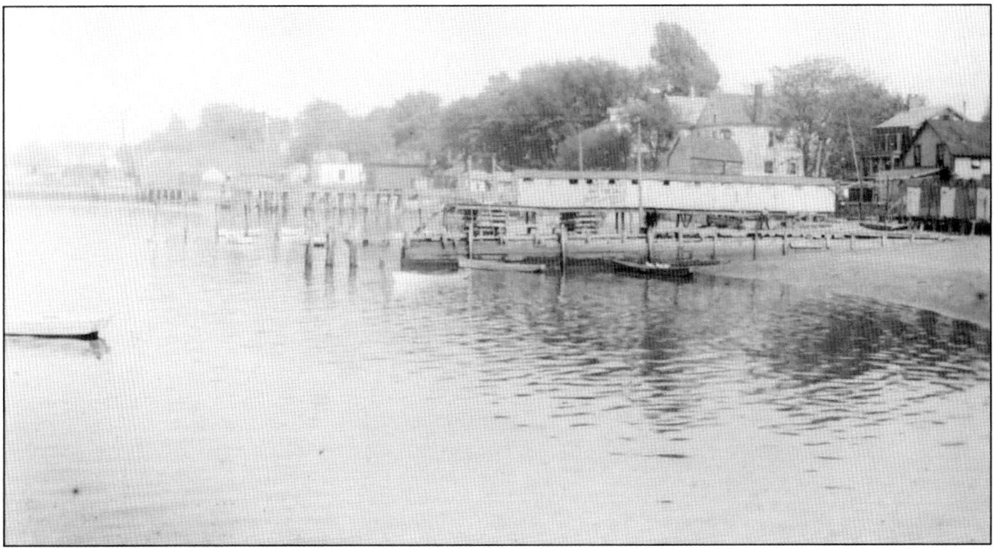

Keyport became an important business center in the third quarter of the 19th century as steam ships increased the reliability of water-borne transport. A c. 1911 Garraway photo looks east on Raritan Bay.

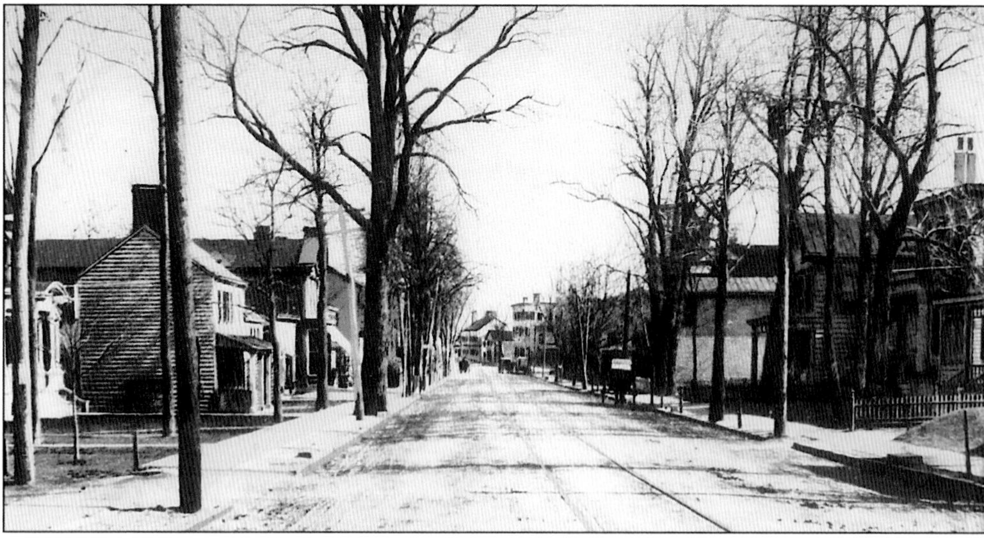

Matawan developed a business center in the second quarter of the 19th century, when known as Middletown Point, then part of Middletown Township. The area was part of the 1848 separation of Raritan Township from Middletown; Matawan was later incorporated as a borough, separating from Matawan Township in 1895. This loss of its early business district is one reason why Middletown, the county's most populous municipality, has no "downtown." This Main Street view is *c.* 1906. (Collection of Robert W. Speck.)

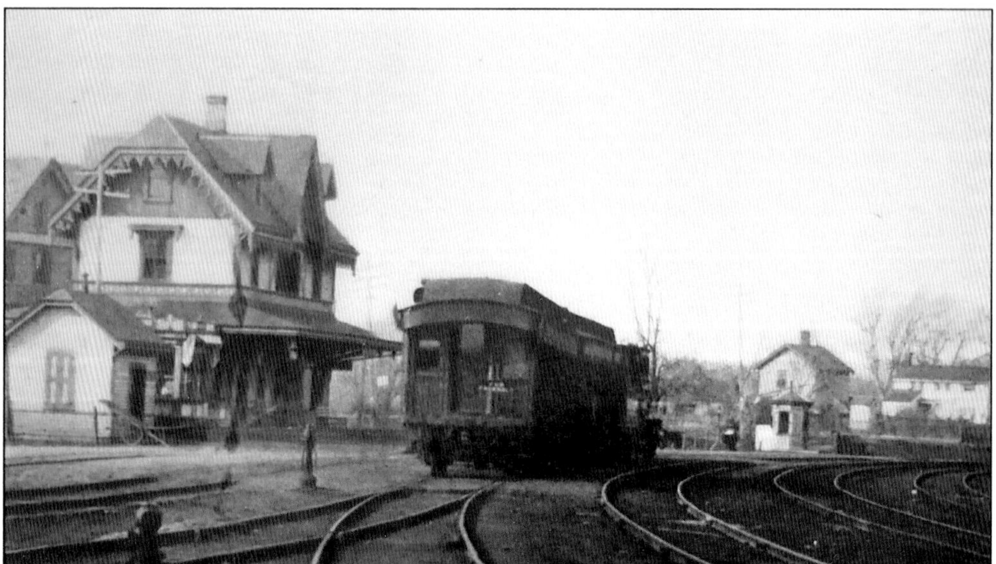

Matawan's commercial role was eclipsed in the third quarter of the 19th century by Keyport. That town's waterfront locale secured it much commerce during the steamship's ascendancy in local transport. Matawan sought to reverse its fortunes by securing the area's station on the New York and Long Branch Railroad. Their station dates from the line's 1875 opening, replacing a temporary structure built earlier that year. Matawan was an important rail juncture, linking the shore's main road with the Central Railroad's Freehold and Atlantic Highlands branches. The structure stands, but station functions were replaced by a new building in 1983.

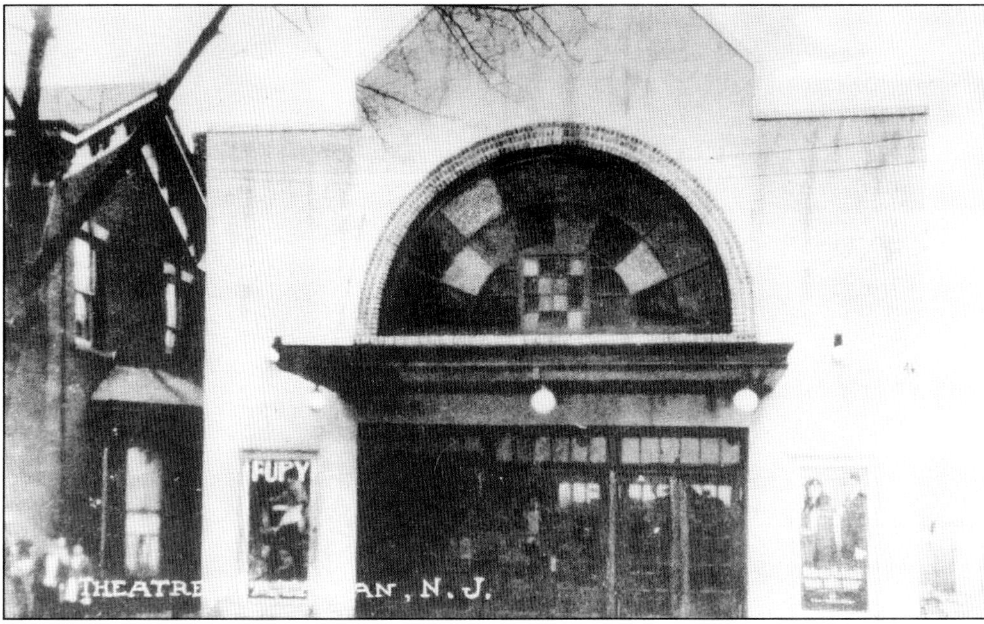

The Rivoli Theater on the east side of Main Street was built in 1929, an appealing small-town example from the age of great motion picture houses. The building survives, now a dry cleaners. The card dates from 1936, admittedly out of the volume's time guide, placed here for its old look. (Collection of John Rhody.)

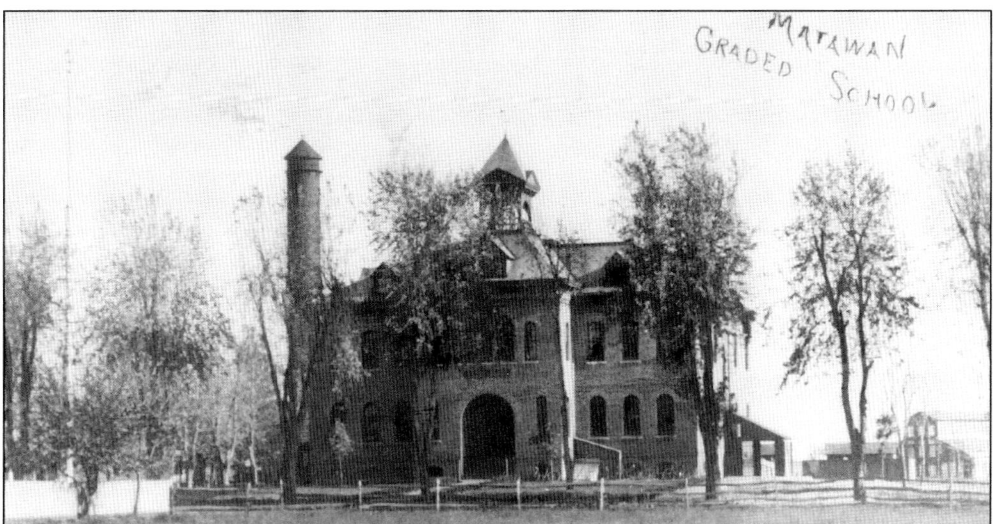

The 1895 Matawan Graded School was built in response to the 1894 school consolidation law that marked the waning of the one-room school. This example was postmarked in 1905, three years prior to construction of an addition on the right. (Collection of John Rhody.)

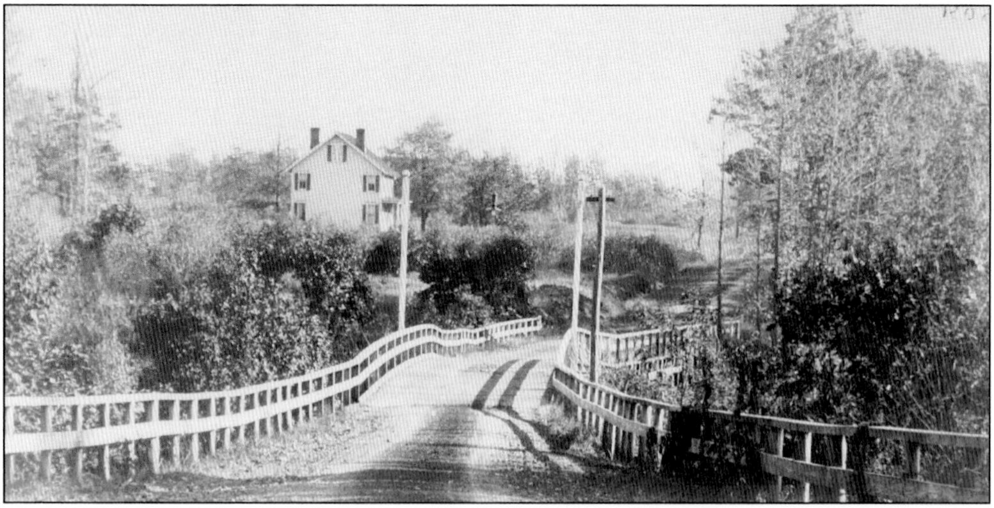

Holmdel Road is a forerunner of Highway 34, built in the early 1930s. It is believed this *c.* 1905 image is the crossing of Gravelly Brook. (Collection of John Rhody.)

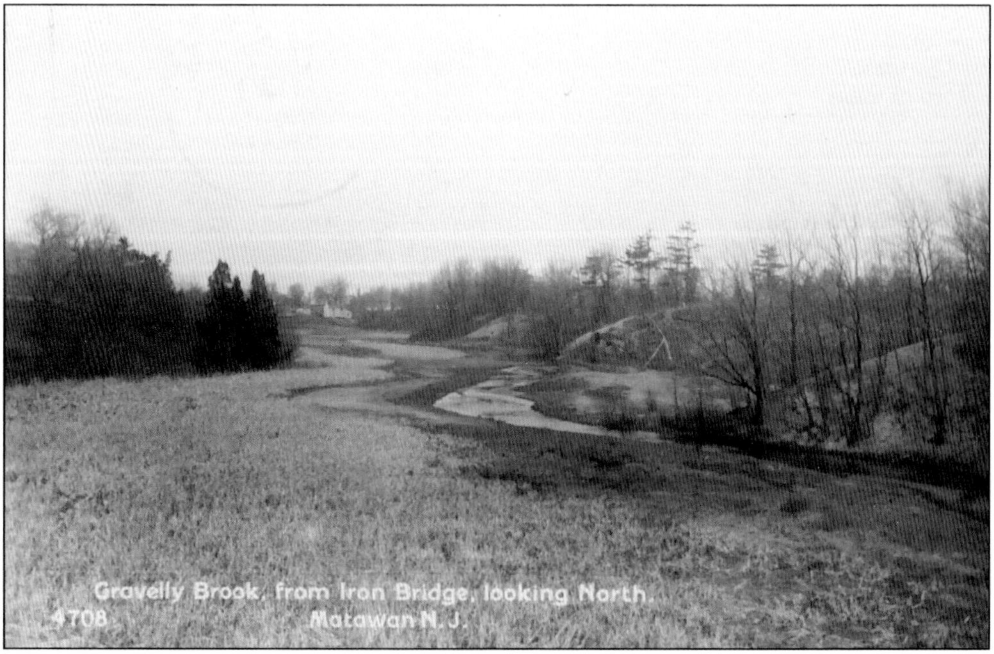

Gravelly Brook looking north from Iron Bridge appears to be the site of Lake Matawan, a man-made body formed by damming the brook. This Garraway example was postmarked in 1911.

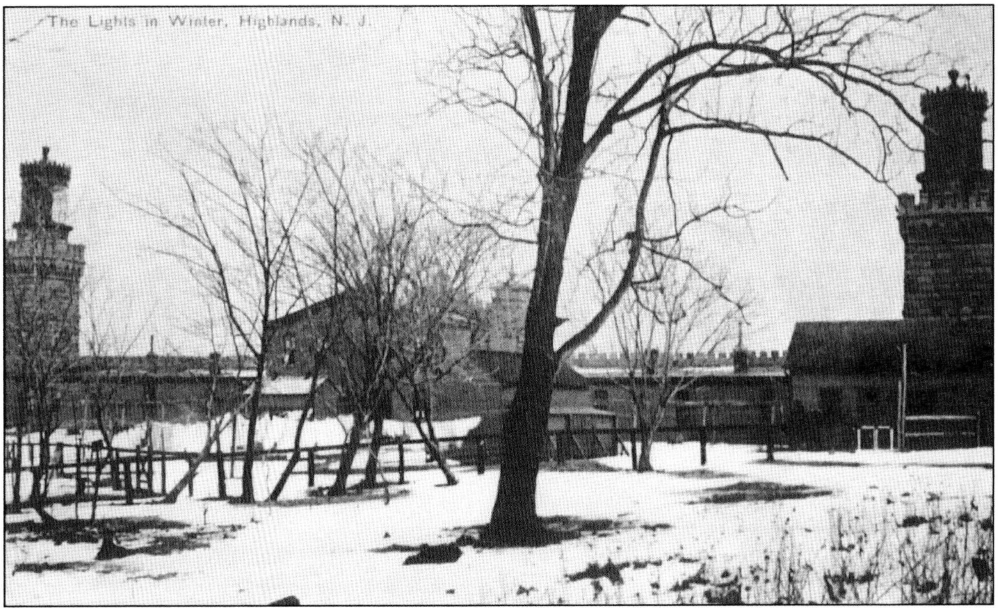

The lighthouse at Highlands, the town's most significant and frequently illustrated site, is known as Twin Lights, a name reminiscent of identical frame towers erected in 1828. The present stone Romanesque Revival towers, designed by government architect Joseph Ledele, are 53 feet tall and stand 246 feet above sea level, but are not "twins"; one is square, the other octagonal. Twins Lights' lengthy, distinguished history includes the installation of the first of the innovative, powerful Fresnel lenses in 1841 and receiving the first ship-to-shore wireless telegraph message, broadcast by inventor Marconi, in 1899. Keepers' quarters were between the towers. The site, decommissioned as a lighthouse in 1949, is a state park open year-round.

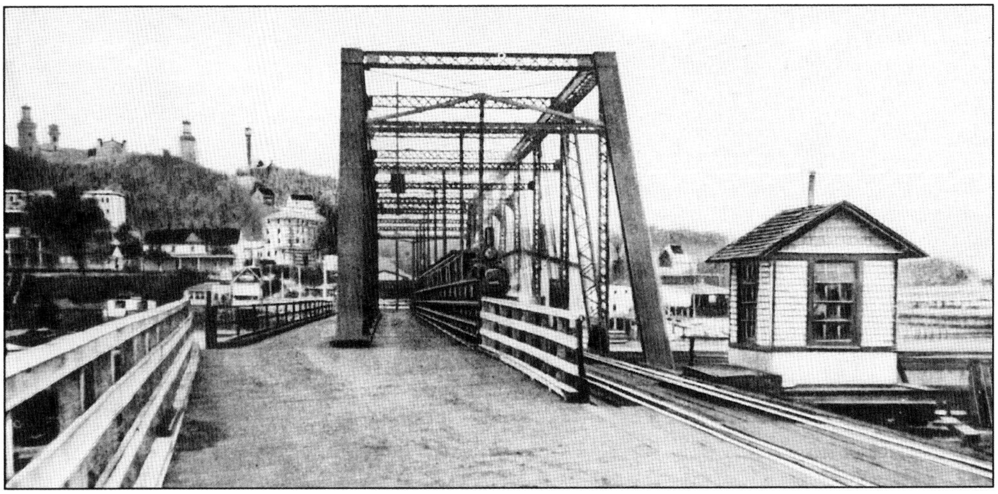

The combined highway-railroad draw bridge at Highlands was built in 1892 to obviate the necessity of two bridges. A new rail line was built between Atlantic Highlands and Sea Bright because the federal government expelled the Central Railroad steamers from their traditional Sandy Hook dock. The road crossed the rails at the spot in the foreground, a highly dangerous design. Later an army engineer would brand the bridge the worst of its kind in the country. This image is c. 1907. The bridge no longer stands, but some of its foundation is visible in the water (see p. 95).

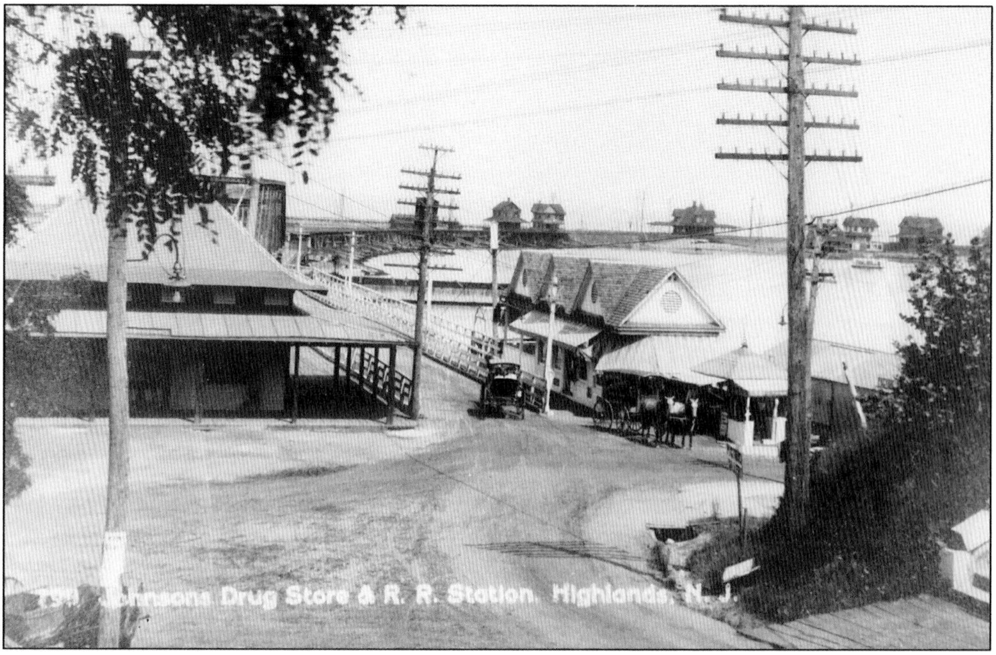

The Highlands railroad station was presumably built in 1900, replacing one that burned in January. Grandin V. Johnson's pharmacy was on Miller Street; the station store was largely a refreshment stand. Behind it is the bridge seen on the previous page. The houses in the background are on the shore in the North Beach section of Sea Bright. (Photo courtesy of Glenn Vogel.)

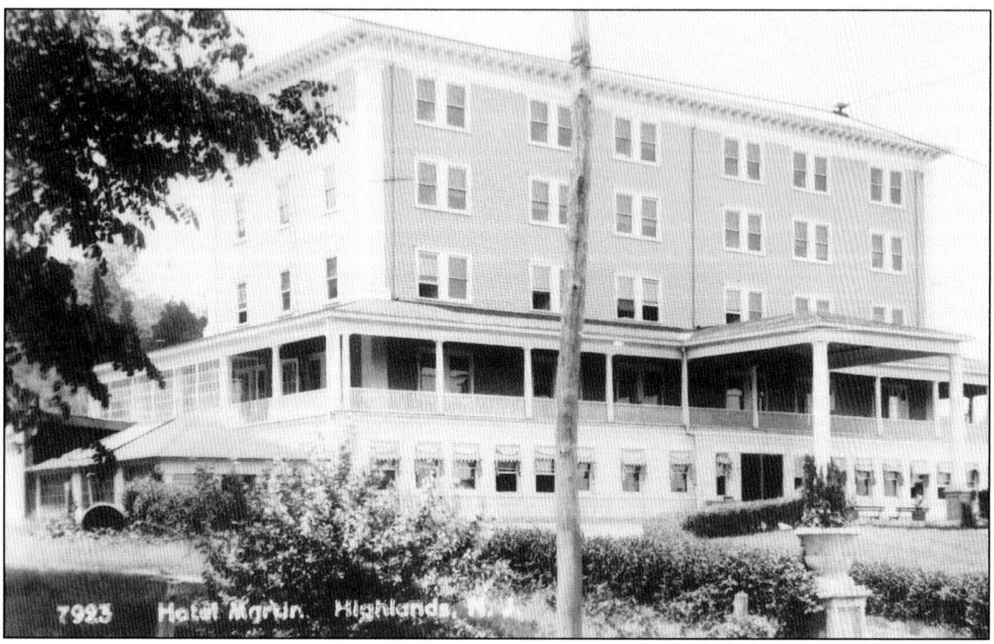

The 200-person Hotel Martin, one of Highlands' largest, was located at Portland and Highlands Roads. Owned by Martin Gerlach, it is seen *c.* 1911 on a Garraway card.

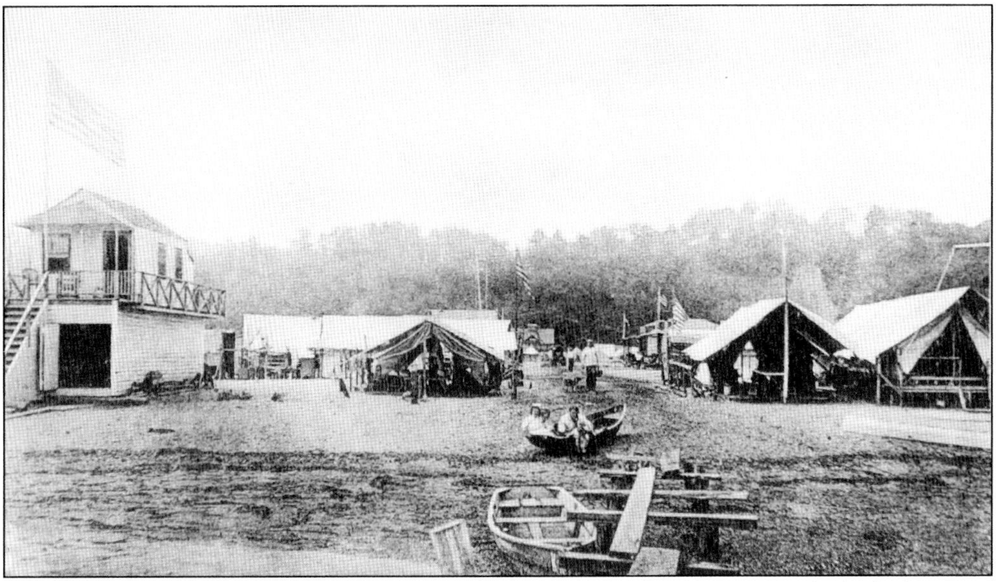

Gravelly Point was an isolated spot in Highlands on Sandy Hook Bay, around which the camp life developed. Summer quarters for many were these simple tents. Their dwellers were seasonal regulars; a warehousemen, Calvin W. Miller, started his Atlantic Highlands business storing their tents between seasons. Clamming, fishing, and life on the water were regular pursuits at Gravelly Point.

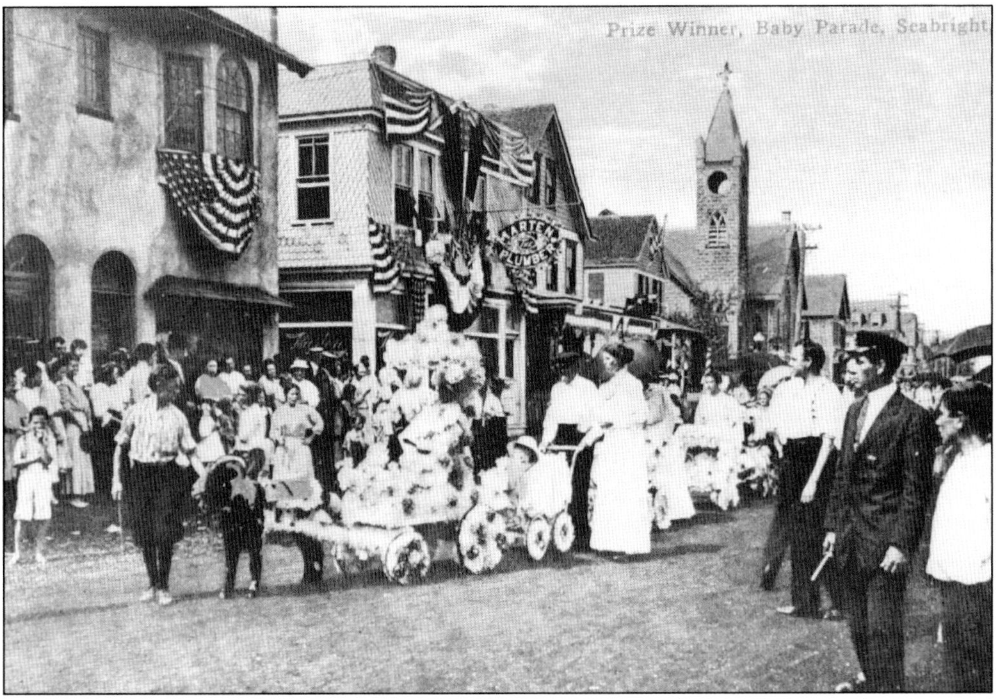

The Highlands' three-day carnival on September 1–3, 1910, included a baby parade. This card states the event is "Sea Bright," but a researcher learns not to trust everything on postcards. The scene is Bay Avenue; the tower of the Methodist church is in the background. (Collection of Michael Steinhorn.)

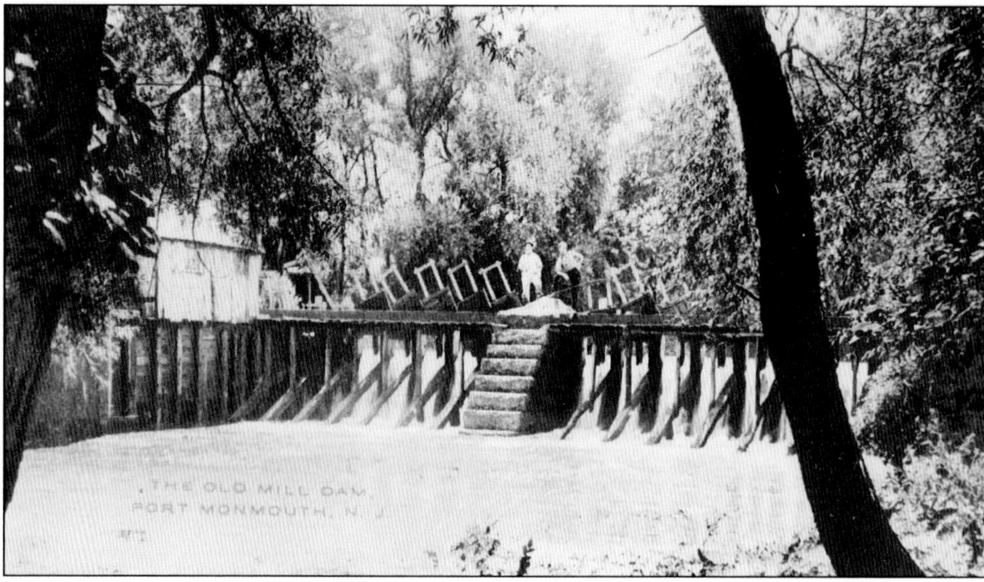

The old mill dam labeled on this c. 1907 card as Port Monmouth is believed to be the Arrowsmith Mill, founded by Thomas Arrowsmith in the 18th century, located west of Palmer Avenue (in what became Holmdel Township). The grist and sawmill was later Phillips Mill, named for owner Alexander Phillips. Milling waned with the loss of local timber and reduction in the wheat crop. The long-vacant mill was deliberately burned in 1928 for demolition purposes.

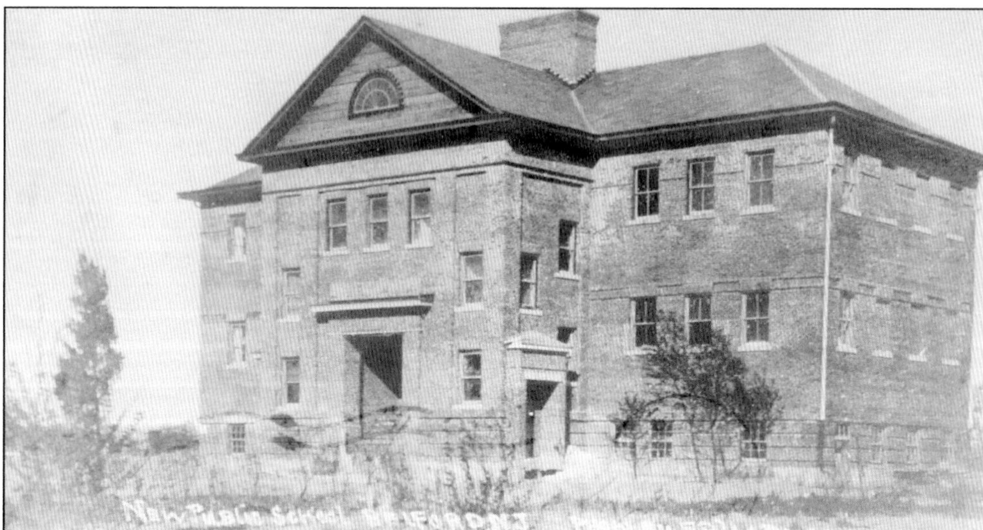

Middletown Township built two new, substantial brick schools in 1907, during the heart of the postcard era, signaling the beginning of the end of its one-room schoolhouses. This one in Belford was a frequent postcard subject; the author has never seen a card of the Middletown village school. The photograph is by the township's premier postcard photographer, Frank Yarnall, whose work is on a par with, but less known than, that of Foxwell or Merriman. A collection of Belford School cards can be placed in chronological order by the presence of finishing objects, including the fire escape, flag pole, drain pipe, and shrubs. The Church Street building is occupied by the Middletown Elks now. (Collection of John Rhody.)

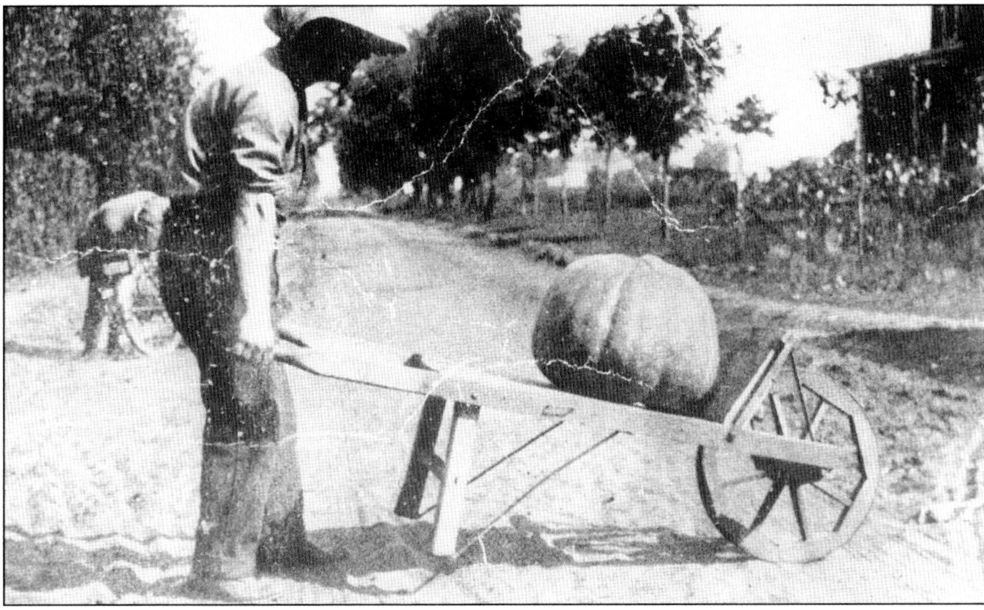

At least one of the two country squashes is recognizable, but we call them pumpkins. One can learn much from postcards, including unfamiliar slang. (Collection of John Rhody.)

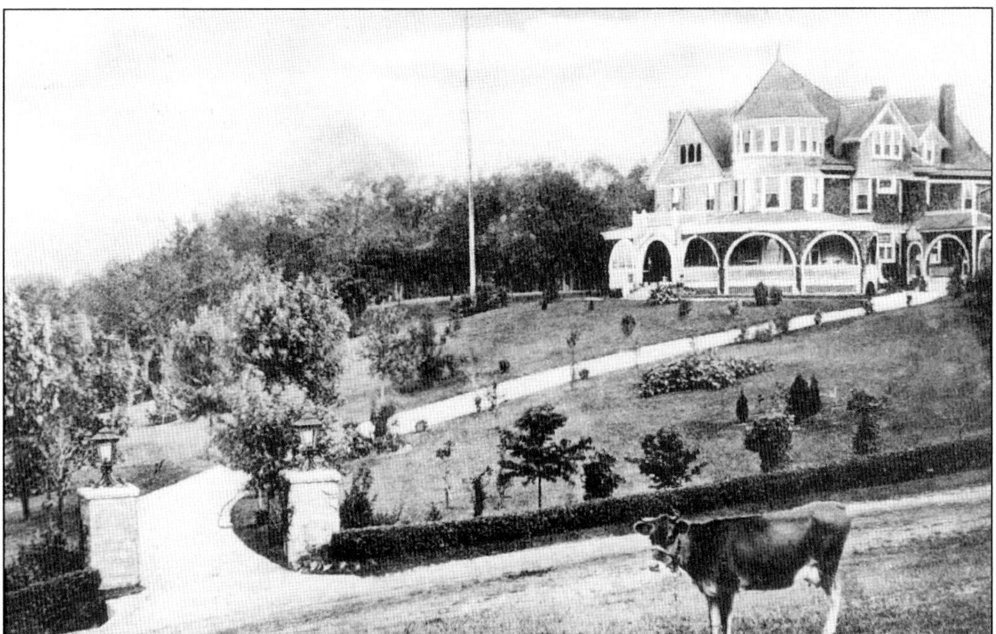

Colonel Ephraim Tillotson of Chicago built this large Queen Anne-style house in 1894 on Serpentine Drive in the Hillside section of Middletown. The identity of his Chicago architect is unknown. The assemblage of his property included the purchase of the lot belonging to the A.M.E. Zion Church, to whom he paid an additional $100 for removing remains from the graveyard. Tillotson had scant time to enjoy the new house, as he died in January 1895. A newly identical view was published in a 1903 book. This one includes a cow, presumably added by an artist. (Collection of John Rhody.)

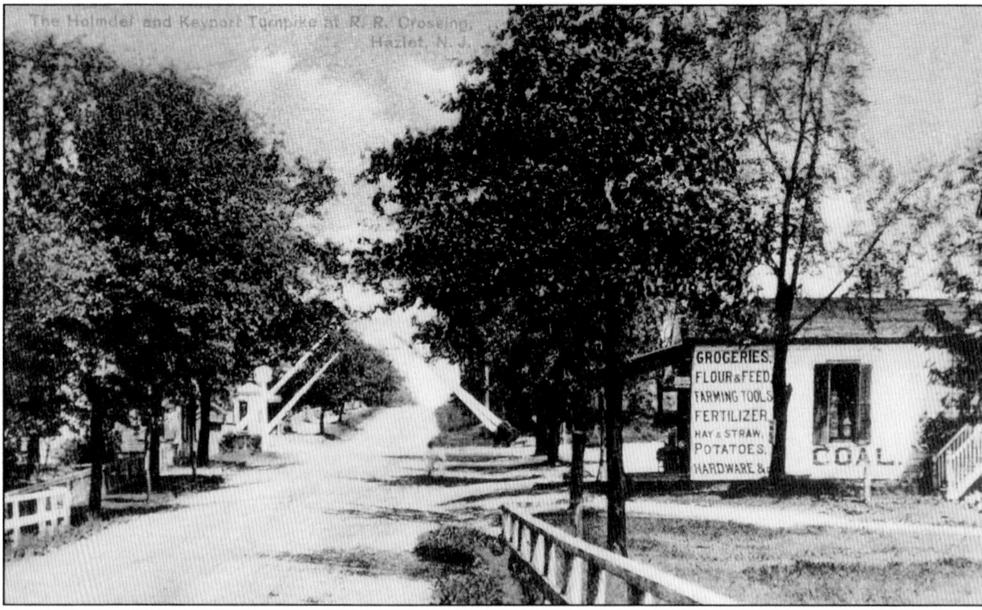

Hazlet apparently was first used for the name of the New York and Long Branch Railroad station in 1875, one year prior to the opening of a post office. The locality was a rural spot in the Township of Raritan, which changed its name to Hazlet in 1967. Little is known of its namesake, Dr. John Hazlet, who is a deserved research subject, especially this year, the 150th anniversary of the township's separation from Middletown. The station was removed in 1952; train passengers are "served" by a shelter. (Collection of John Rhody.)

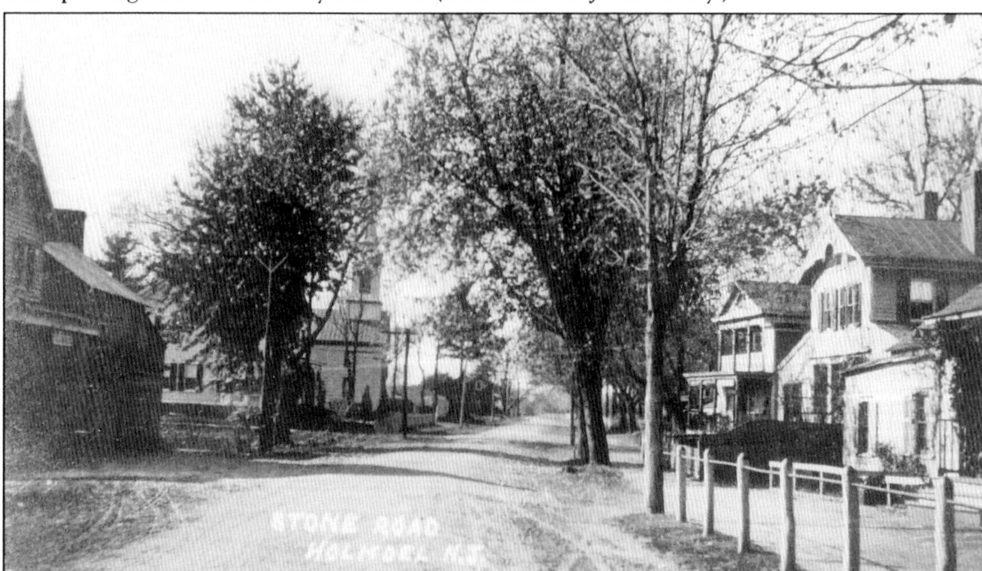

This Main Street, Holmdel view looks west from outside the Village Hotel at its northwest corner with Holmdel Road. The 1838 Greek Revival Dutch Reformed Church in the left background provides current identification of the *c.* 1905 image. The corner hotel was demolished in 1960 for construction of the Village Shopping Center, while the Hance store, left foreground, was also demolished around that time for erection of a Shadow Lawn Savings & Loan branch on the opposite corner.

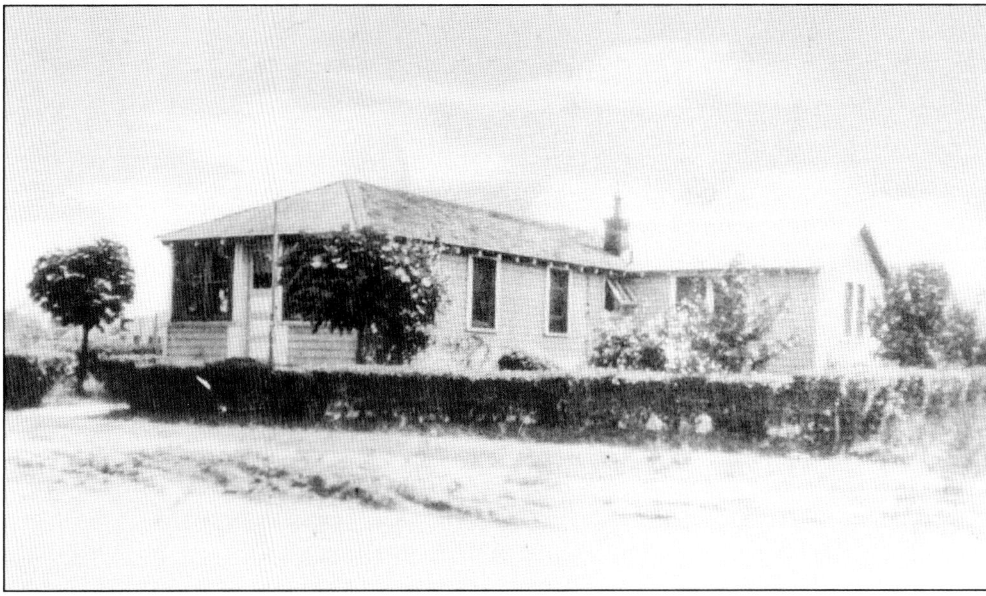

This undated image is of Mrs. Krause's Union Beach hospital.

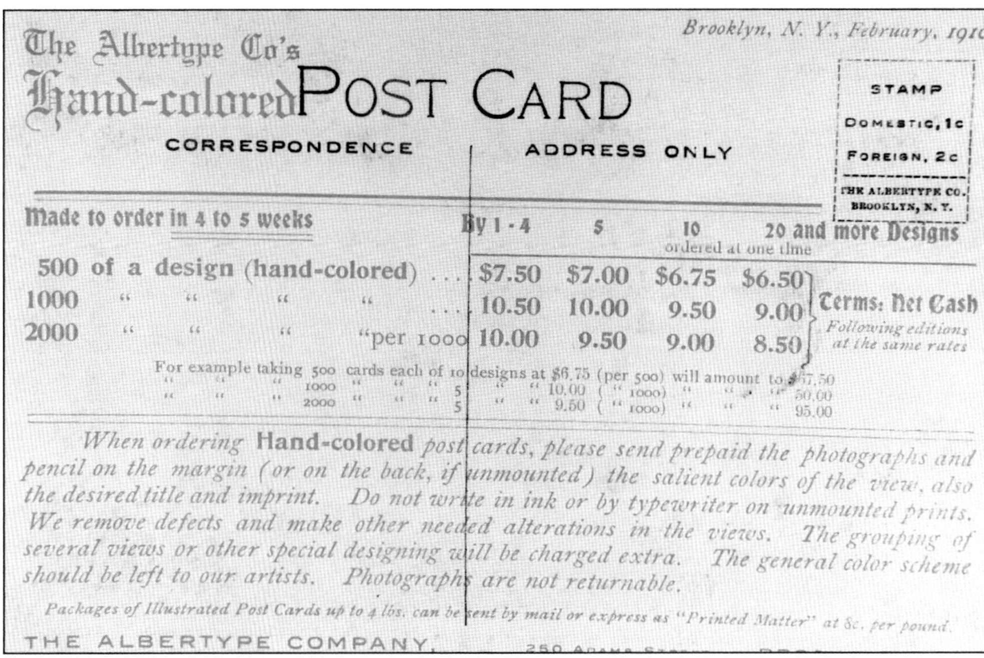

Brooklyn, N. Y., February, 1910

The Albertype Co's
Hand-colored POST CARD

CORRESPONDENCE | ADDRESS ONLY

STAMP
DOMESTIC, 1c
FOREIGN, 2c
THE ALBERTYPE CO.
BROOKLYN, N. Y.

Made to order in 4 to 5 weeks

	By 1 - 4	5	10	20 and more Designs
			ordered at one time	
500 of a design (hand-colored) ...	$7.50	$7.00	$6.75	$6.50
1000 " " " " ...	10.50	10.00	9.50	9.00
2000 " " " "per 1000	10.00	9.50	9.00	8.50

Terms: Net Cash
Following editions at the same rates

For example taking 500 cards each of 10 designs at $6.75 (per 500) will amount to $67.50
" " " 1000 " " " 5 " " 10.00 (" 1000) " " " 50.00
" " " 2000 " " " 5 " " 9.50 (" 1000) " " " 95.00

When ordering **Hand-colored** *post cards, please send prepaid the photographs and pencil on the margin (or on the back, if unmounted) the salient colors of the view, also the desired title and imprint. Do not write in ink or by typewriter on unmounted prints. We remove defects and make other needed alterations in the views. The grouping of several views or other special designing will be charged extra. The general color scheme should be left to our artists. Photographs are not returnable.*

Packages of Illustrated Post Cards up to 4 lbs. can be sent by mail or express as "Printed Matter" at 8c. per pound.

THE ALBERTYPE COMPANY, 250 A

The Albertype Company is distinguished as a longtime American producer of quality cards. This 1910 price list gives an idea of the economics of postcard retailing, when the cards typically sold at two or three for 5¢. Their cards of the period were also printed in monochrome, with a small price difference.

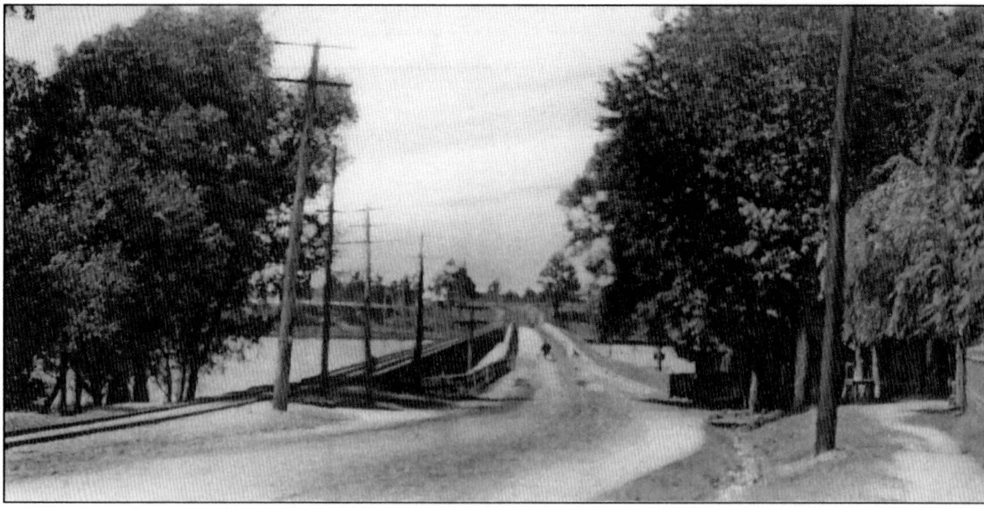

This pastoral scene is today's busy Highway 35's Coopers Bridge over the Navesink River, linking Red Bank with Middletown (at top). The *c.* 1905 Rotograph card also depicts the trolley bridge at left. The first bridge was built *c.* 1835, while this span dates from *c.* 1862. The present bridge opened May 5, 1926, with its replacement now in the planning stage.

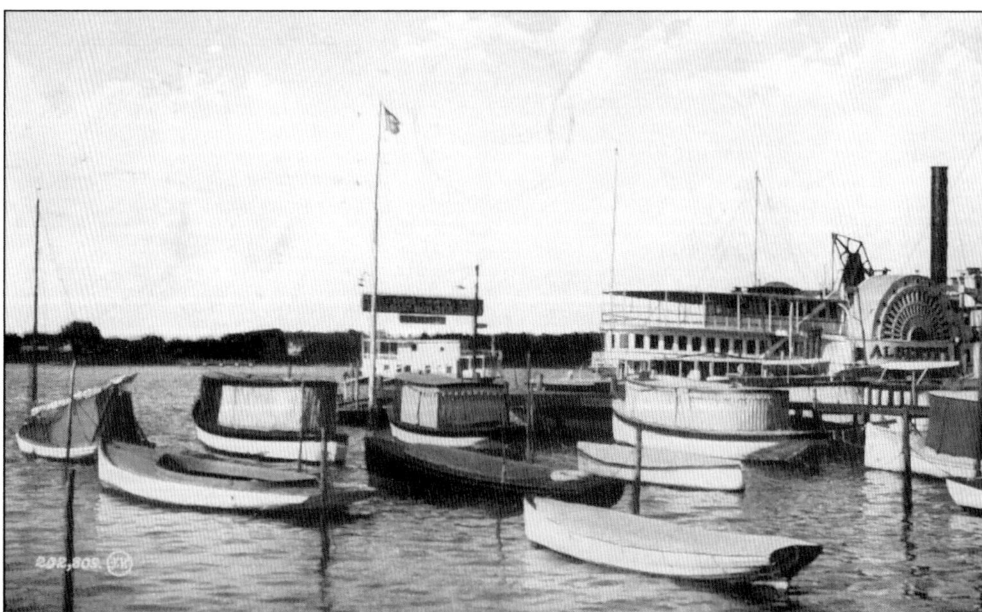

Steamships helped build Red Bank in its early development period from about 1840 to the 1860s and continued running into the 1930s, long after rail took the major share of traffic. The steamboat dock was at the foot of Wharf Avenue. The *Albertina*, built in 1882 for the Merchants Steamboat Company, its 165-foot length expanded by 9 feet in the 1880s, was one of the Navesink River's legendary craft. This Valentine card is *c.* 1905.

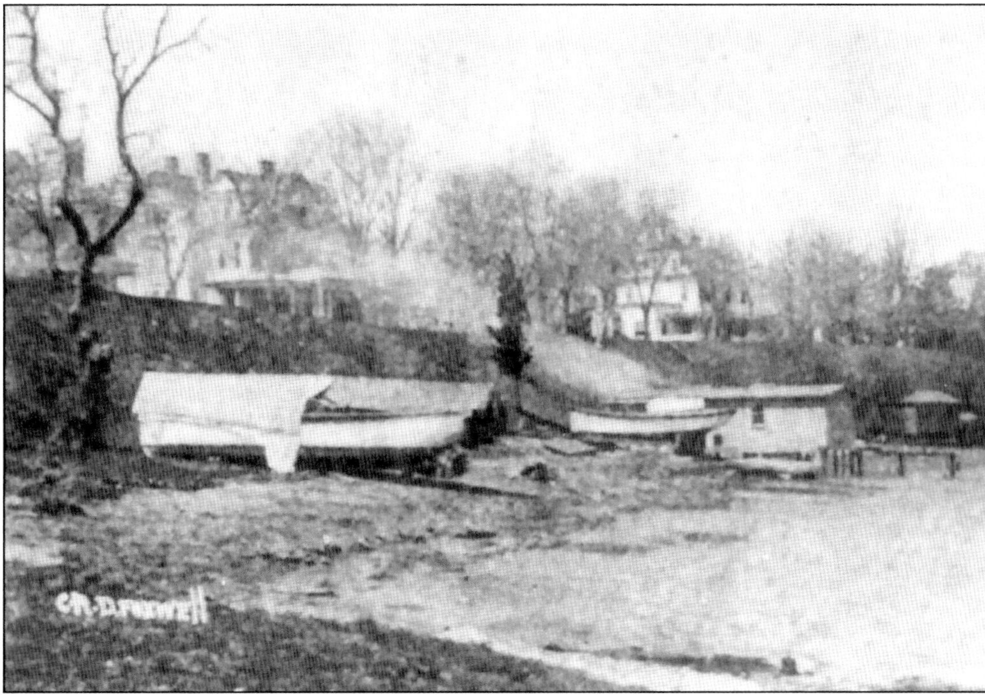

This Foxwell image, also found on a standard card, was lifted from a postcard invitation with the text adjacent to the illustration, "You are cordially invited to visit Red Bank, N.J., during Jubilee Week, August 7th to 10th, 1907. Red Bank is the most beautiful city along the North Jersey coast. The Jubilee Week attractions will include a mardi gras, a Grand Parade of Sunday-Schools, Motor Boat Races, Carnival of Venice, & c. Come!" The jubilee was a virtual town-wide summer celebration. The back included a "Welcome to Red Bank" greeting. The scene is the shore of the Navesink River.

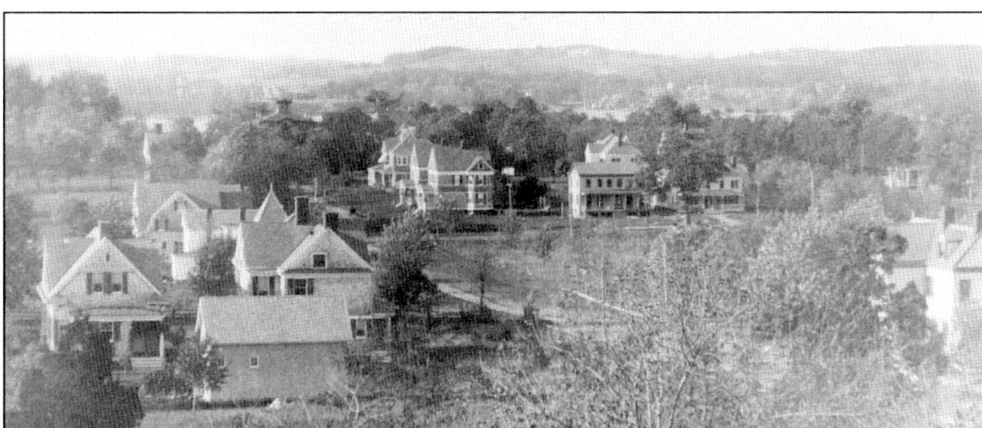

This view from Red Bank's Tower Hill is labeled "view from Bordens Hill" on the undivided back photo card, the older name stemming from a Borden-owned boarding house near the top of Prospect Avenue. The Navesink River and the hills of Middletown are in the background.

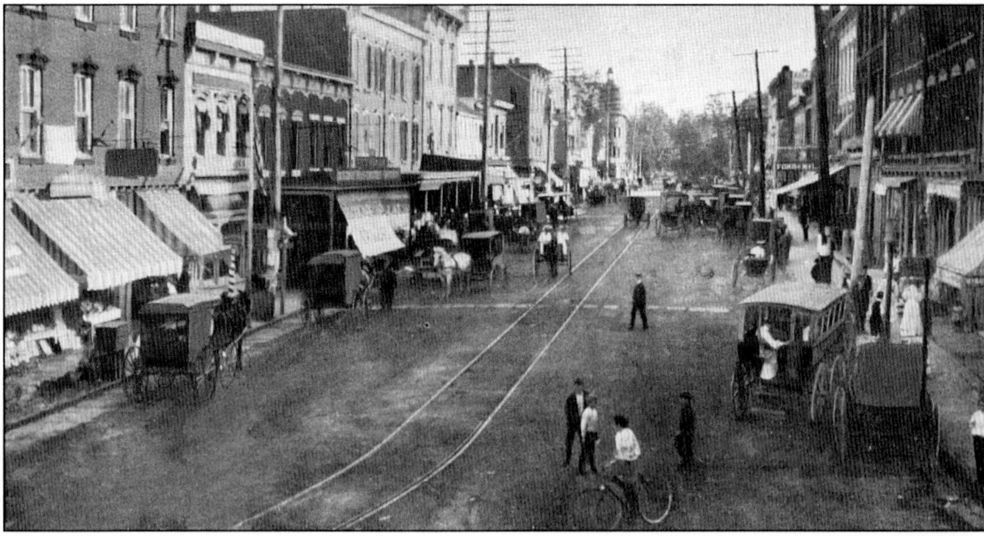

The 1898 Mercantile Bank Building, with the tower in the background and the 1903 Salz store (under the nearer of the cross-armed poles) also at left, are two dating aids for the numerous Broad Street, Red Bank scenes, including those "pre-postcard." However, one expects an undivided back to be in the 1903–1907 period. This example is from Raphael Tuck & Sons PC series 2404. Most of lower Broad Street is in the Commercial Italianate style, the buildings having been erected following a series of fires in the early 1880s.

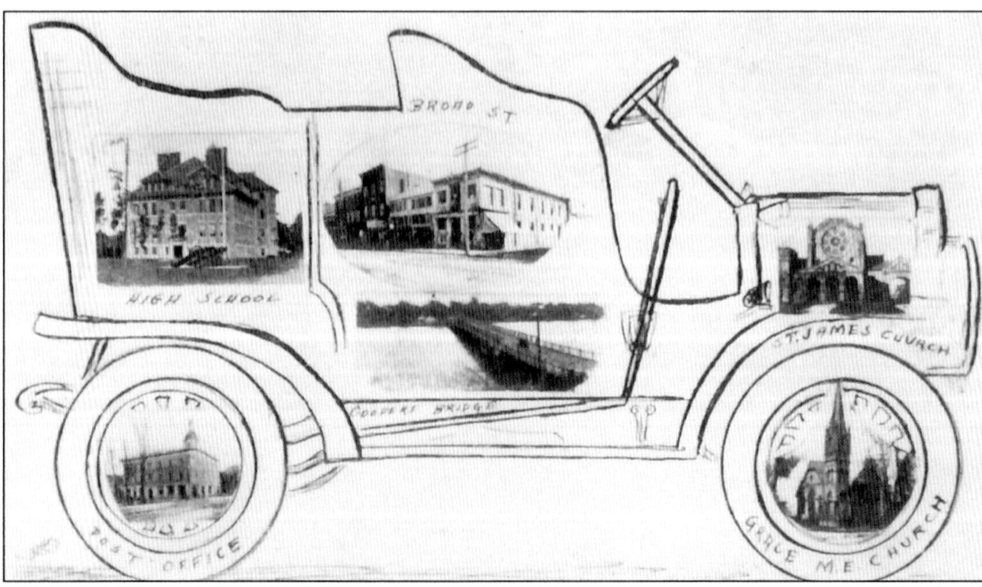

This *c.* 1905 novelty was published by Joseph Salz, a well-known Red Bank clothier, whose store is seen under the pole in the Broad Street view at top center. He produced few cards, probably because his early efforts were surpassed by local skilled photographer-postcard publishers Charles Foxwell and Joseph Dickopf.

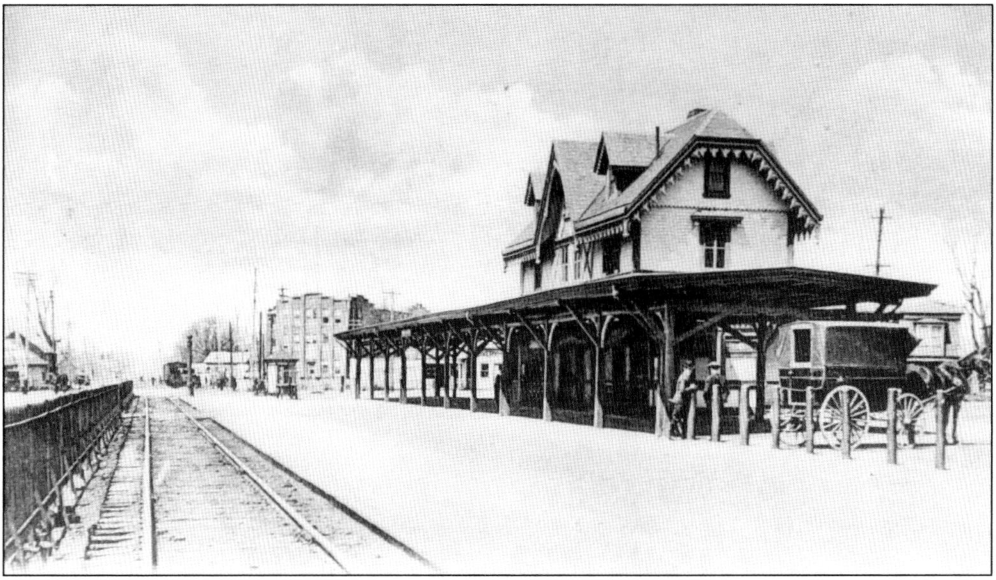

This view from the Red Bank station on the New York and Long Branch line looks north *c.* 1905. The station was built when the line opened in 1875; the large canopy was added *c.* 1900. The large brick building in the background is the Sigmund Eisner garment factory; it later attained prominence as arguably the world's largest uniform manufacturer. Both station and factory stand, although the latter has been remodeled as the Galleria shops. (Collection of John Rhody.)

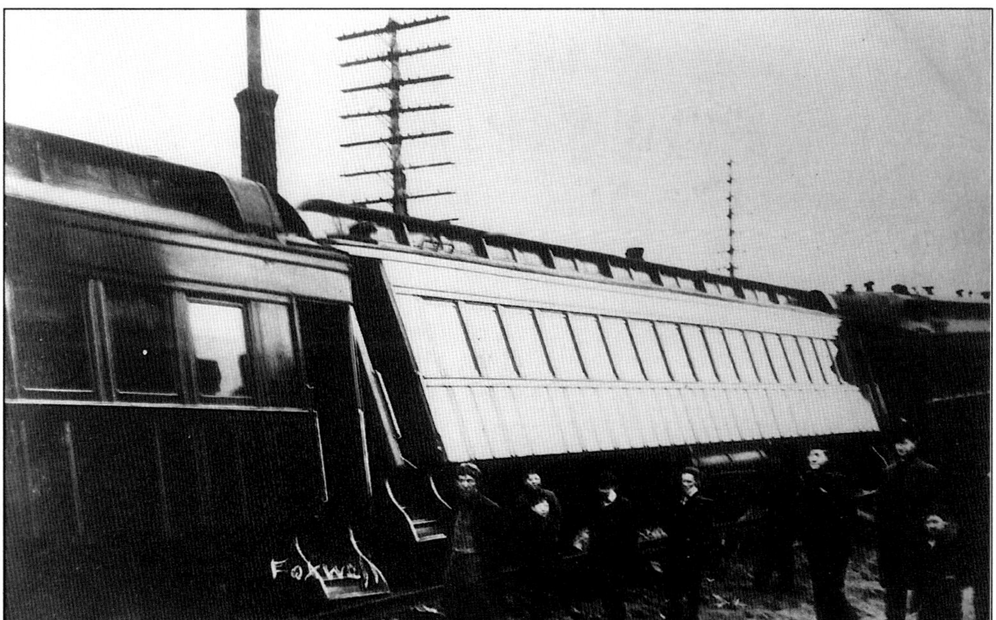

Charles Foxwell photographed the March 19, 1909 derailment in Red Bank of a north-bound Pennsylvania Railroad train. Conductor John Moore was reported as the only injury, cut and bruised when thrown from the platform of the car at right. This is a fine example of postcards serving as news photographs of their day.

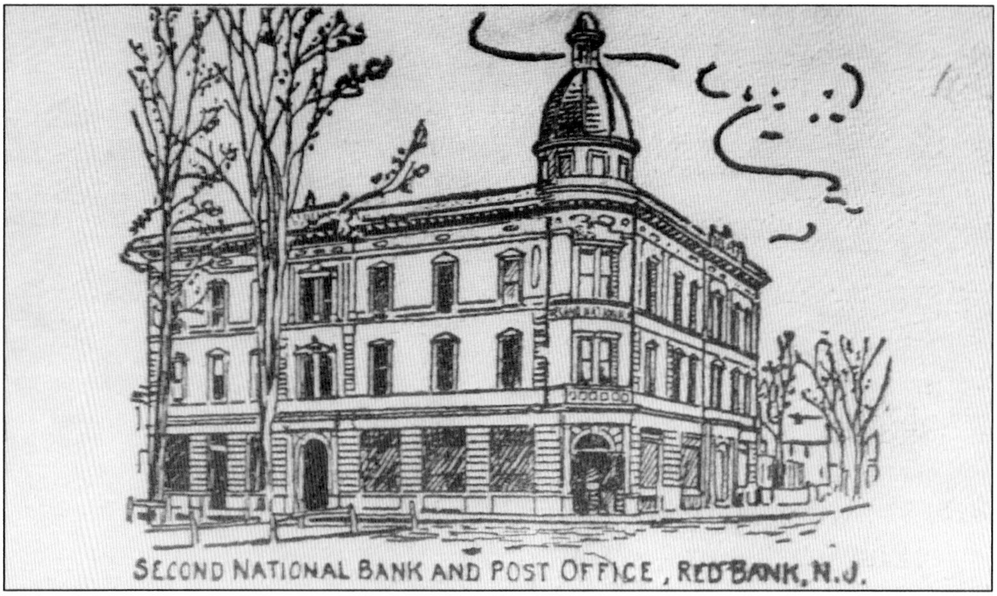

The postcard era saw all manner of novelties produced as cards, including use of unusual materials, such as this example in leather. The Second National Bank acquired the Mercantile Bank Building on the southeast corner of Broad and Wallace Streets in 1905. It was a likely subject for a special issue as the building was regarded as Red Bank's most attractive. Its remnants stand, but fire reduced it to a one-story, but rebuilt, shell. (Collection of John Rhody.)

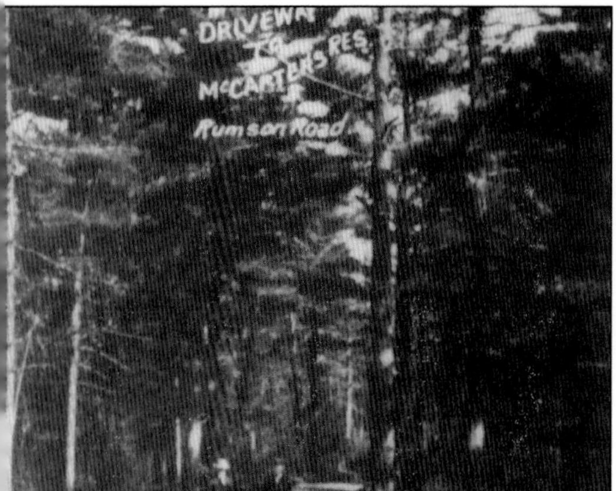

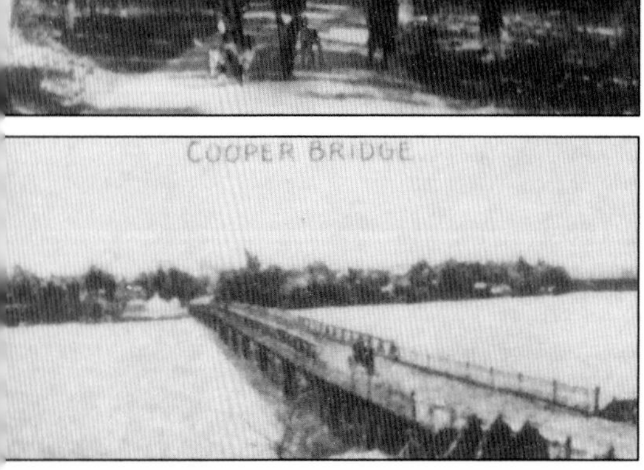

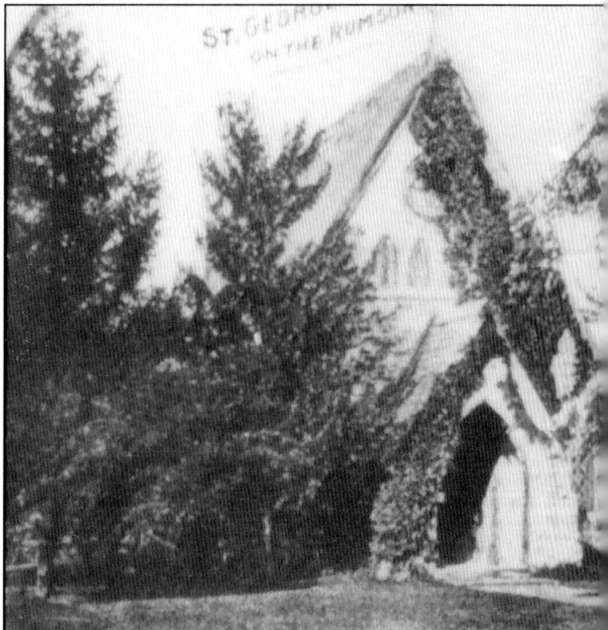

This multiple view card "Souvenir of Red Bank" has Rumson scenes on its two full-sized panels. The four small cards showing eight Red Bank views can be seen flip-style after pulling out one of the large panels.

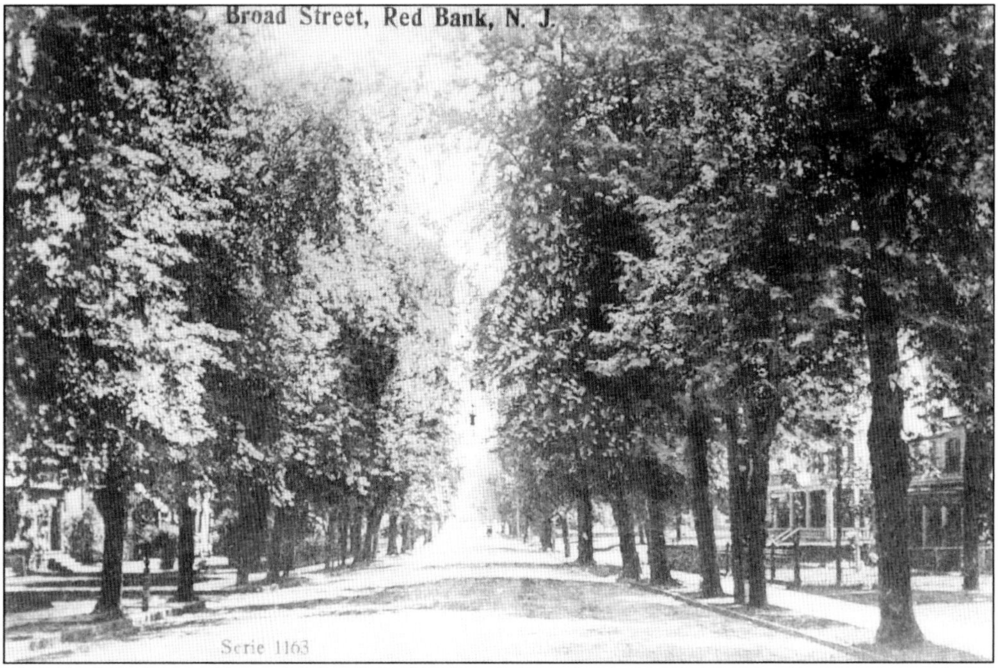

This prosaic upper Broad Street, Red Bank scene is the front of an enclosure for 12 pull-out 3-by-2-inch views of sites also known on individual cards. It was published by the Union News Company. Broad was residential south of Monmouth Street in the postcard era. The replacement of every building makes identification of old pictures nearly impossible for a three-block span.

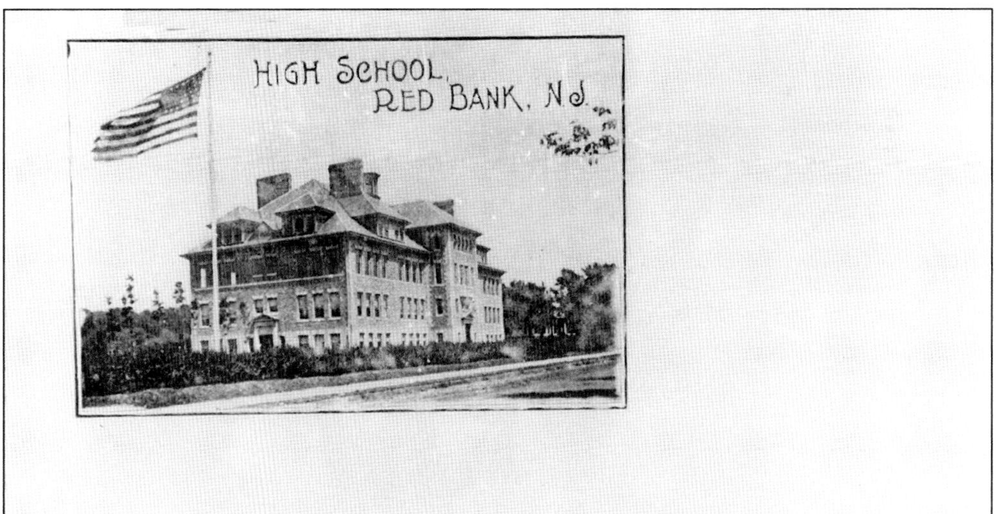

Red Bank High School was built in 1901 on the east side of Branch Avenue at its juncture with Harding Road. One of few in the county at the time, its stature merited special materials card treatment, such as this example in aluminum, which required a separate mailer. The school was demolished in March 1977, following the erection of Red Bank Regional High School on Ridge Road, just east of the Red Bank border in Little Silver. (Collection of John Rhody.)

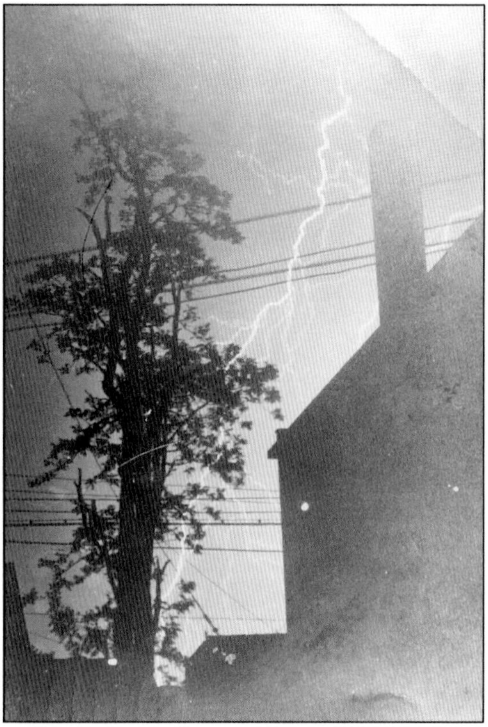

Charles R.D. Foxwell, Red Bank's outstanding postcard photographer, made numerous real photo (to use the common redundancy the author dislikes) street scenes that are among the most eagerly sought of Red Bank cards. He had a large body of casual work, such as this fine illustration of a lightening strike. Printing on postcard stock elevated a great photograph that might otherwise have been lost into a deltiological collectible. (Collection of John Rhody; photo courtesy of Glenn Vogel.)

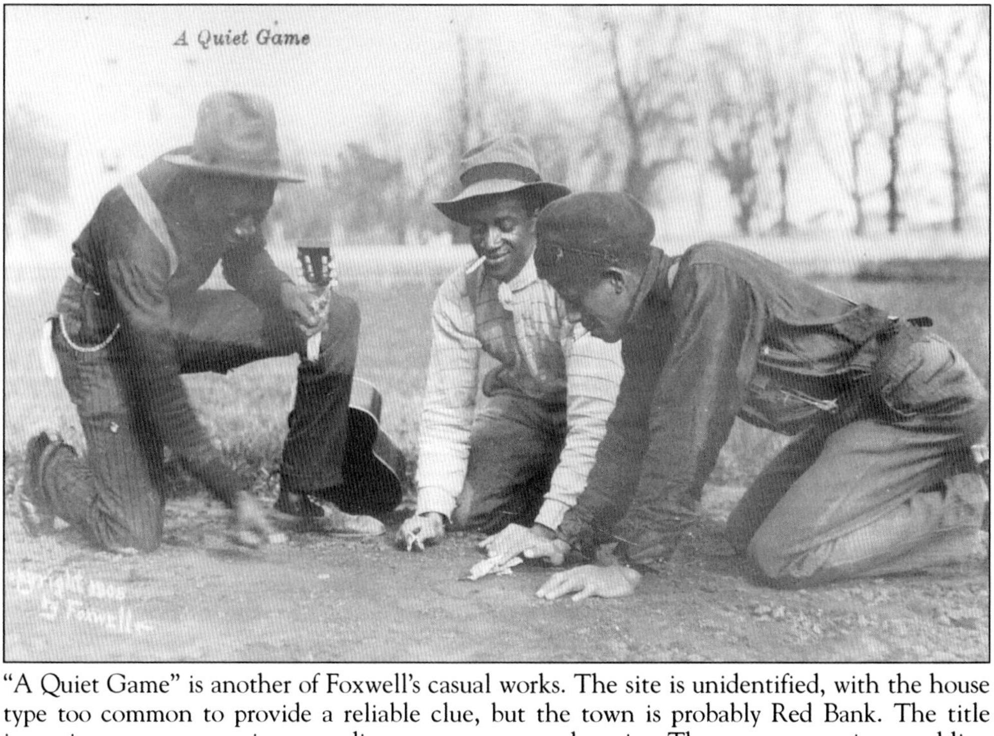

"A Quiet Game" is another of Foxwell's casual works. The site is unidentified, with the house type too common to provide a reliable clue, but the town is probably Red Bank. The title is a misnomer or an enigma, as dice games were rarely quiet. There was an active gambling culture in Red Bank's west side, notably at "The Pit," around Bridge Avenue and Bergen Place. (Collection of John Rhody; photo courtesy of Glenn Vogel.)

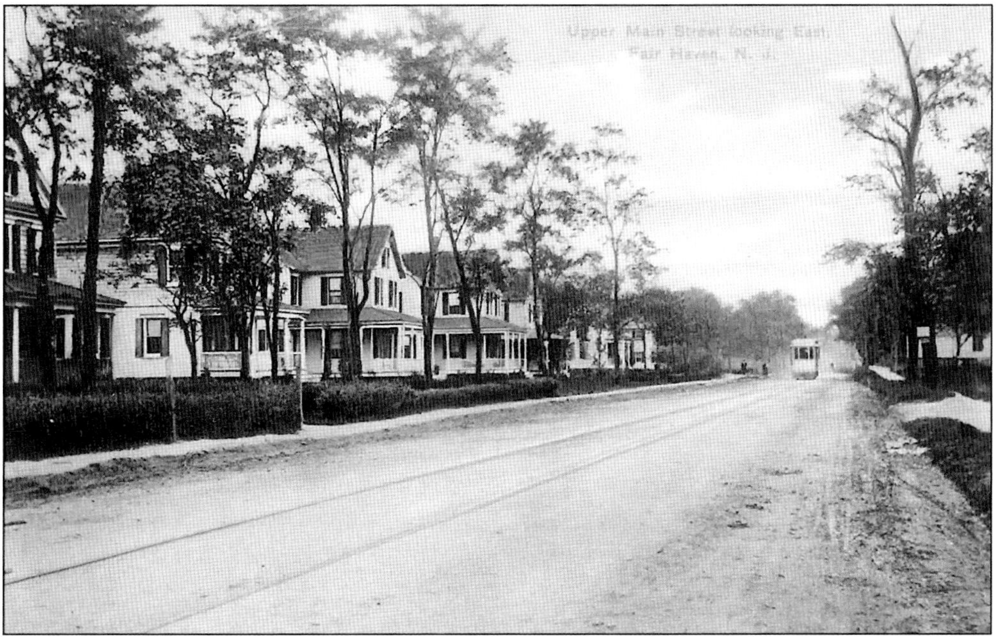

Access to a print from Christopher Chandler's 1907 glass plate provides two clues to postcard production. The scene is the southeast corner of River Road and Maple Avenue, Fair Haven, showing 673–685 River Road at left. The printed card obscures the brick pavement along the roadbed, accounting for the distant pedestrian's presence in the middle of the road. More interestingly, the street's telephone poles were removed for the postcard version! (See *Fair Haven*, p. 49.)

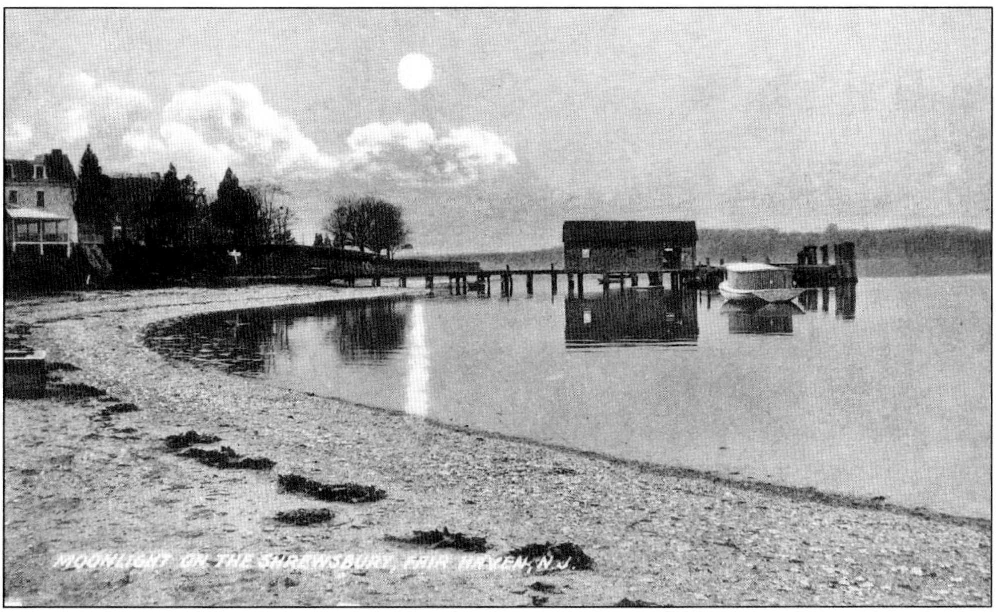

The building of a steamboat dock in Fair Haven, located at the foot of today's Fair Haven Road, c. late 1840s, propelled the development of the town. A daylight version of this view looking west exists, but coloring it as night dramatizes a mundane scene. At left is the Grand View Hotel, demolished following its 1935 purchase by adjoining estate owner Jerome Rice.

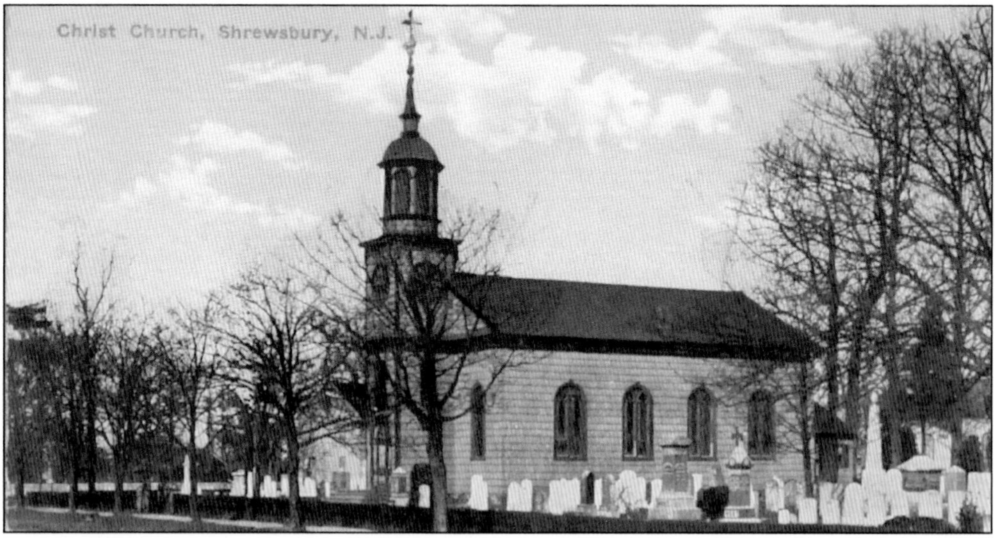

Christ Church, on the southeast corner of Broad Street and Sycamore Avenue, Shrewsbury, dates its origin to 1702. The present edifice was designed by prominent Philadelphia architect-builder Robert Smith and built between 1769 and 1774 near the foundation of a 1732 brick church. The 10-foot square clock tower was added in 1874, on which builder Lambert Borden mounted the cupola, initially erected on the roof. The clock, from the E. Howard Clock Co. of Boston, with faces on the north, west, and south sides, was provided by private subscription. It is still operative and is wound weekly by hand.

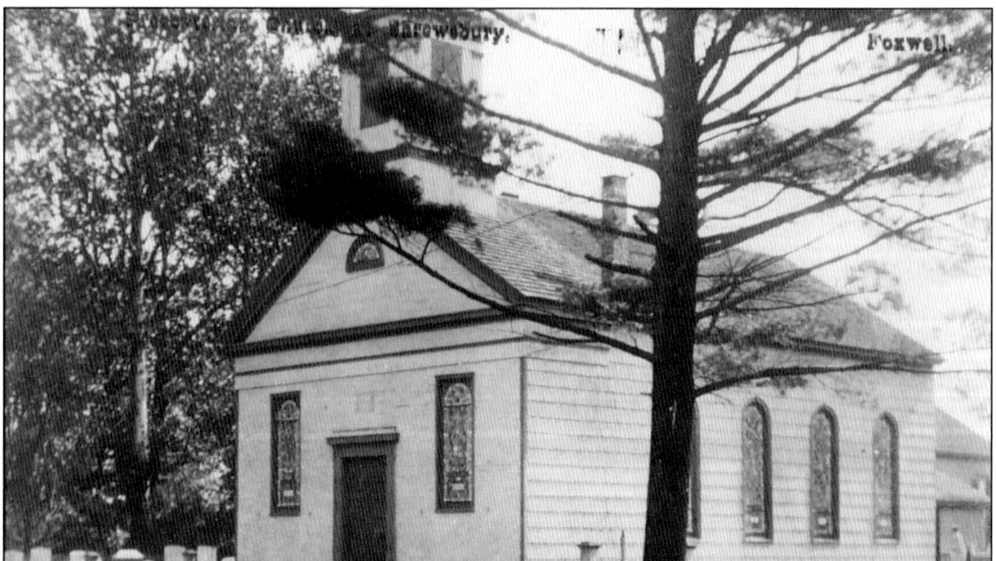

The Presbyterian Church at Shrewsbury has established its founding as 1732, but notes that Presbyterian activity in the area can be traced at least to 1705, when John Boyd was licensed as the first minister to be ordained by the first Presbytery in this country. A charter was obtained in 1750; an early church was built, deteriorated, and was torn down. Services were held elsewhere, including Christ Church. Funds for a new church were raised in 1821, with the present Greek Revival edifice dedicated on September 29, 1822. This Foxwell photo shows the church c. 1905. (Collection of John Rhody.)

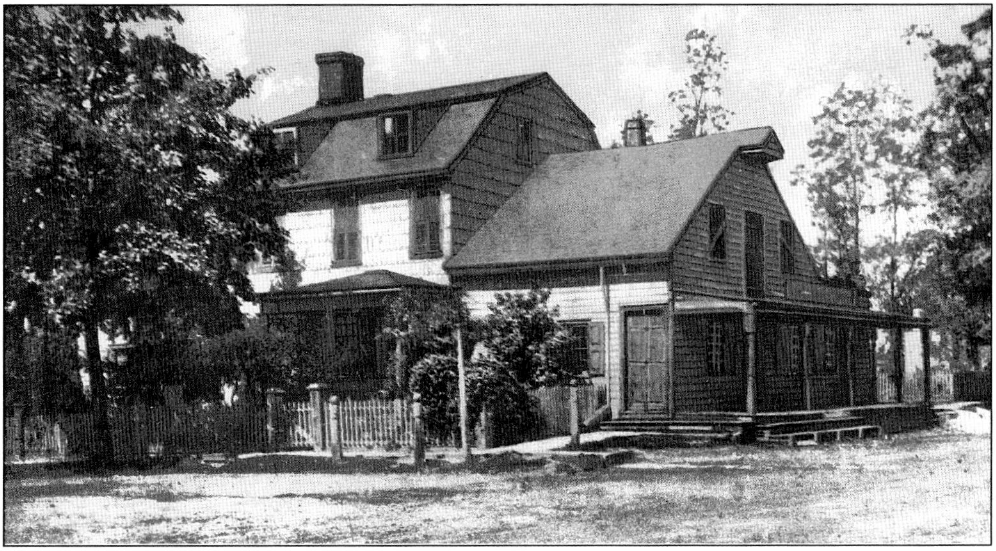

The Allen House at Broad & Sycamore's northwest corner , with its origin likely during the first half of the 18th century as a smaller building, was a typical colonial-era town gathering spot known as the Blue Ball Tavern. A store section at right was built c. 1814. This c. 1905 view dates from its early tenure as A. Holmes Borden's store, a business destroyed by fire on April 17, 1914. The Monmouth County Historical Association restored the building, aided by a local group, the Shrewsbury Association for the Restoration of the Allen House, or SARAH, and operates it as a museum.

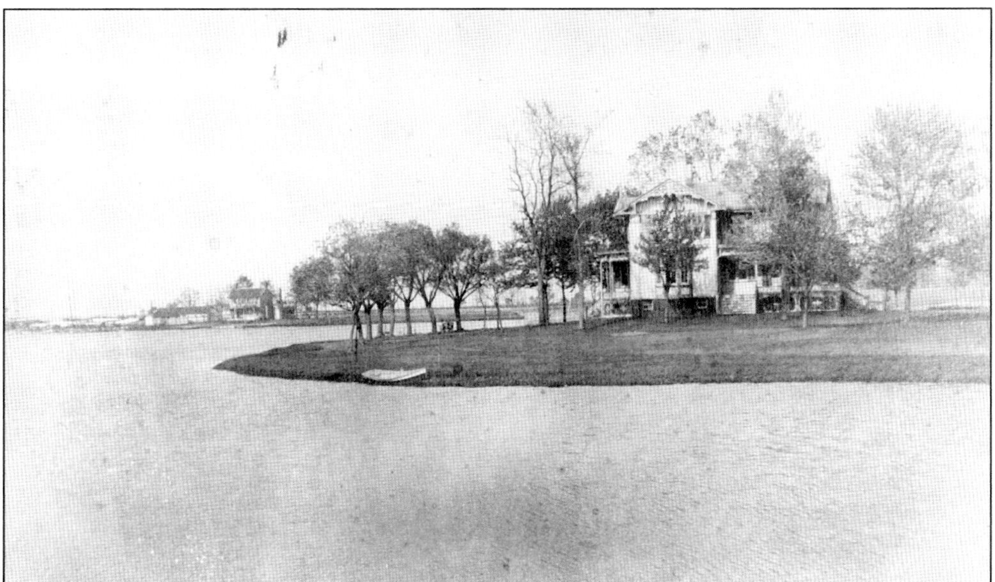

Identification and description of the no-longer-standing Judge Fitzgerald House is difficult, but it appears to have been built in two major sections, with the gable end facing the viewer possessing attractive c. 1870s vergeboard decoration. The site is in today's Old Wharf Park. (Collection of John Rhody.)

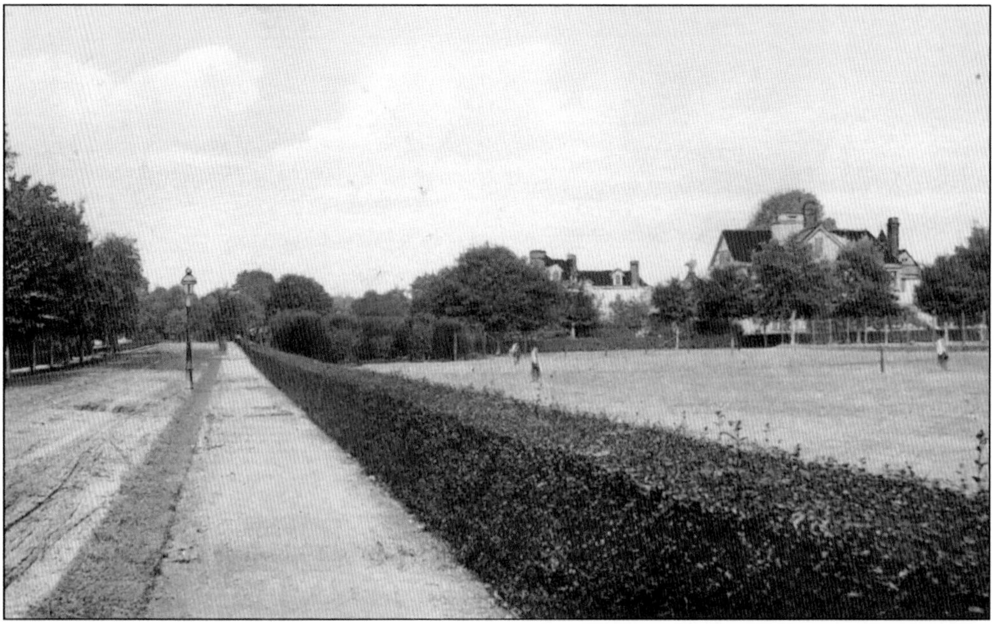

The card's title, "Rumson Road, Sea Bright, N.J.," confuses modern viewers, but not early senders, as eastern Rumson was known as Sea Bright prior to either place incorporating as boroughs. The view looks west outside the grass courts of the Seabright Lawn Tennis and Cricket Club, a scene changed only by pavement, much taller hedges, and the fencing of the courts.

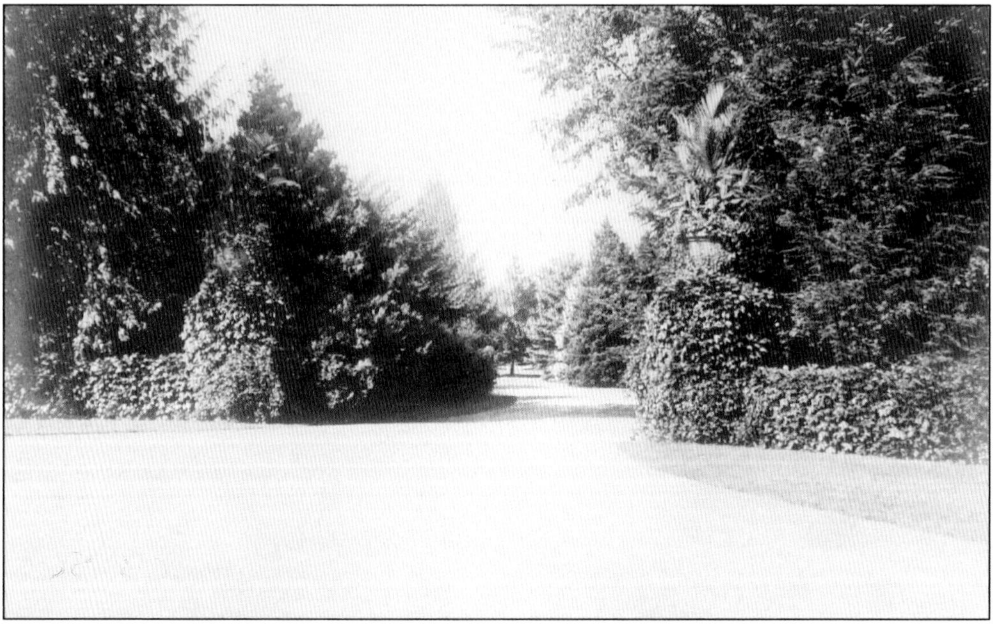

Rumson Road cards are so common because its fame as early as 1890 as one of the nation's finest country drives made postcard buyers eager to send and own them. It attained that stature in 20 years, as the thoroughfare was little more than a sandy path when the Sea Bright-Rumson Bridge was opened in 1870. The card is titled "Red Bank" in a not-unusual case of publisher use of a nearby better-known town. The image is *c*. 1910. (Collection of John Rhody.)

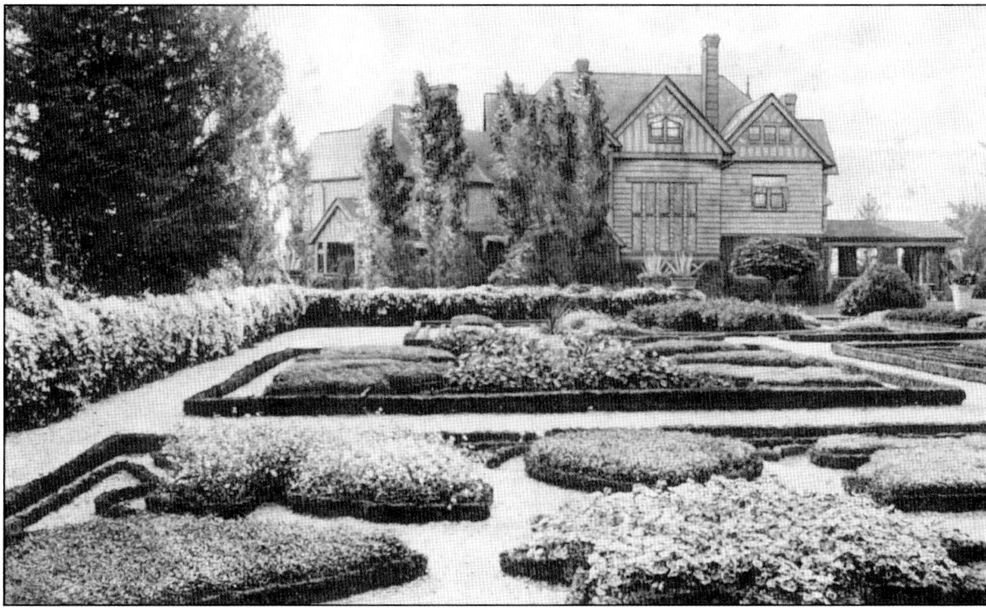

William F. Havemeyer, of the New York sugar trust family, built in 1890 a large Queen Anne-style house with strong Tudor Revival elements, designed by New York's Brunner and Tryon, on the north side of Rumson Road, near Kemp Avenue. Nathan F. Barrett designed the grounds, including its noteworthy Italian garden. The house, known as The Beeches, was demolished for construction of new houses. The former grandeur of their grounds is suggested by The Beeches' still-standing wrought iron fence on Rumson Road.

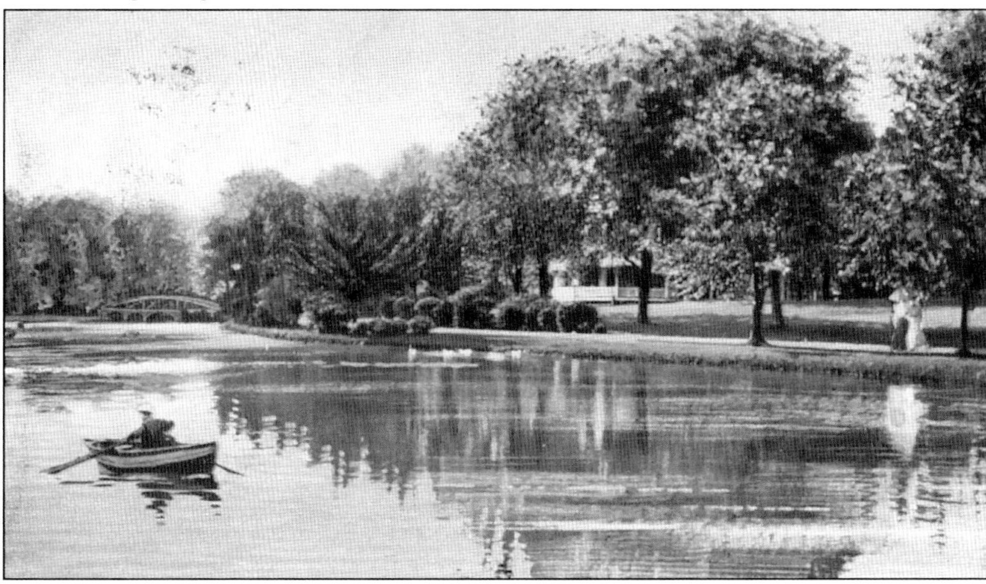

The book's second example from the Tuck Red Bank series 2404 shows the lake west of the John Harper Bonnell House on the northwest corner of Rumson Road and Buena Vista Avenue, Rumson. The back is filled with misinformation about the body of water, which was man-made by David B. Keeler, who owned a large tract that included his house on the southwest corner. This example was mailed to New York in 1906 to confirm an appointment, a reminder of the high reliability once placed on prompt mail delivery.

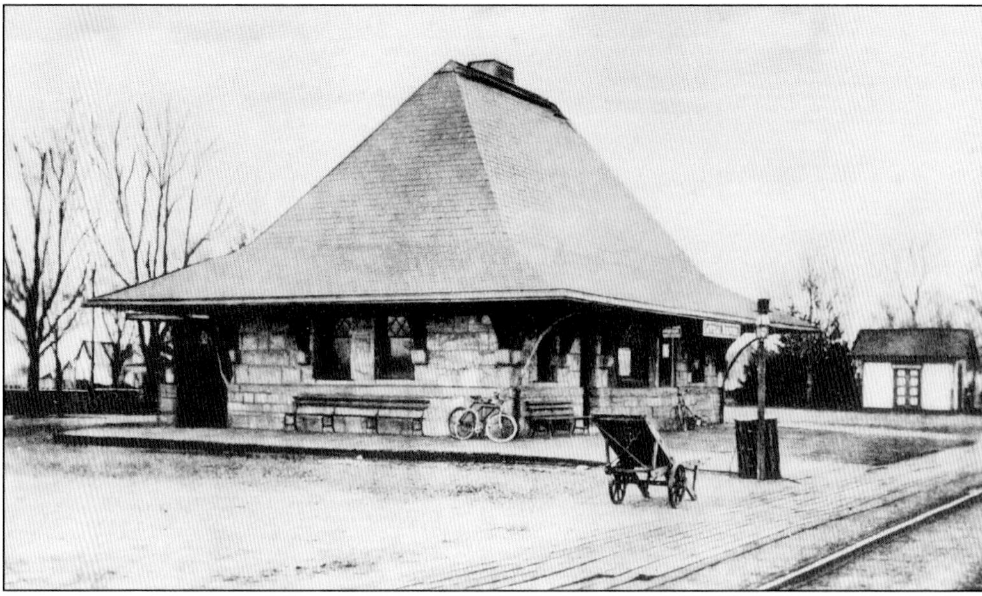

Little Silver's railroad station, a Vernacular Victorian design by Boston architects Peabody and Stearns, was built in 1889 by R.V. Breece of Long Branch. The depot's distinctive design is dominated by the steeply pitched roof; its stone walls suggest the influence of the Romanesque Revival. The curiosity of a Boston architect designing a country station in New Jersey is addressed by awareness that the firm designed the Central Railroad's office in downtown New York. (Collection of Keith Wells.)

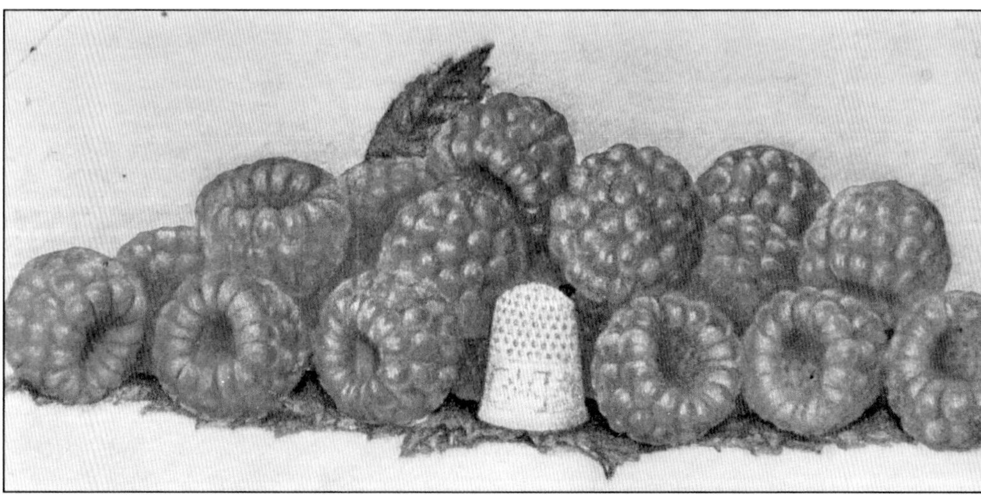

J.T. Lovett's Monmouth Nursery developed many varieties of fruits and berries with distinctions likely unnoticed by the average consumer. The St. Regis raspberry boasted size, which if larger than a thimble, perhaps presented a choking hazard if swallowed whole! This image is c. 1910. An earlier Lovett raspberry, the Hansell, was claimed to be the earliest of the fruit. The front of this card also offered the Himalaya Giant Berry, the Silver Coin Strawberry, and the Perfection Currant. (Collection of John Rhody.)

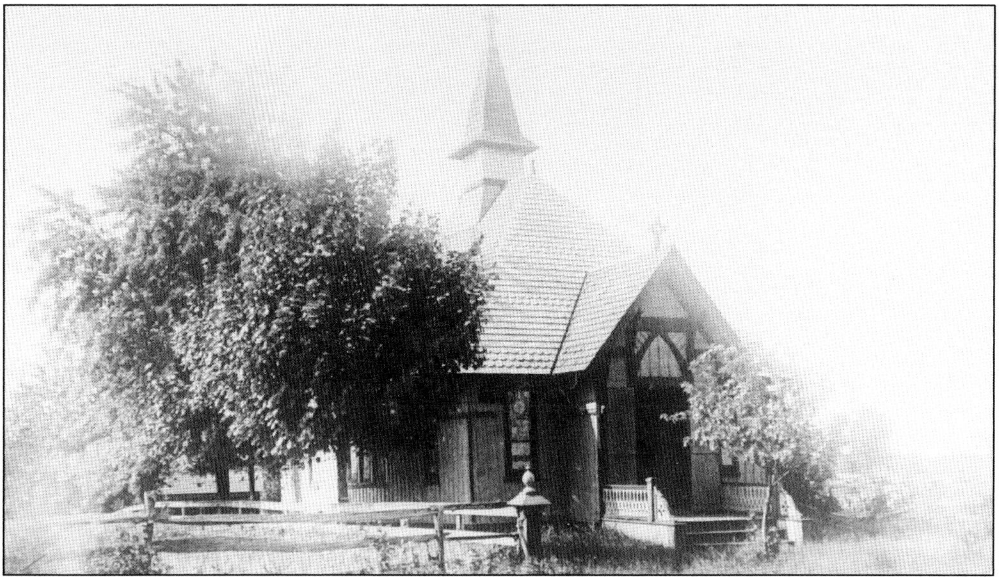

St. John's P.E. Church, on the north side of Little Silver Point Road, east of Prospect Avenue, Little Silver, was built in 1876 as a chapel part of Red Bank's Trinity Church. Designed by John E. Sidman of New York, the Stick Style building, clad in board and batten and fish scale shingles, retains a high degree of integrity, despite the presence of additions. Minor changes made since this *c.* 1910 image include fiberglass roof shingles, replacement of the carved entry rails, the construction of a handicapped ramp, and the covering of wood trim with paint. The chapel was designated a church in 1959; St. John's is listed on the National Register of Historic Places. (Collection of Keith Wells.)

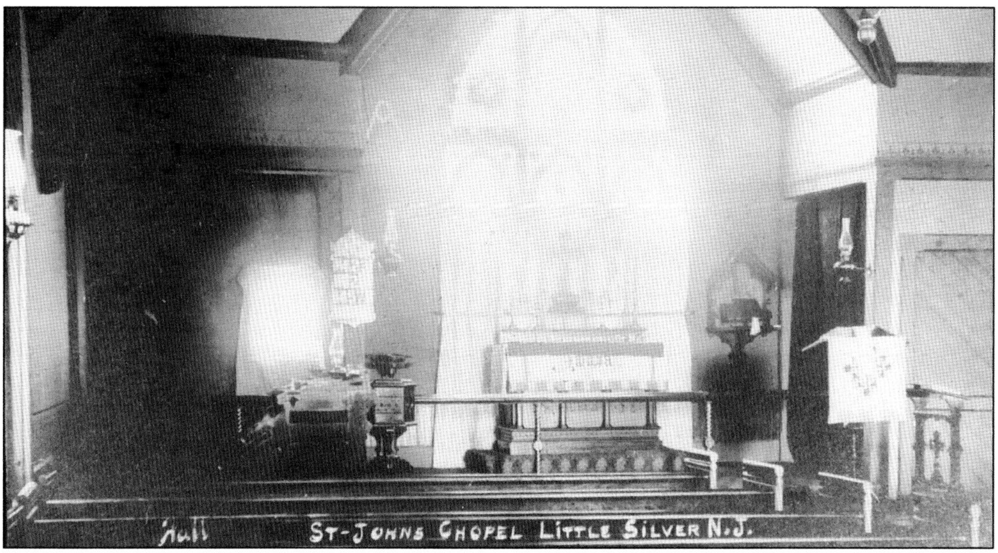

St. John's interior also maintains its integrity and the furnishings from this *c.* 1910 image, including the altar carved by John Bates. The small window at left is now backed by a hall added to a side of the north elevation. The first three pews were removed, shortened, and positioned on the west to face the aisle, to permit placement of a piano and organ on the east. The space at right is now open and most of the beams, other than the roof's, are painted white. (Collection of Keith Wells.)

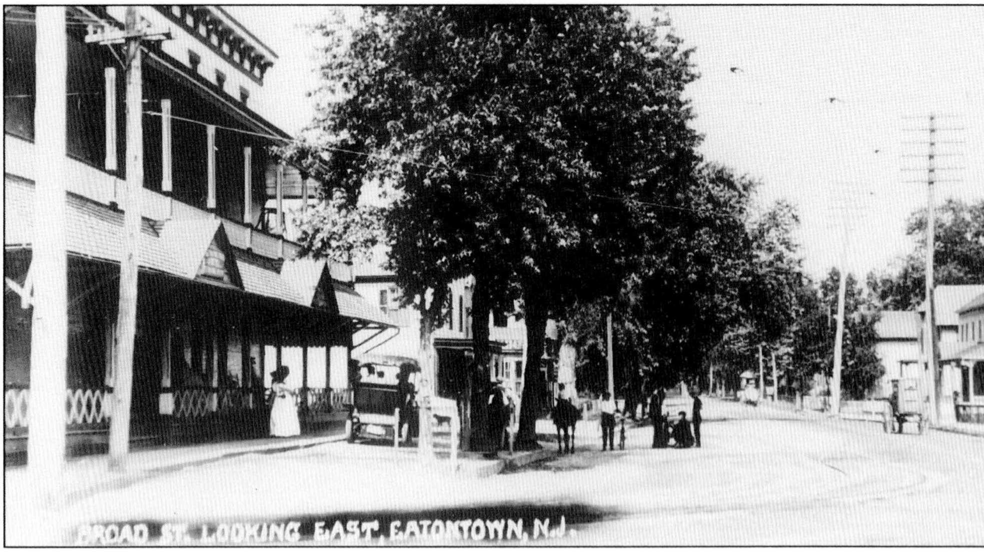

Broad Street is seen looking east c. 1910 from Main, Eatontown's principal juncture, the two better known as Highways 71 and 35 respectively. Many historic structures are along this stem, but the Metropolitan Hotel, the former center of Eatontown's social life, is gone, replaced by an office building. The hotel, when built in the 1870s, catered to a substantial racing following from nearby Monmouth Park. Its fall upon hard times was reflected in its 1919 sheriff's sale for a mere $6,000, a fraction of its construction cost, the price reflecting Prohibition's coming and the decline in stature of country hotels. (Collection of Glenn Vogel.)

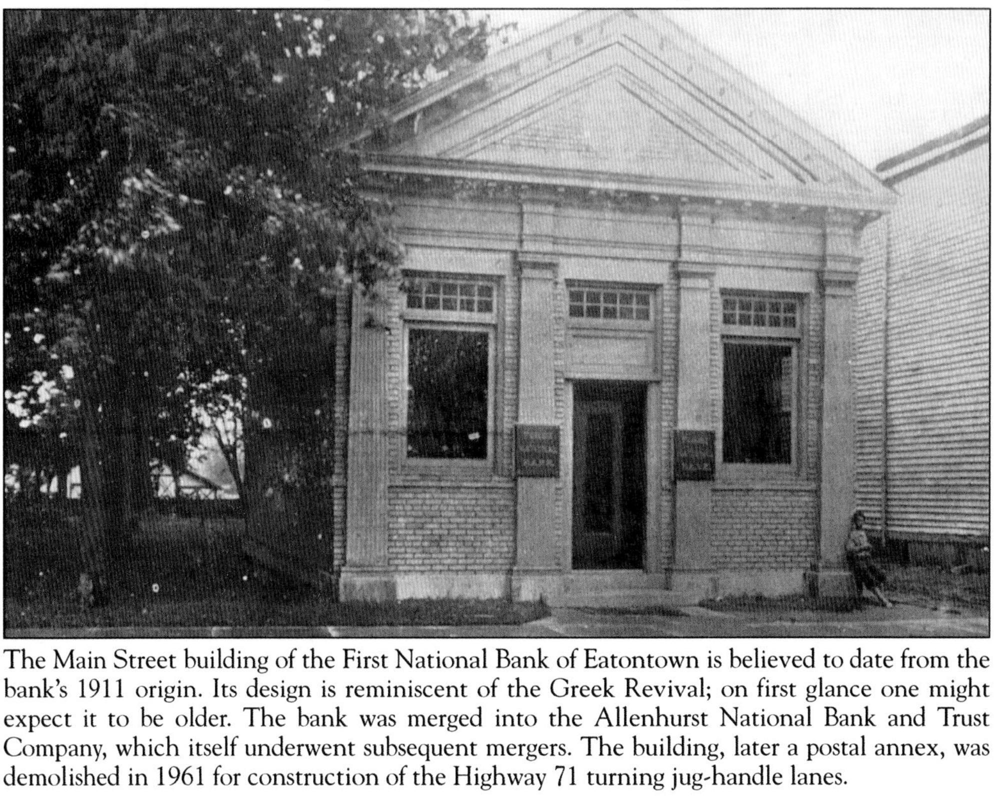

The Main Street building of the First National Bank of Eatontown is believed to date from the bank's 1911 origin. Its design is reminiscent of the Greek Revival; on first glance one might expect it to be older. The bank was merged into the Allenhurst National Bank and Trust Company, which itself underwent subsequent mergers. The building, later a postal annex, was demolished in 1961 for construction of the Highway 71 turning jug-handle lanes.

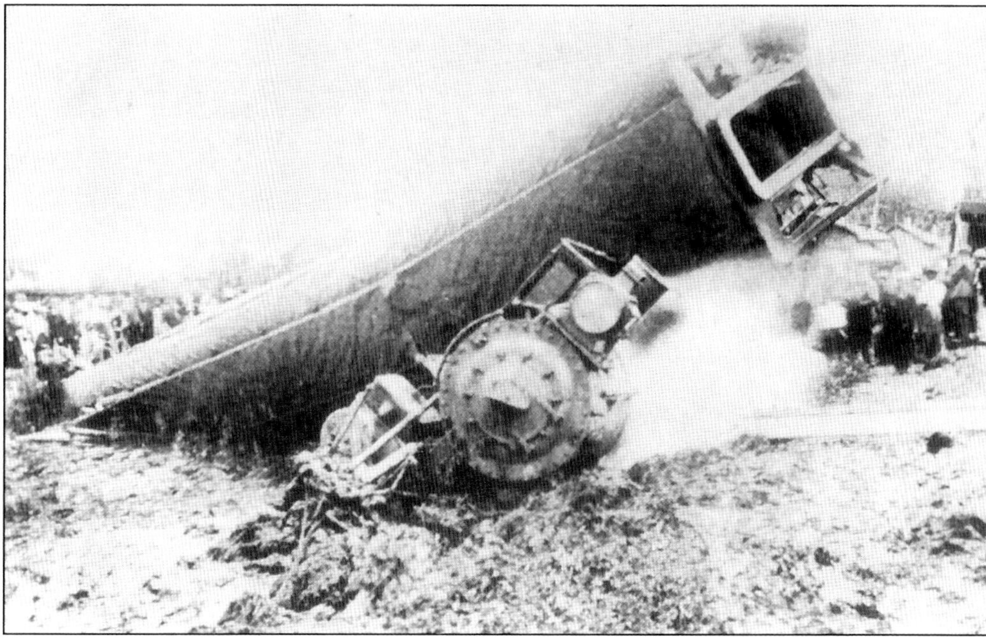

Due to an improperly fastened switch, a northbound Central Railroad Atlantic City Flyer derailed at Eatontown on June 11, 1906, on tracks where trains from the Lakewood stem turned slightly to the northwest to reach the main line to Red Bank. The locomotive passed safely over the switch, but its coupling gave way after rear cars left the tracks, sending the locomotive into the adjoining marsh. George D. Van Duser of New York, after jumping from a derailed car, was pinned into mud by a car moving after it derailed; he was killed and about 50 persons were injured.

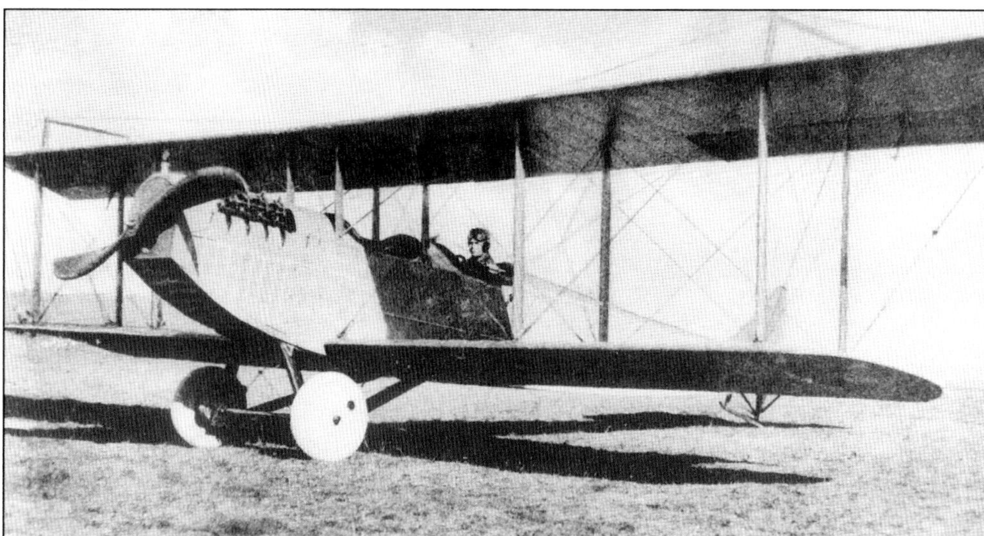

Camp Alfred Vail, the origin of Fort Monmouth, was designated in September 1917, a renaming to reflect the permanency of a signal corps development center, established that May as Camp Little Silver. The early camp, located in Eatontown Township on land that became Oceanport in 1920, embraced the site of the first Monmouth Park. The area's first air strip was built here. The plane is a Curtiss JN-4, better known as a Jenny. (Collection of John Rhody.)

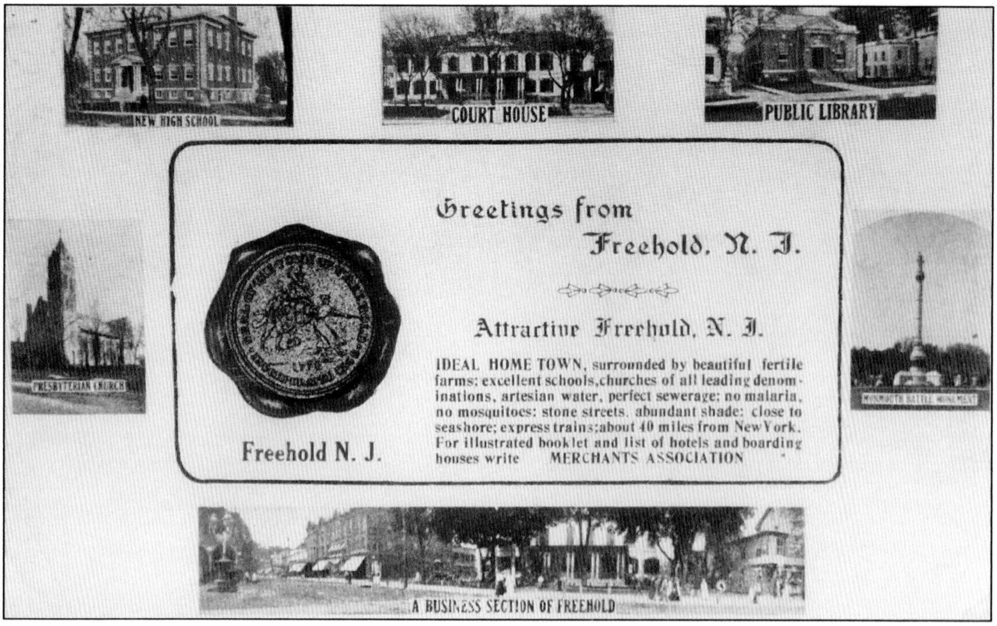

Freehold's example of New York publisher Franz Huld Company's 1909 View Seal series promotes Monmouth's county seat with still familiar images. Many of the business buildings are intact, creating one of Monmouth County's finest downtown streetscapes. The Court House, replaced in 1955, is now the Hall of Records, with a map room and deed records of essential help to researchers. The school has been replaced, but the library and Presbyterian church are Main Street landmarks.

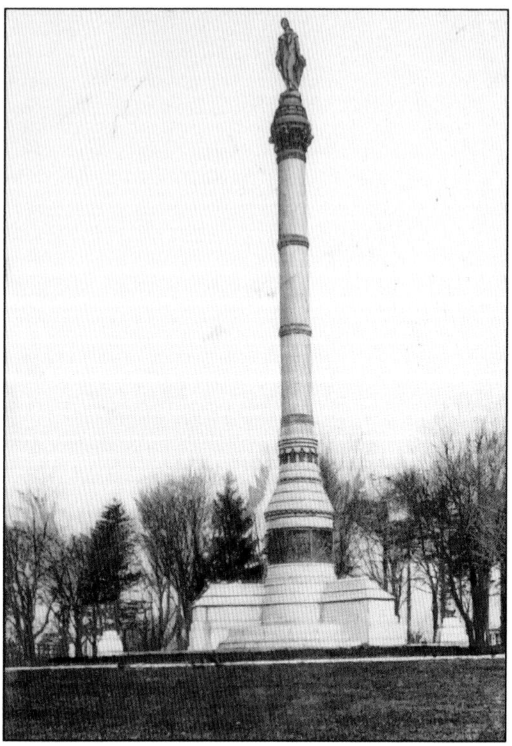

The cornerstone of the Monmouth Battle Monument was laid on June 28, 1878, the centennial of the battle it commemorates. The triangular base corresponds with a triangular plot of ground on the east side of Court Street. The granite monument was designed by Emelin T. Little and Douglas Smyth. Liberty Triumphant stands atop the shaft's cap, rising about 94 feet in height. The five bronze bas reliefs with battle scenes that surround the column were sculpted by James E. Kelly. Federal and state funds, together with public subscription, paid the approximate $40,000 cost. At long last, the monument was unveiled in November 1884.

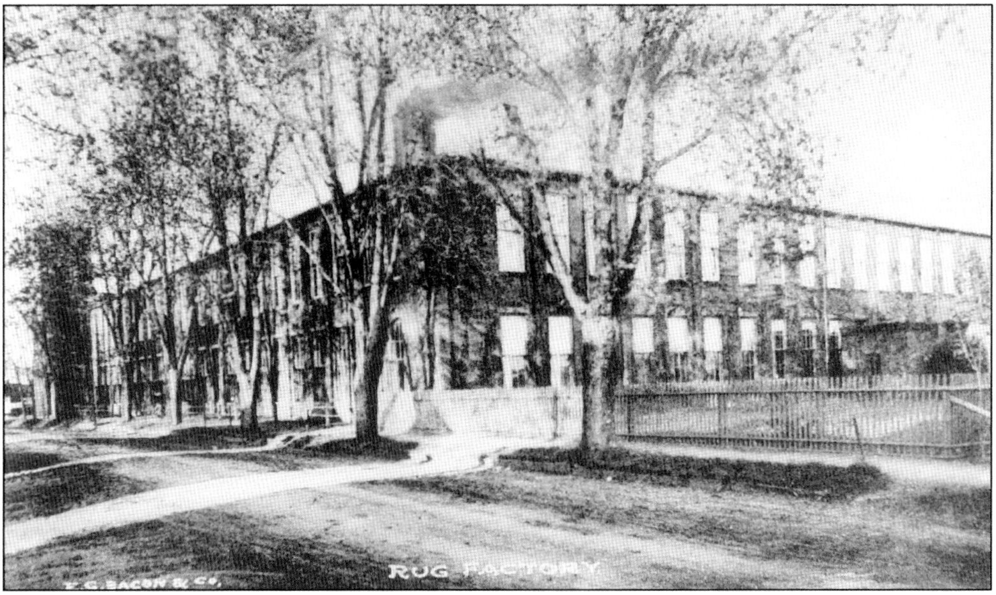

A. & M. Karaguheusian Inc. began rug weaving in an existing factory on Jackson Street c. 1904, building one the country's largest and substantial carpet operations. This original two-story building, erected in 1894, is pictured on a c. 1906 card. The expanding plant soon loomed over this with four and five-story buildings. Mixed occupancies succeeded rug weaving in 1961. Fires have left the structures in major disrepair, but redevelopment plans are proceeding. (Collection of Michael Steinhorn.)

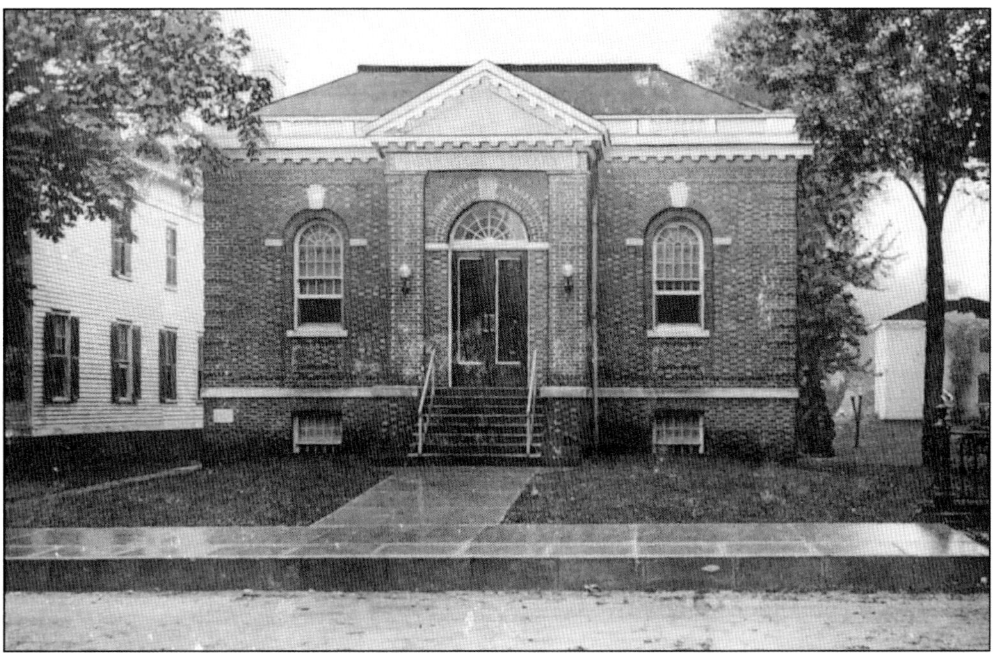

The Freehold Borough Public Library at 28 East Main Street was built in 1903, assisted by a Carnegie grant. Its attractive Colonial Revival design was the work of New York architects Jackson and Rosencrans. The well-preserved library is still in use, looking today much the way it does in this c. 1906 card.

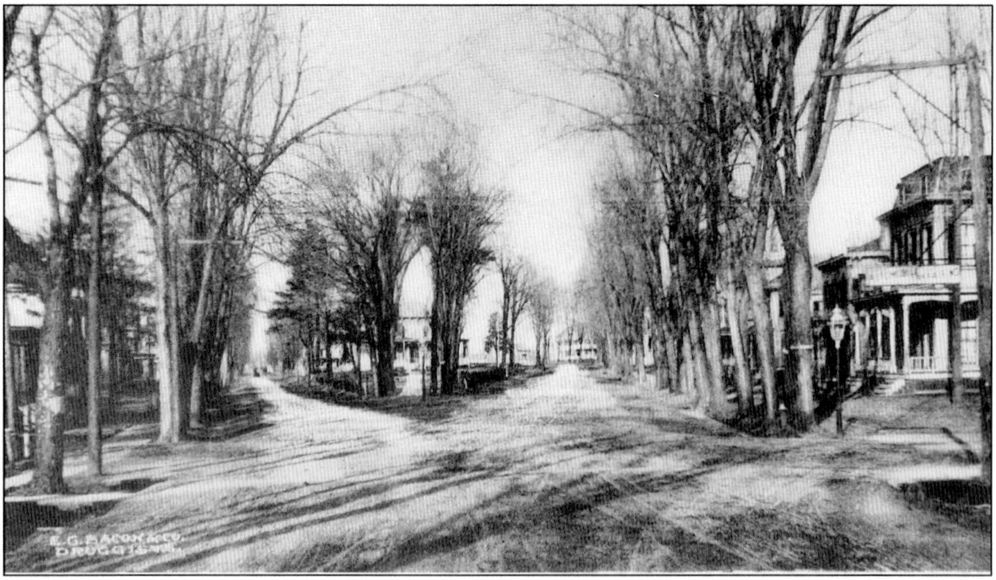

Once quiet country roads and townscapes familiar today as traffic bottlenecks are among the most startling images of early cards, such as this *c.* 1905 Albertype view of Broadway (at left) intersecting with Freehold's Main Street. Many of the houses are intact; some have been converted to offices, but a gas station is now at left and a telephone company building is at right. The view is north and east. (Collection of Michael Steinhorn.)

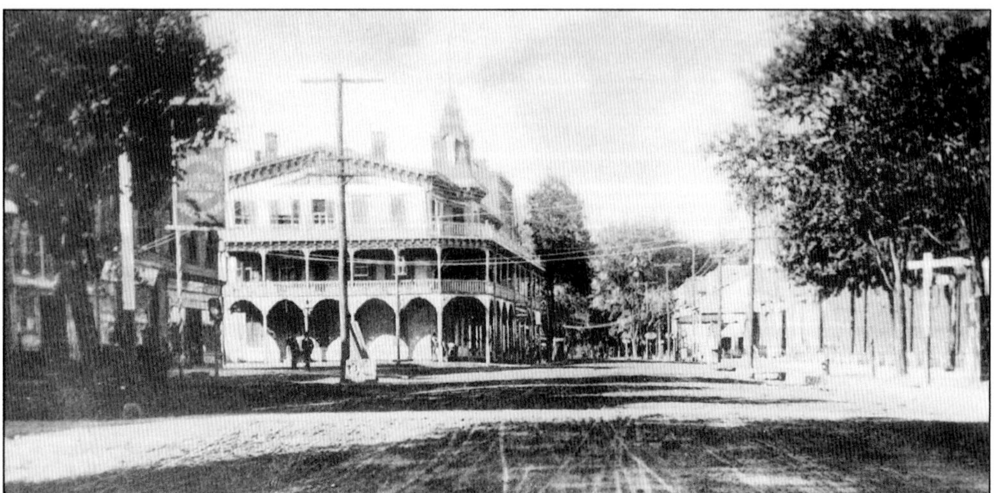

Main Street is viewed looking west *c.* 1905 toward the juncture of South Street (at left). The 1887 Belmont Hotel, which occupied the corner, was destroyed by fire in February 1933. A pharmacy is on the site now. Many of the buildings on this stem of Main Street are intact. The sign of the no longer extant Monmouth House is at left. (Collection of Michael Steinhorn.)

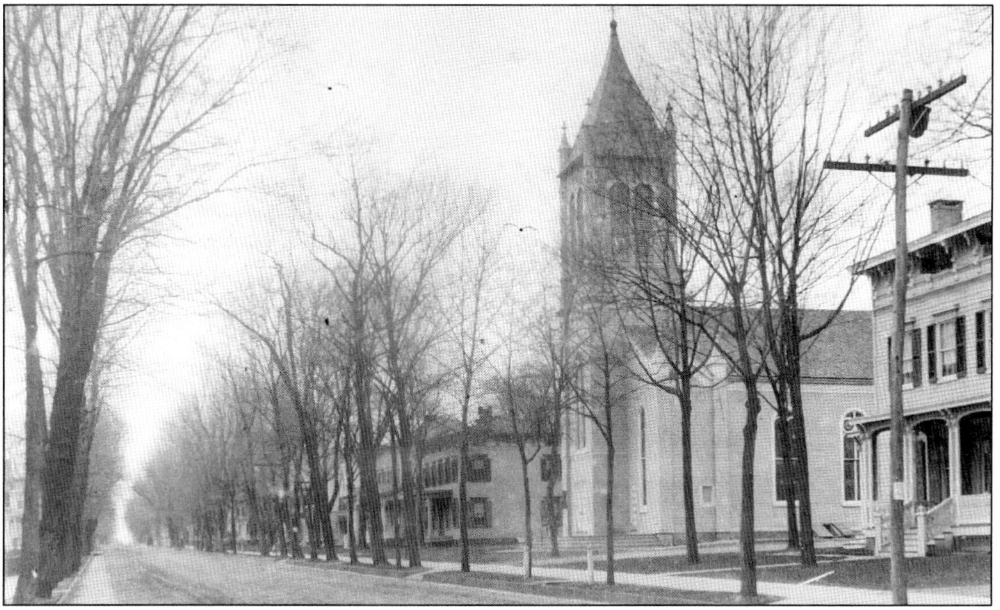

The Woodhull Building (at right) and the Reformed Church, numbers 63 and 67 West Main Street, are readily recognizable today, although the former now has only a small entry porch. A new building, however, has replaced the two houses west of the church. The card is *c.* 1912. (Collection of Michael Steinhorn.)

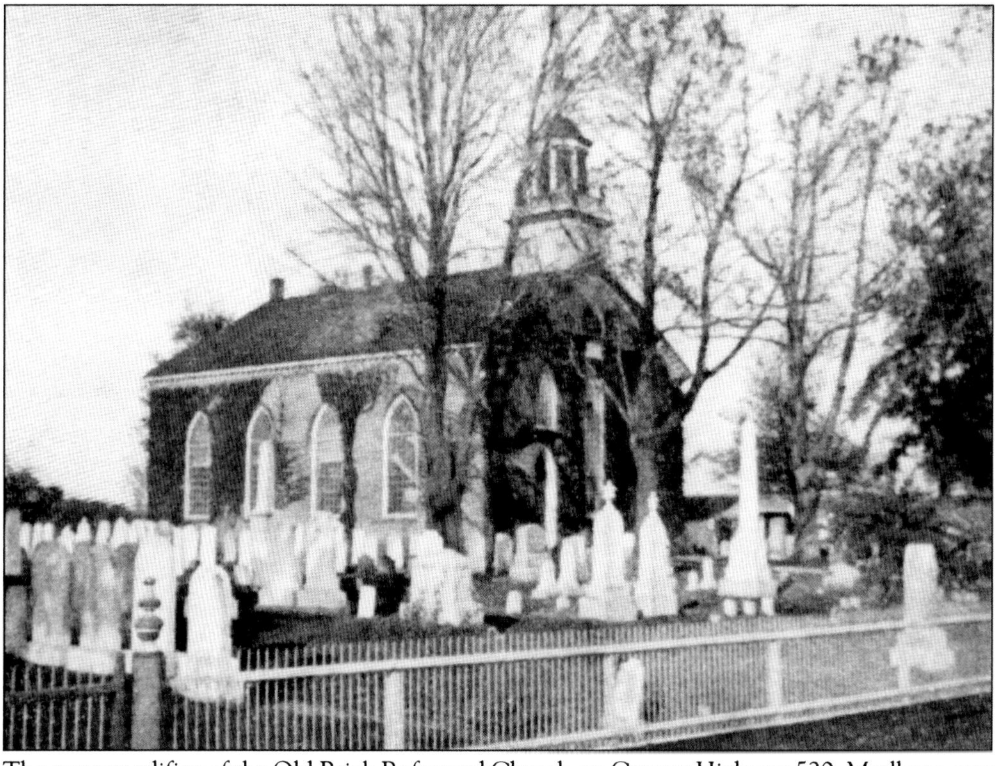

The present edifice of the Old Brick Reformed Church on County Highway 520, Marlboro, was built in 1826–27; first services were held on August 23, 1827.

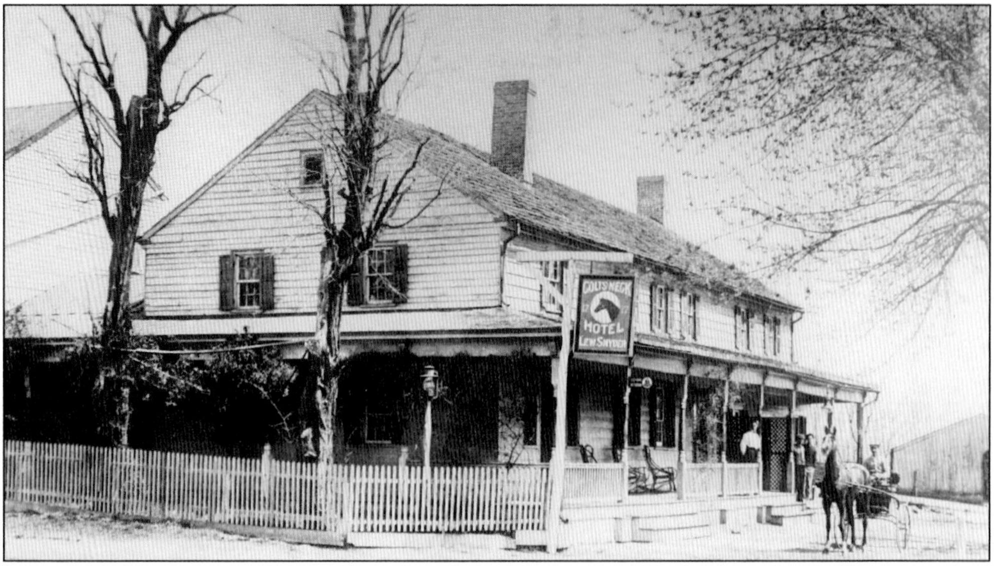

The Colts Neck Inn, tracing its origins to 1717, was a hotbed of activity in the Revolution. Once owned by Lairds, the apple jack business originated on the site in a no-longer standing building. Located on County Highway 537, west of Highway 34, one of the county's most historic names in hospitality was discarded in 1997 when the place was renamed Maxwell's. (Collection of Michael F. Bremer.)

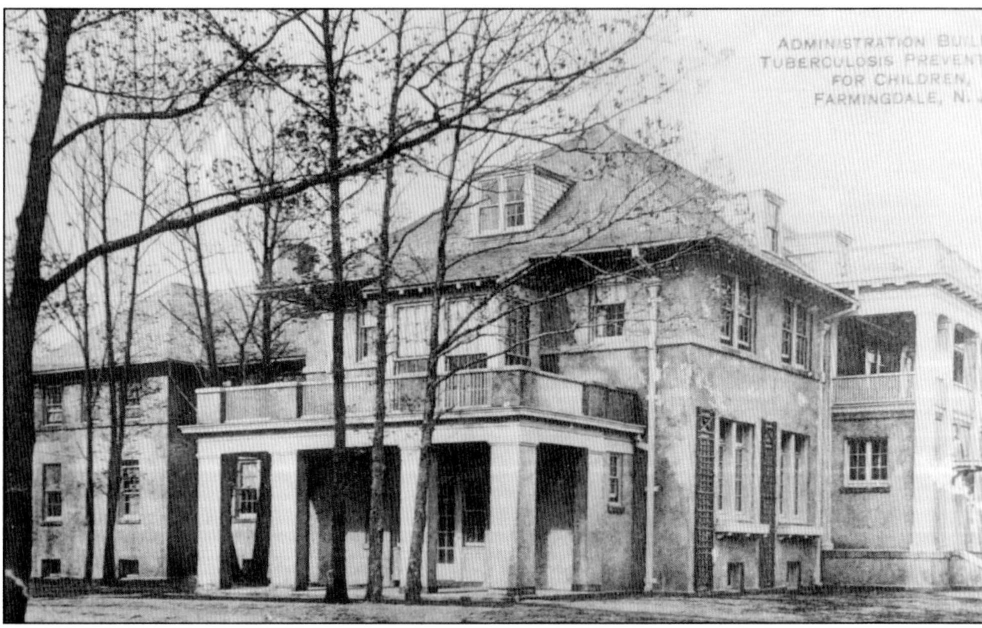

The Preventorium, an institution intended to prevent consumption in children, was built in 1912 on a 170-acre site in Howell Township, 2 miles from Farmingdale. Children slept in the open air (under roofs) in buildings with no ventilating ducts. Facilities for community life were present, including a hospital and school. The administration building is pictured when new. It was remodeled as municipal offices, its present occupancy, and is located at 251 Preventorium Road, part of a complex that combines new construction harmonious with the old buildings. (Collection of John Rhody.)

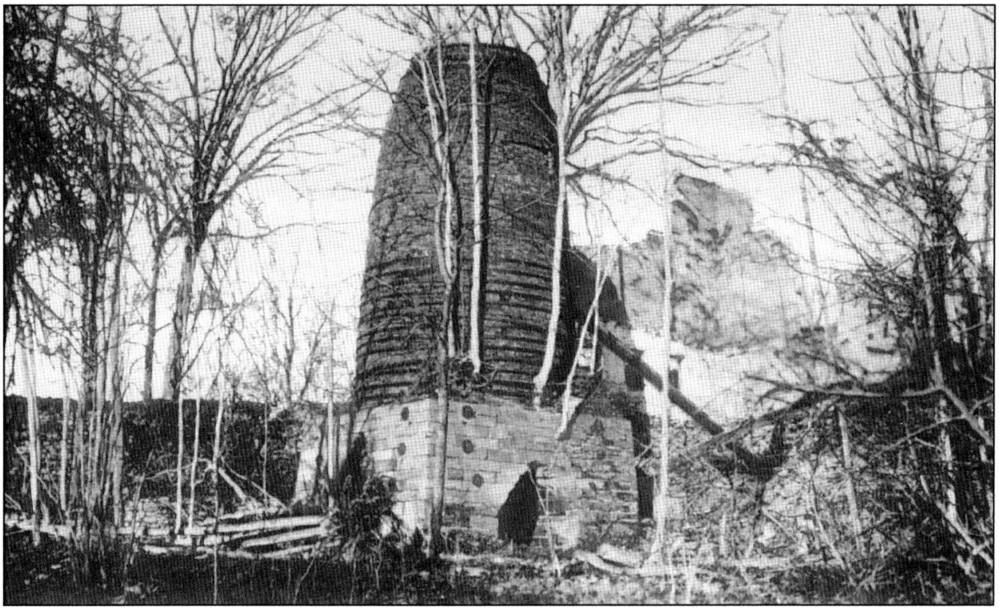

Although bog iron mining and refining preceded James P. Allaire by many years, it was his 1822 purchase and expansion of the central Monmouth County site of Howell Furnace that gave the place its greatest prosperity and notoriety. The facility was not called Allaire until after his death; it ceased operation in 1846 as other forms supplanted bog iron. The iron works and community Allaire built fell into a state of decline and was known by the turn of the century as the Deserted Village.

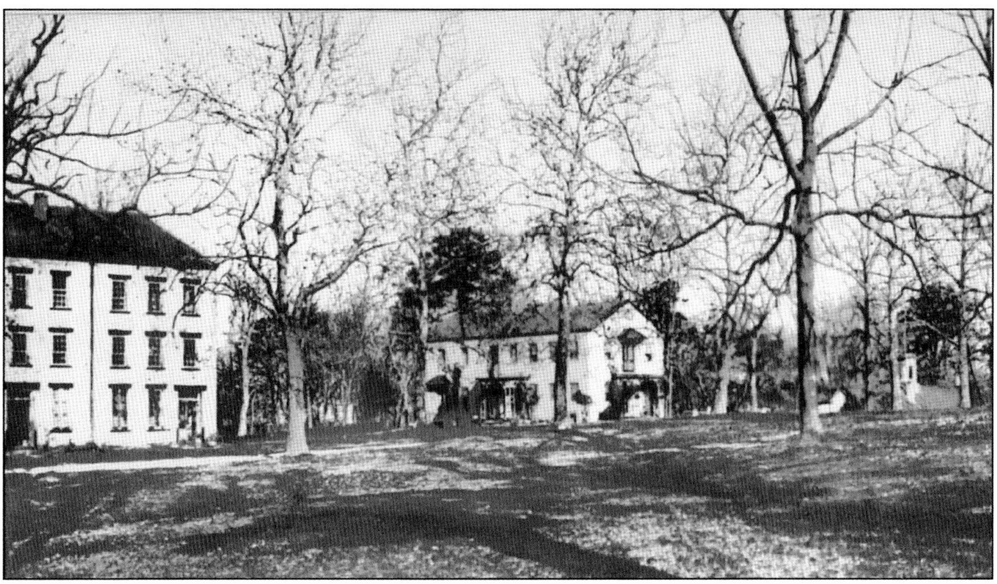

The village at Allaire, including the three-and-one-half-story general store at left, crumbled, but stood. Noted newspaper editor Arthur Brisbane purchased 5,000 acres and the village in 1907, later building a substantial country house here. He planned to transfer much of the property to the State of New Jersey prior to his death in 1936, but it was not until 1941 that his widow deeded 1,200 acres. The village is an active state park today, hosting various historical and other activities.

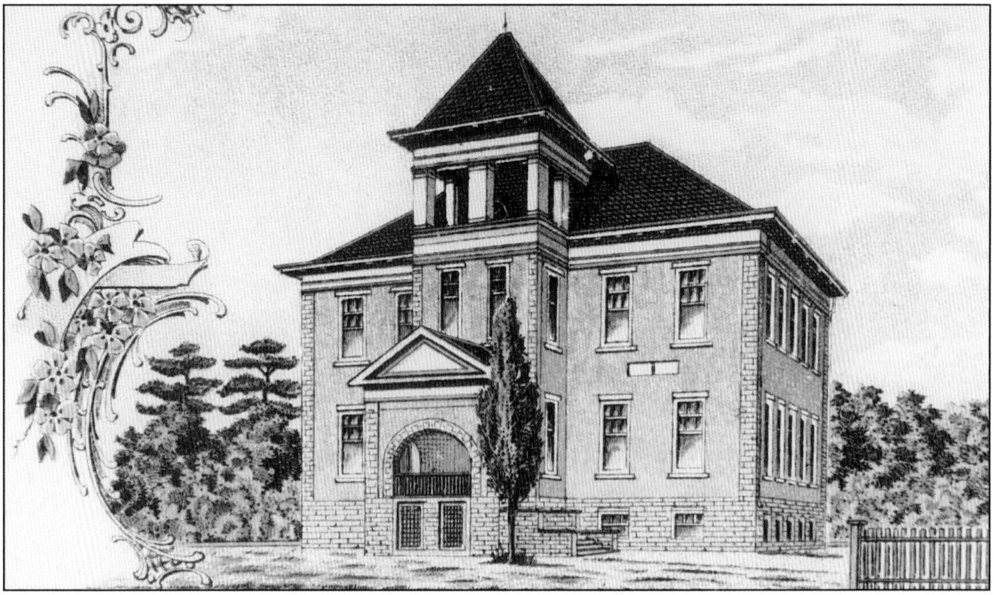

The Oakhurst elementary school was built in 1900, the substantial brick building reflecting Ocean Township's need to consolidate its one-room schools. Expansions were made later. The school served as classrooms until 1978, when it was converted to the Ocean Township Board of Education's administrative offices. The building at 163 Monmouth Road also houses the township's historical museum. This *c.* 1904 card is an unusual design, employing an artistic style rare in the United States, one typically found on German cards. (Collection of John Rhody.)

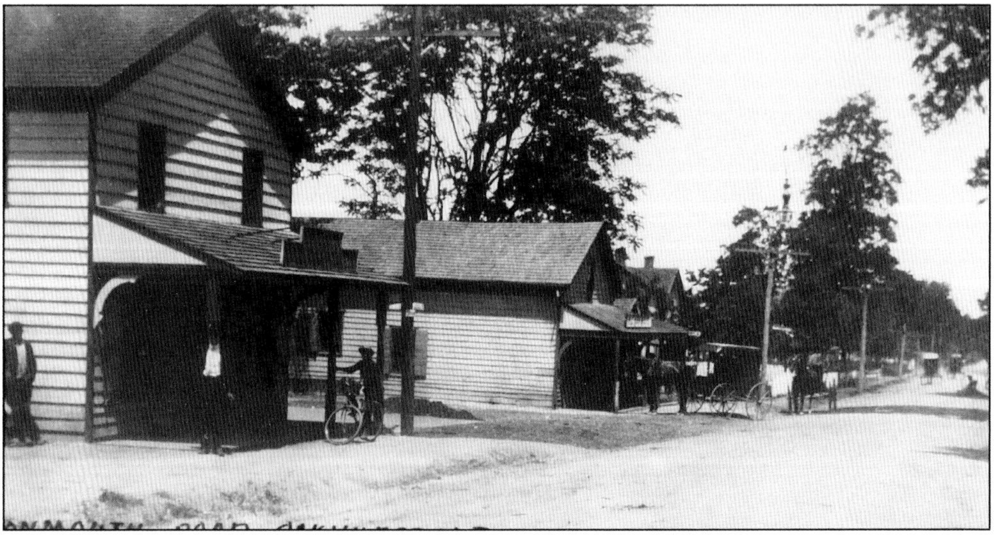

Black Bill (standing at left) occupied the rooms over the store on the east side of Monmouth Road, Oakhurst, opposite its juncture with West Park Avenue, a site unrecognizable for its change of buildings since this *c.* 1907 image was taken. The chimney in the background appears to belong to the still-standing structure at 71 Monmouth Road. (Collection of John Rhody.)

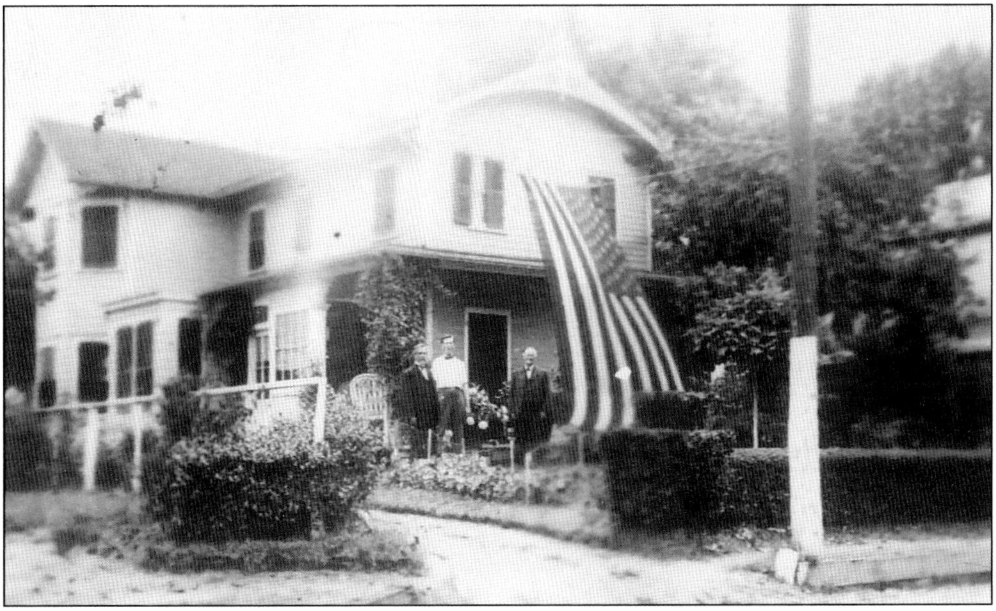

Keith Well's reacted visibly while looking through John Rhody's Oakhurst cards, expressing surprise and delight at seeing this image, his childhood home at 370 West Park Avenue. The Vernacular Victorian house still stands, its porch enclosed. This view dates from July 4, 1908, the card annotated to identify, from left to right, Charles Bowden, Isaac Bowden, and the photographer, Albert J. White. Keith's grandparents bought the house from White. Acknowledging that some experiences are priceless, John gladly gave Keith the card. (Collection of Keith Wells.)

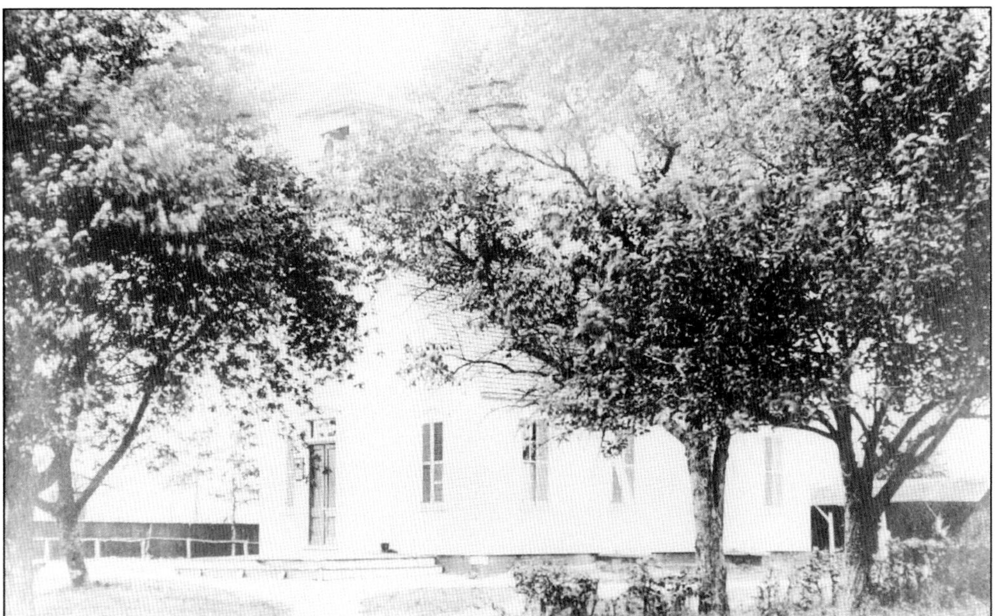

The Centerville Methodist Church, costing $ 1,400, was built in 1882 and dedicated on September 20 of that year. It is located at 1215 West Park Avenue in Wayside, Ocean Township, and has been renamed for that locality. (Collection of Glenn Vogel.)

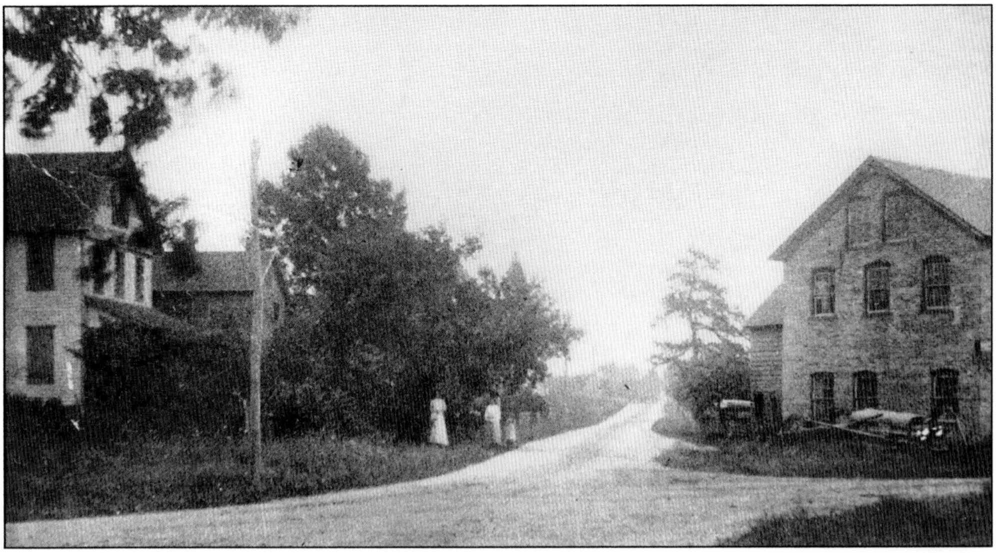

"Downtown" Allenwood is seen c. 1905 looking from Ramshorn Drive east on Atlantic Avenue. The brick building at right, formerly a blacksmith's shop, provides recognizable identity to the scene, as it is now an office. The steeple of the Allenwood church, initially a Methodist congregation, is visible in the center. The corner building at left was removed, helping sight lines at an angled intersection better suited to the era of the horse than motor traffic. (Collection of John Rhody.)

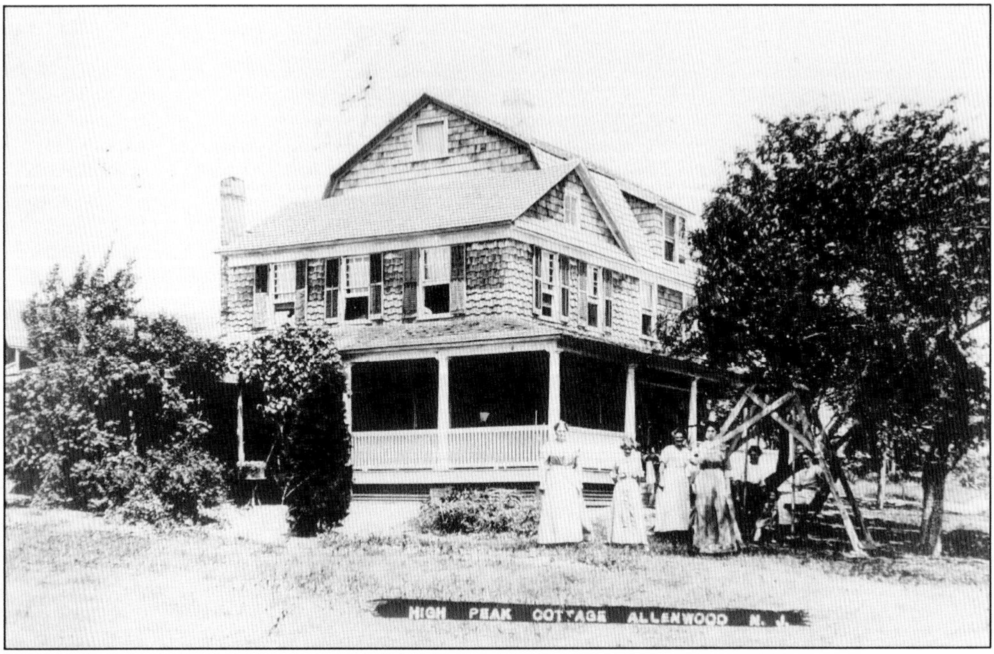

A quintet of onlookers appears ready for a relaxing time at the High Peak Cottage in Allenwood. Is the term a title or descriptive? The Merriman photo is c. 1911. (Collection of John Rhody.)

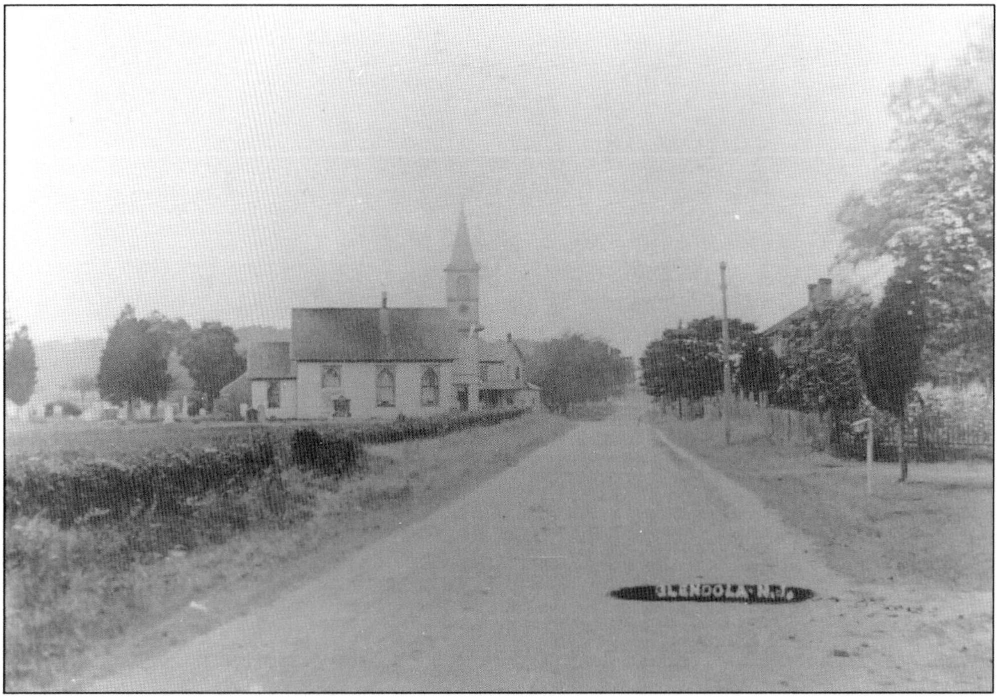

A Merriman trip to rural settlements usually included one or more views of the main road, such as this Glendola scene and the locality's prominent structures.

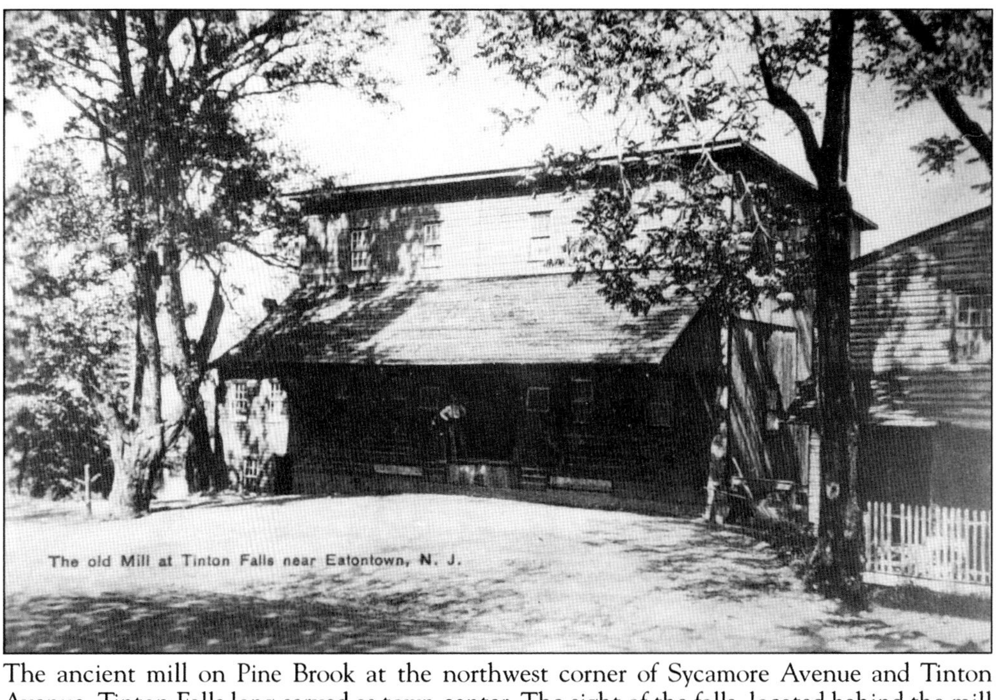

The ancient mill on Pine Brook at the northwest corner of Sycamore Avenue and Tinton Avenue, Tinton Falls long-served as town center. The sight of the falls, located behind the mill structure and not visible from the road, is worth the stop required to view them. The mill, once an artist's studio, has long-been a restaurant. (Collection of Glenn Vogel.)

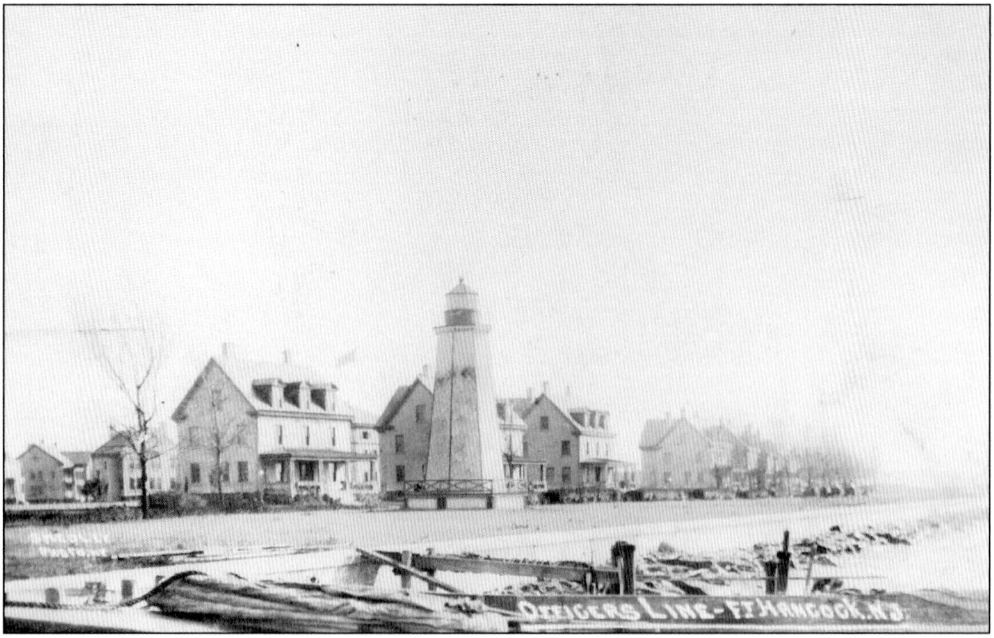

The Sandy Hook Lighthouse (see p. 115) is one of the best-known landmarks on the East Coast; the no-longer standing West Beacon is one of the Hook's more obscure structures. Marking a shipping channel, it is thought to have been removed in the early 1930s. It is seen in front of Officers Row, the line of 1898–99 Colonial Revival-design housing constructed for base personnel. The buildings are little changed; most are vacant and available for long-term lease to tenants who will restore them. The Smedley photo is *c.* 1910.

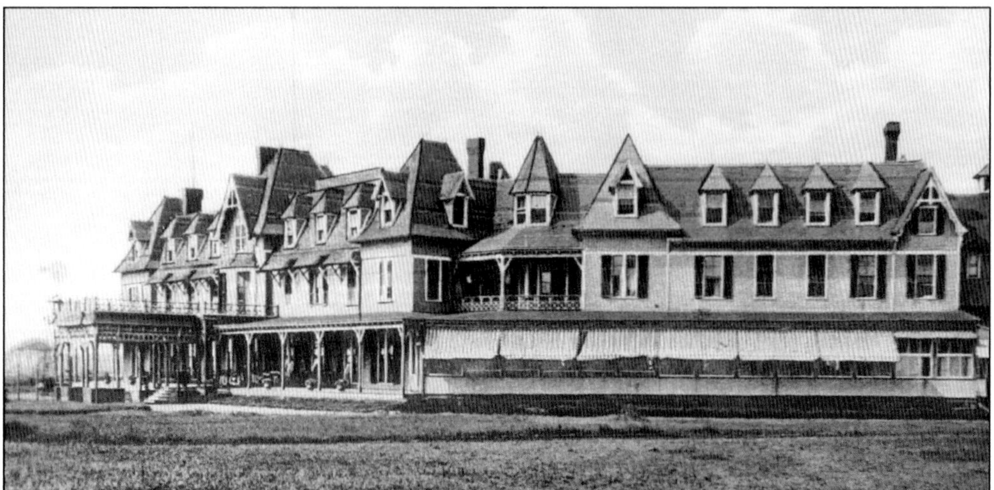

The Normandie section of Sea Bright was named for the railroad station that took the name of the Normandie-by-the-Sea Hotel, which originated as the Hotel Bellevue, believed to have been built by Lemuel Smith *c.* 1876 and renamed by its 1887 buyer, Frederick P. Earle, for a hotel he owned in New York. Earle enlarged the place, which faced both ocean and river and included a dock on the latter. The site was near the old Ocean House, the first hotel in the area, built *c.* 1840s. The Normandie was destroyed by fire in 1916. The card is *c.* 1910. (Collection of Keith Wells.)

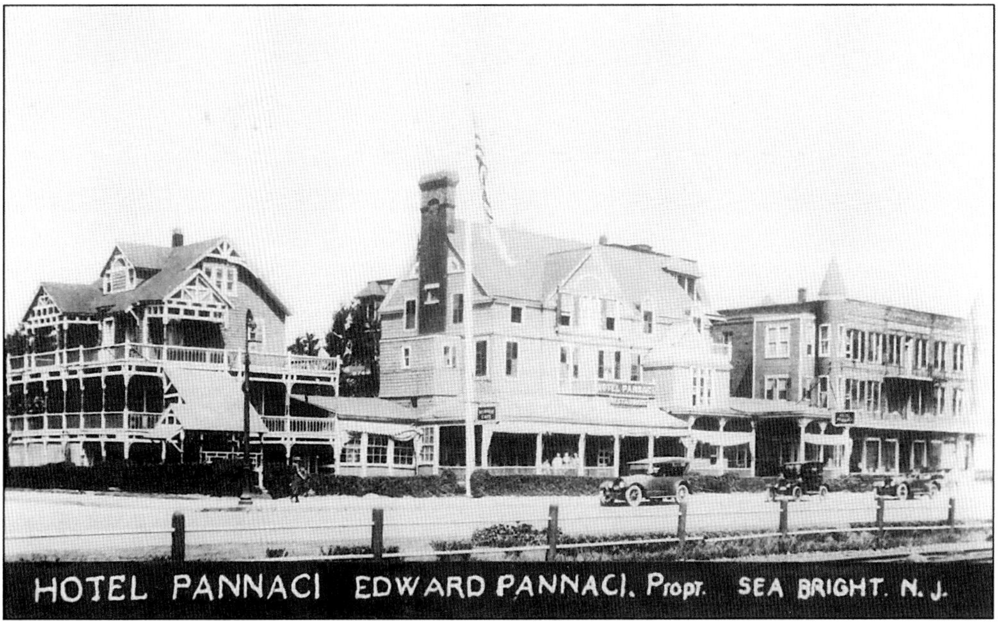

Edward Pannaci bought Harmony Hall, a hotel built in 1881 by famed pipe organ builder Hilbourne L. Roosevelt, and renamed it for himself. The Pannaci was known as the Sea Bright Inn when it was destroyed by fire on October 31, 1953, a blaze that also destroyed the Charles Manor, the Parker Real Estate Agency, and the Sea Bright Post Office, which was in the building at right. That structure was repaired, minus the turrets and top floor. The house at left, part of the Pannaci, was demolished in the 1990s.

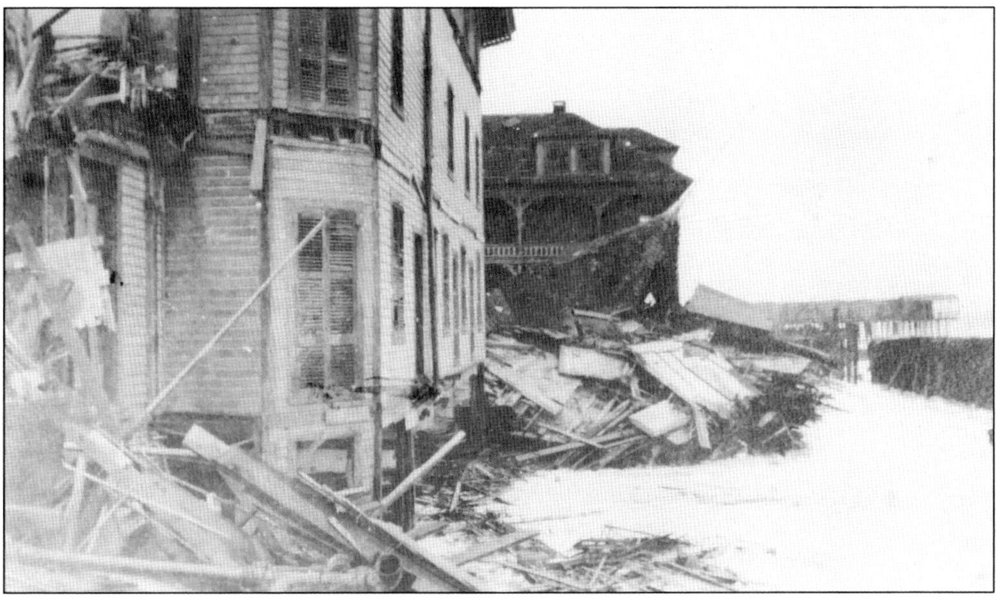

Sea Bright, a fragile barrier beach, has long been and continues to be buffeted by storms, which have claimed many structures and forced the moving of others. The storms of December 1913 and January 1914 were particularly devastating, making a total loss of the Octagon Hotel, among many others. This photo card was postmarked January 12, 1914. (Special Collections & Archives, Rutgers University Libraries.)

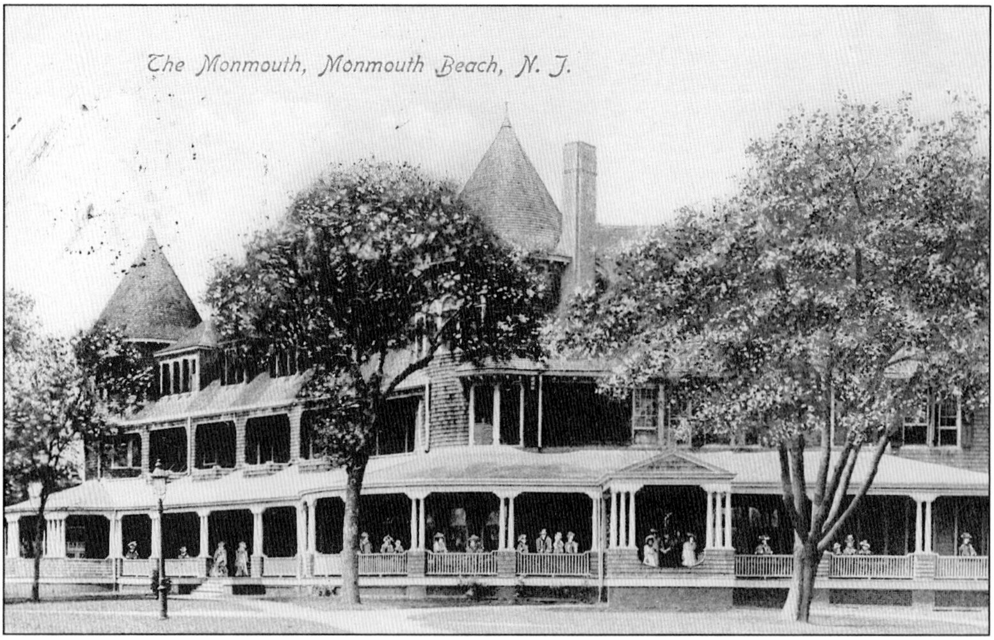

Most of the shorefront land in Monmouth Beach was owned by an association that erected a clubhouse on the Beach Road site of the old Wardell House. They also built a number of summer houses around the club and sold land to those known to them, or who were well recommended. The clubhouse, pictured *c.* 1907, later known as the Monmouth Beach Inn, was operated in conjunction with the bath house on Ocean Avenue which is now the Monmouth Beach Bath and Tennis Club. The inn was destroyed by fire in December 1929. A private house is on the site now.

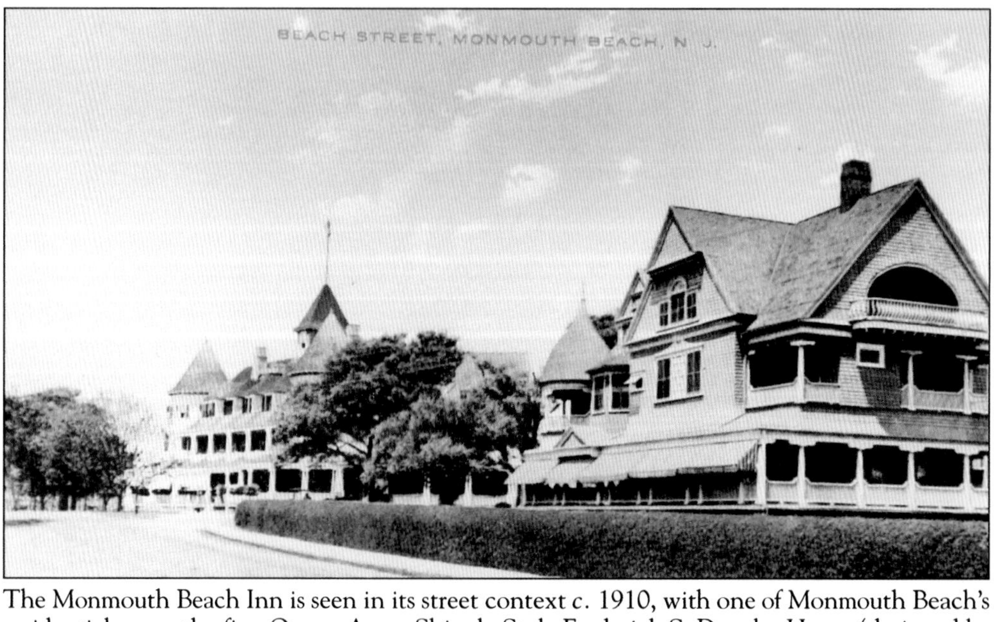

The Monmouth Beach Inn is seen in its street context *c.* 1910, with one of Monmouth Beach's residential gems, the fine Queen Anne-Shingle Style Frederick S. Douglas House (designed by Long Branch architect Allen L. Hartwell). Club Road, the circular drive of Monmouth Beach Association houses, separates the two. (Collection of John Rhody.)

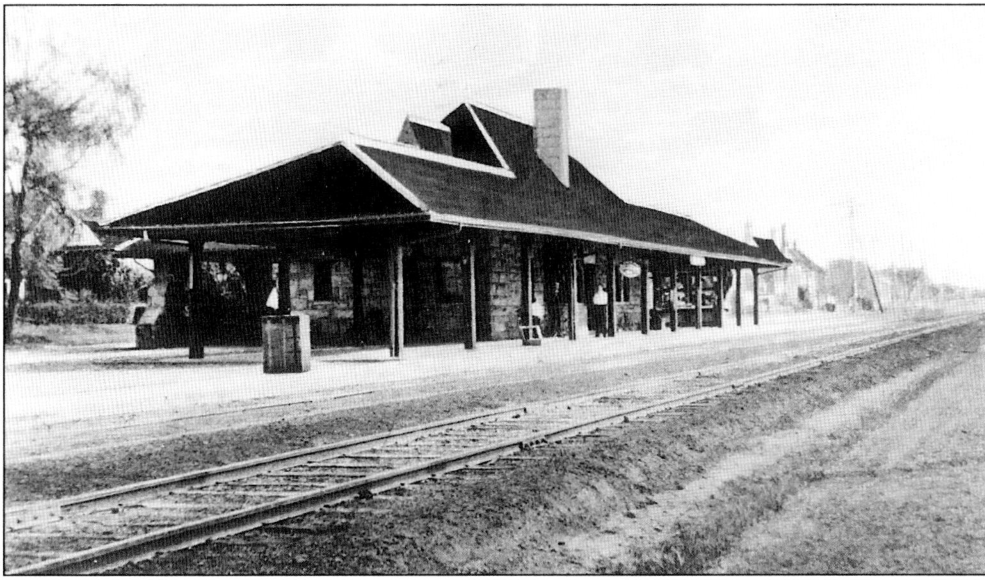

Three stations on the seashore line had Monmouth Beach in their names. This one, showing the Association-supported structure built in the 1890s, retained Monmouth Beach after the others were changed to Low Moor and Galilee. The station, located on Railroad Avenue (now Seaview), south of Beach Road, was demolished after the 1947 termination of rail service on the shore. The image is c. 1906. (Collection of Keith Wells.)

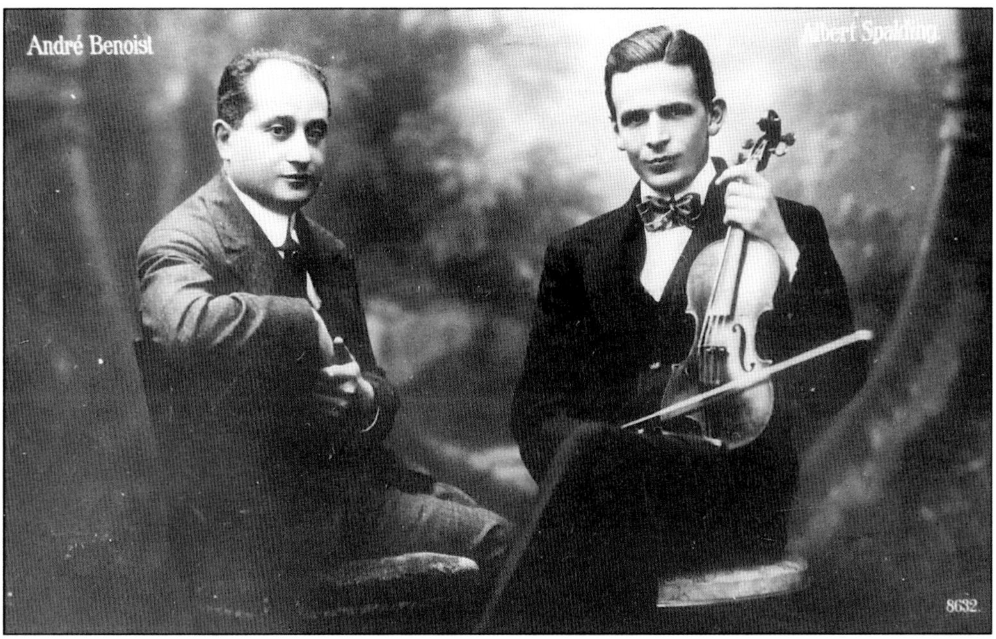

Andre Benoist, born 1880 in Paris, studied at the Conservatoire, graduated in his teens, emigrated to the United States, and chose early in his career the role of accompanist. He was attracted to Monmouth Beach with the prospect of working with Albert Spalding, who became one of America's all-time foremost violinists, and settled there. The relationship of the two was long and rewarding, with Benoist's stature rising to the top of the accompanist field. They are seen in a c. 1910 publicity postcard.

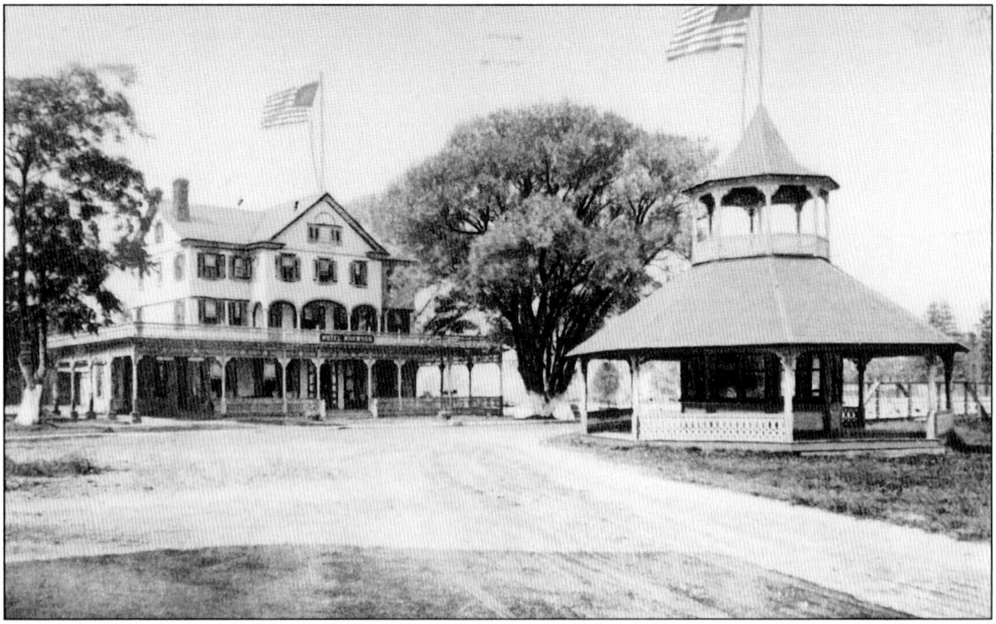

The Hotel Norwood, once the principal guest house of the resort area of Pleasure Bay, is recognizable today in its present incarnation as a restaurant if one gives it a careful look. (Collection of Keith Wells.)

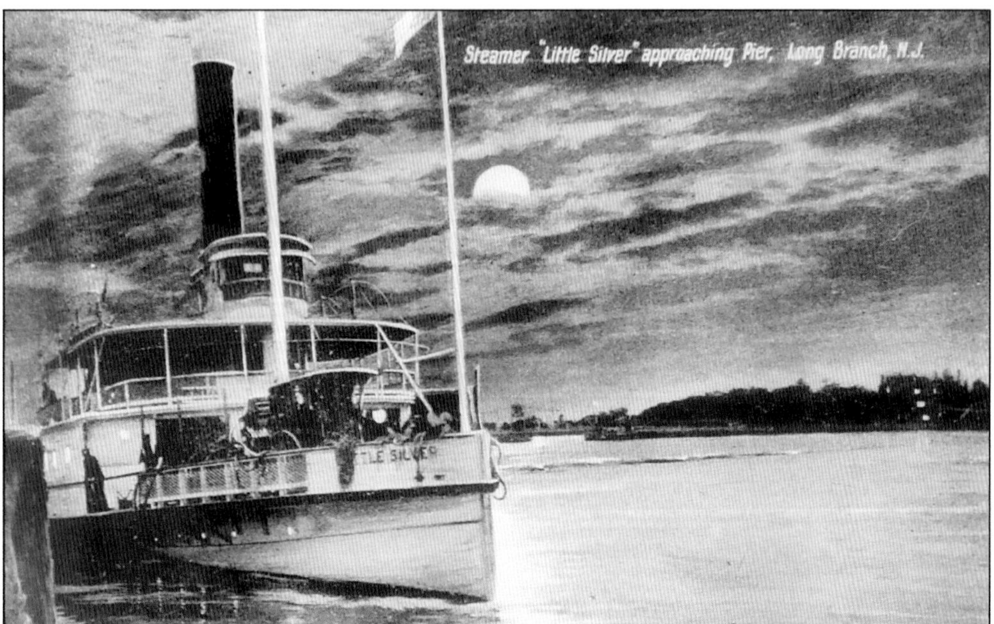

The *Little Silver*, approaching the Long Branch pier, is dramatized by the night colorization. (Collection of Keith Wells.)

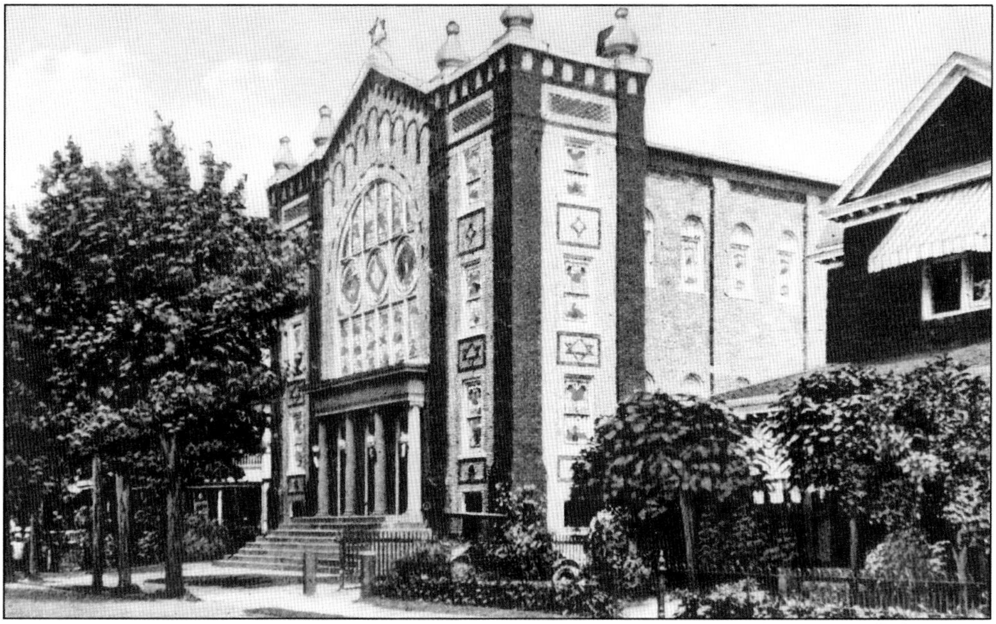

Congregation Brothers of Israel synagogue was founded in 1898, meeting on Jeffery Street, until the 1918 construction of this classically inspired brick edifice at 85 Second Avenue, Long Branch. The I. Lagowitz Hebrew Institute was later built to the north. The congregation moved to Park Avenue, Elberon, in 1977. The substantial, handsome building was vacant for some years prior to its demolition *c.* early 1990s. (Collection of Keith Wells.)

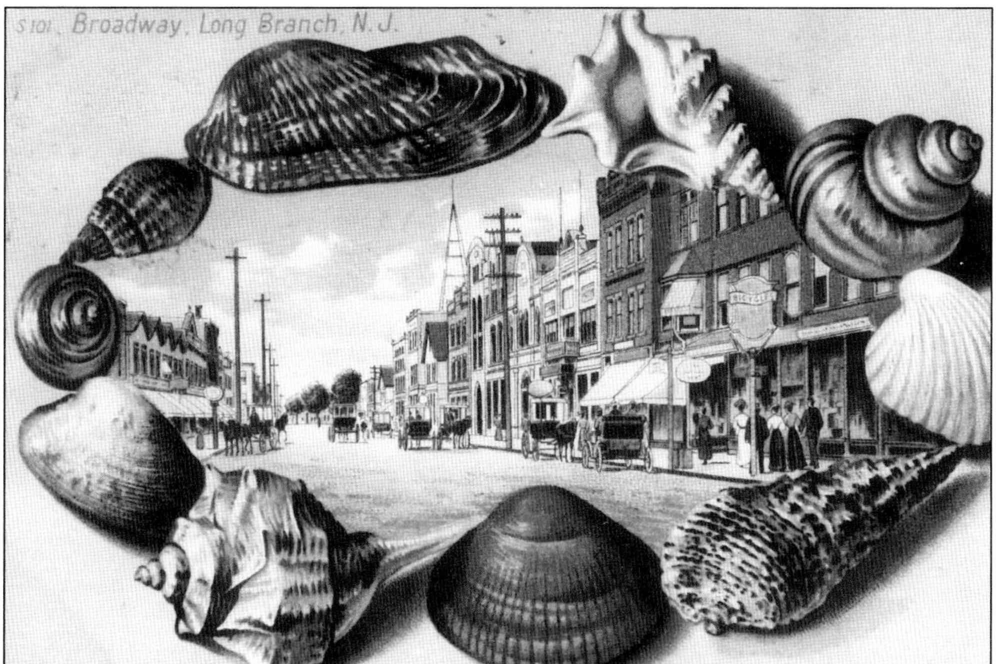

Shell borders were a popular motif for adding visual interest to shore-area cards. The stylized drawing of Broadway, Long Branch, makes up with charm what it lacks in good visual depiction of the important business street. The S. Langsgraf & Co. card is *c.* 1910.

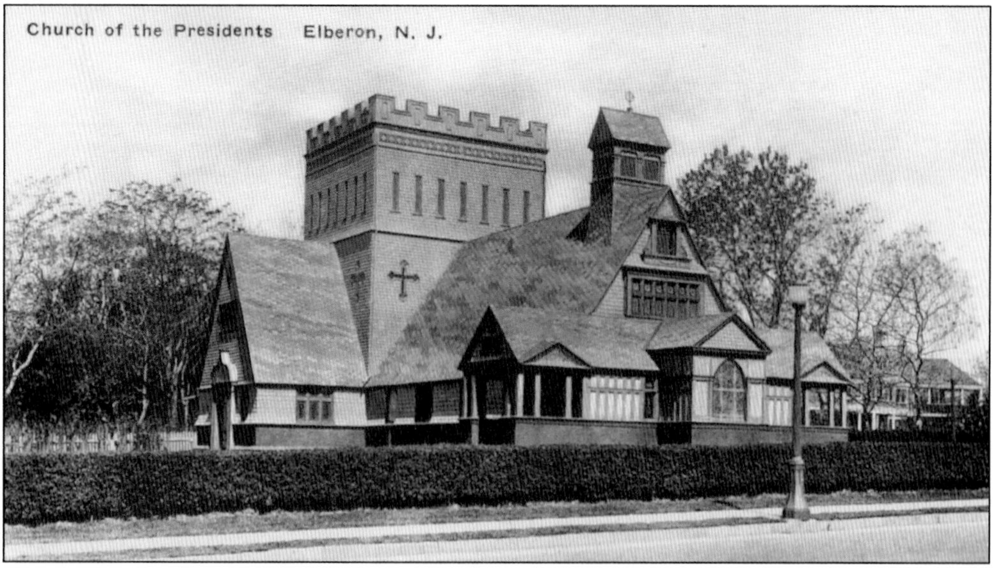

The Church of the Presidents, the popular name of the St. James Chapel, was built in 1879 so Elberon County cottagers need not travel to the Episcopalian church on Broadway. The Shingle Style edifice is the work of noted New York architects Potter and Robertson. A 15-foot addition to the chancel was made in 1893, designed by John Snook & Sons of New York, the part represented by the square tower. The church was sold for museum purposes c. 1953 and was operated for many years as the Long Branch Historical Museum at 1260 Ocean Avenue. It has been unopened for years and is in a deplorable state of decline that threatens the building's survival.

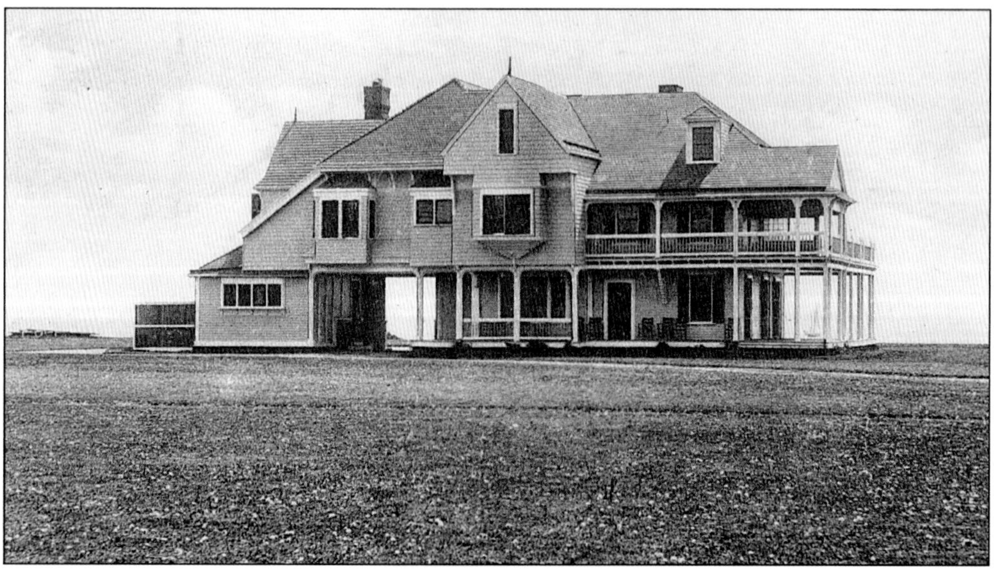

Charles Francklyn's Elberon house, designed by Charles F. McKim and built in 1876, was located on the east side of Ocean Avenue, opposite Lincoln Avenue. It was popularly known as the "Garfield Cottage" after the wounded president was brought here after being struck by an assailant's bullet in July 1881. It was hoped that exposure to the sea would aid his recovery, but he died on September 19 of that same year. The house was seriously damaged in a 1914 fire and was later demolished.

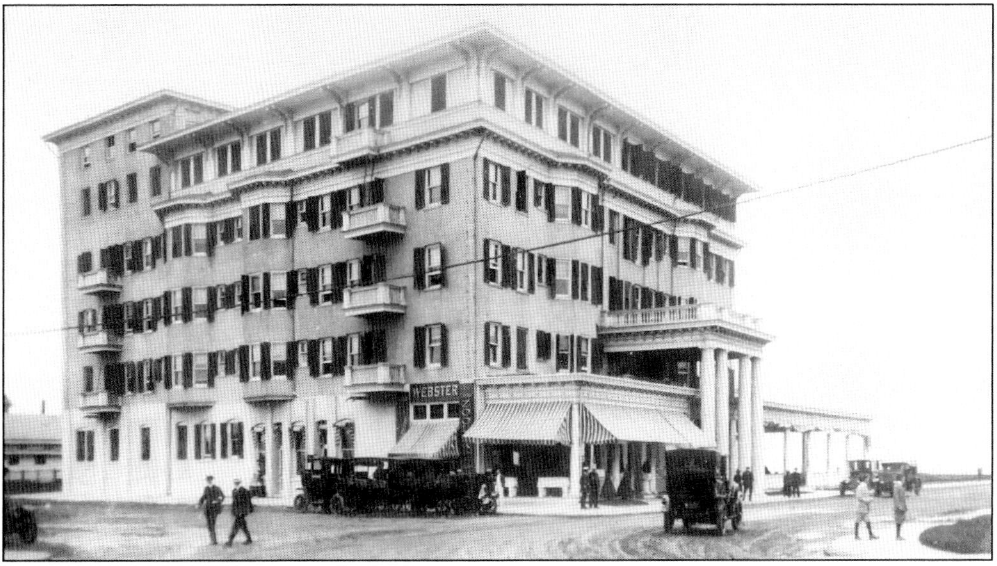

The 150-person Takanassee Hotel was built in 1906 at Ocean and Brighton Avenues in the West End section of Long Branch on the site of the demolished West End Hotel. Although it was for some years Long Branch's newest and most modern hotel, it could not survive the Depression and was demolished in the 1930s. (Collection of John Rhody.)

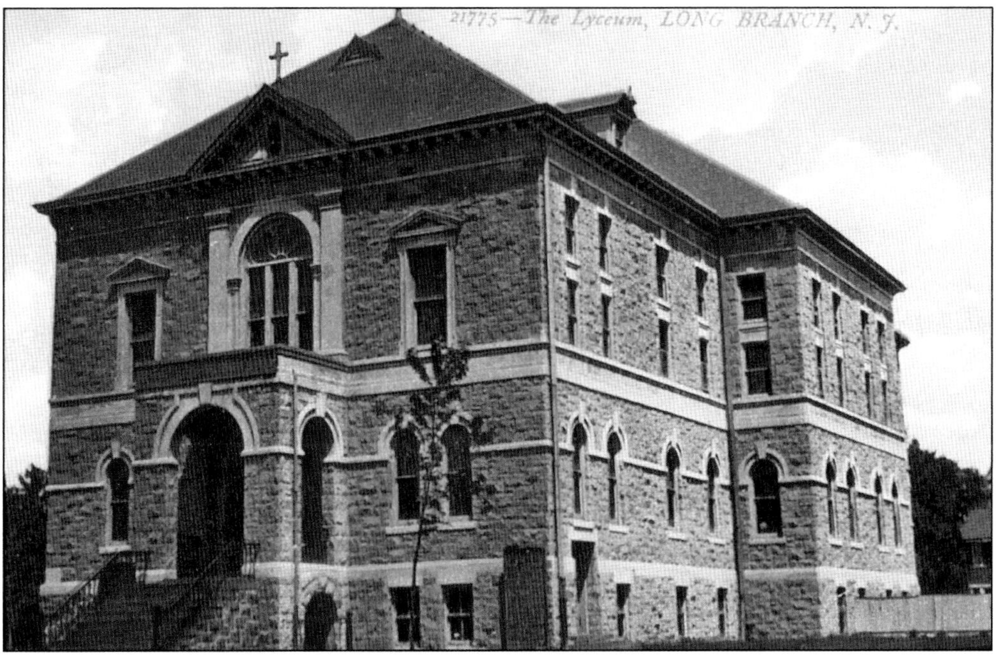

The Star of the Sea Lyceum was built at the northeast corner of Chelsea and Third Avenues in 1900, designed in the Romanesque Revival style by New Jersey's leading Catholic architect of his time, Jeremiah O'Rourke. The building, erected in addition to that church's nearby Academy, reflected the ascendency of Catholic education in the early 20th century. It served as an elementary school, while the Academy was a high school. Declining enrollment forced the Lyceum's closing after the 1985–86 academic year; the building was sold to the Long Branch Board of Education in 1994. This image is *c.* 1910.

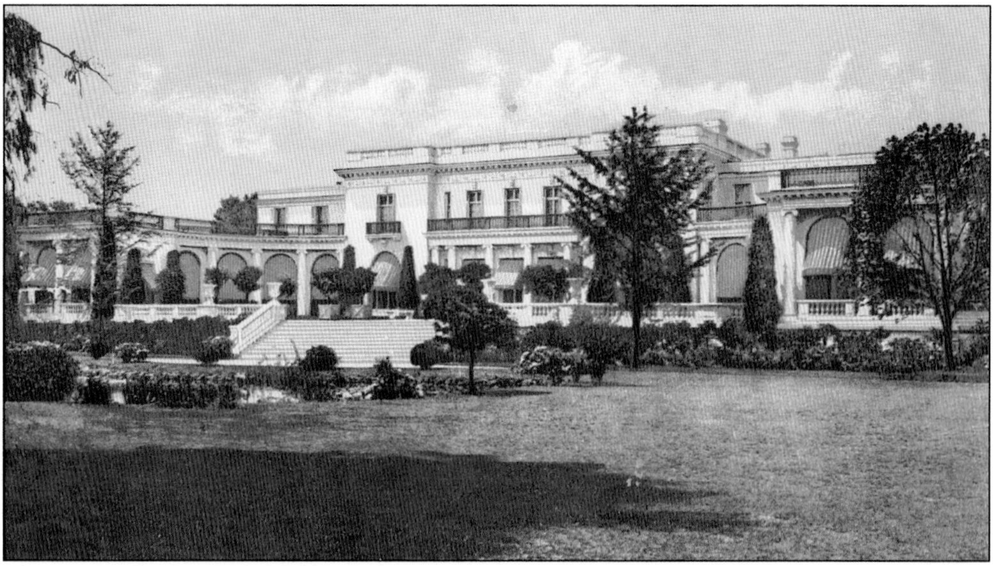

The Guggenheim family made a fortune in mining and smelting. Four of the sons of Meyer bought or built Long Branch-area mansions. Murry commissioned New York architects Carrère and Hastings to design this Neo-Classical house at Norwood and Cedar Avenues, a project that was awarded the 1906 Medal of Honor of the New York Chapter of the American Institute of Architects. Murry died in 1939; his wife, Leonie, survived until 1959. The 8-acre property was donated to the then-Monmouth College by the Murry and Leonie Guggenheim Foundation in 1960 and remodeled for use as a library, its present occupancy. This image is c. 1906.

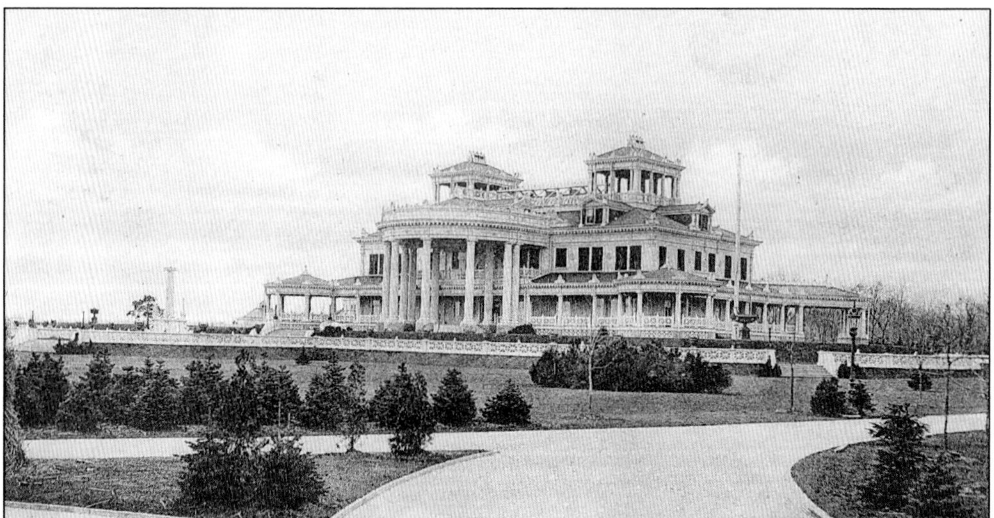

In 1903, John McCall, president of New York Life Insurance Company, built this Italian Renaissance and Neo-Classical mansion, designed by New York architect Henry G. Creiger, on a Hulick farm tract at the southwest corner of Cedar and Norwood Avenues. Joseph Greenhut bought the place following McCall's 1906 death after an insurance scandal, giving it the name Shadow Lawn, and offering it in 1915 to Woodrow Wilson for use as a summer White House. Shadow Lawn, which received national notoriety in 1916 as Wilson conducted his re-election campaign from there, was destroyed by fire in 1917 (see p. 96).

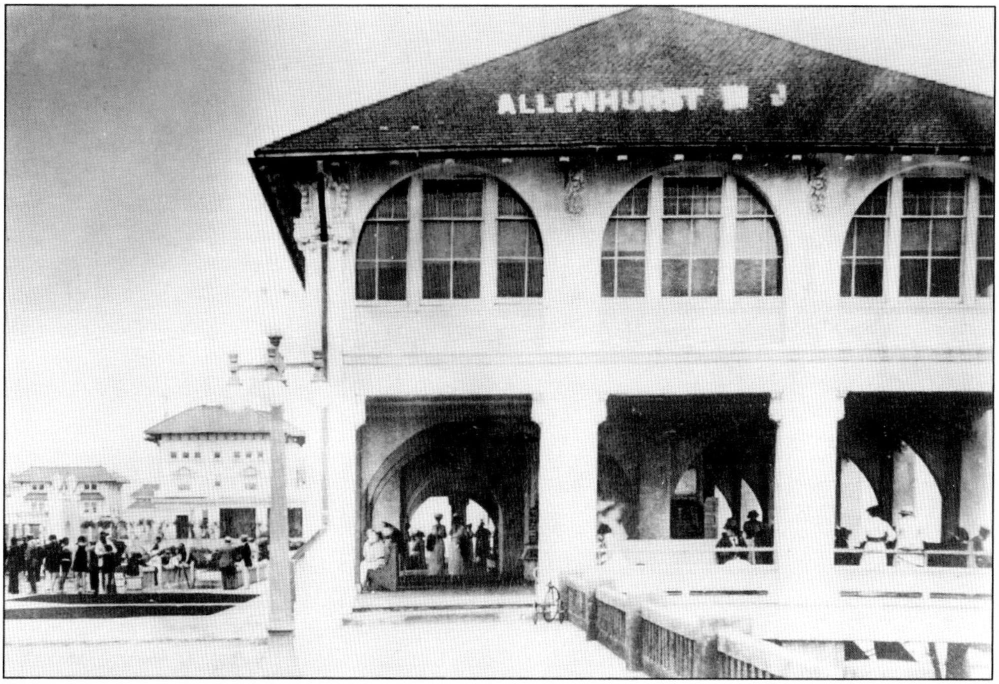

The Allenhurst Bath Club has three pools and an oceanfront beach. The *c.* 1910 image is of the second series of buildings, this reflecting a Mediterranean style, executed in stucco. More modest structures fill the Borough-owned site. (Collection of John Rhody.)

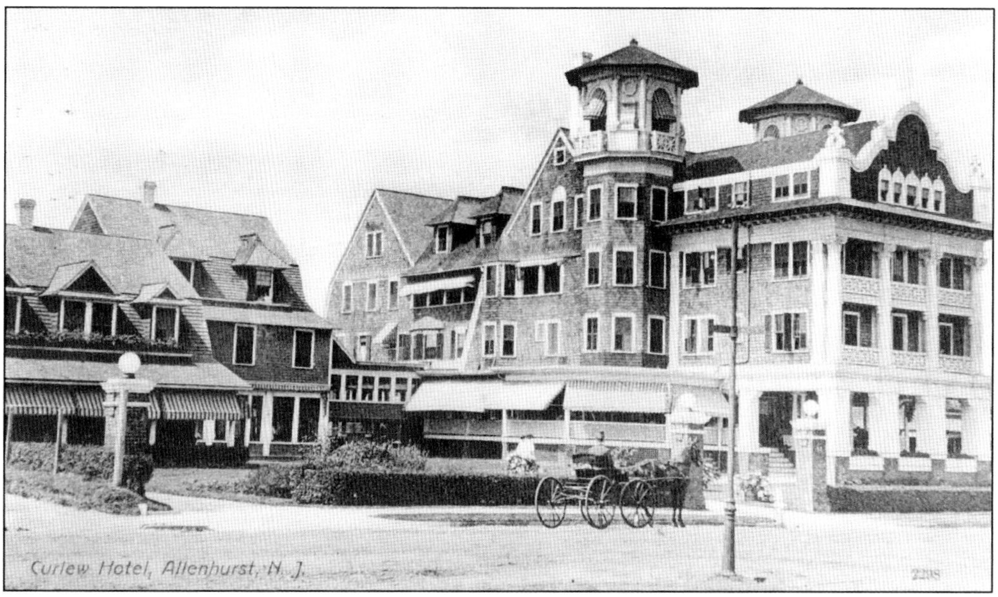

The Curlew and Cottages was a 160-person hotel in Allenhurst, likely built in the 1890s in the Shingle Style. The place was expanded in 1904 when reorganized as the Curlew Realty Company, with the addition of 14 bedrooms and two tower rooms on the front, a time when Colonial Revival motifs were incorporated. They maintained their own horse-driven coach, and had a richly decorated interior, which included amenities such as a billiard room. The hotel was destroyed by fire in 1931.

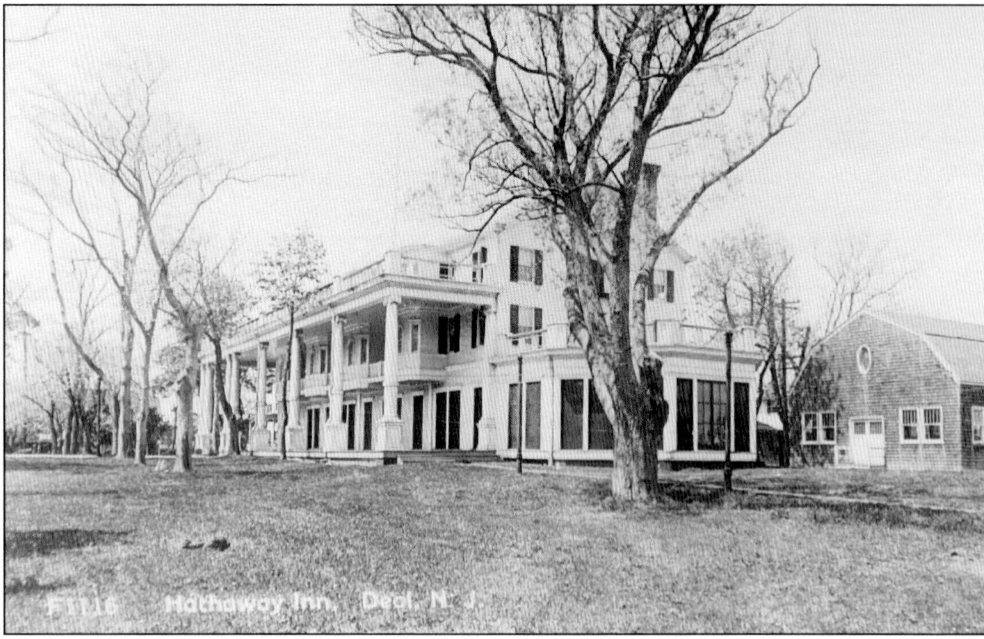

The Hathaway House began as a boarding house built by Thomas C. Borden in 1837. It was purchased by William Hathaway Sr. *c.* 1855 and expanded. Later owners continued to enlarge Deal's famed resort, changing the name to Hathaway Inn. The place appeared to have a large Colonial Revival porch when published by Garraway *c.* 1911. (Collection of John Rhody.)

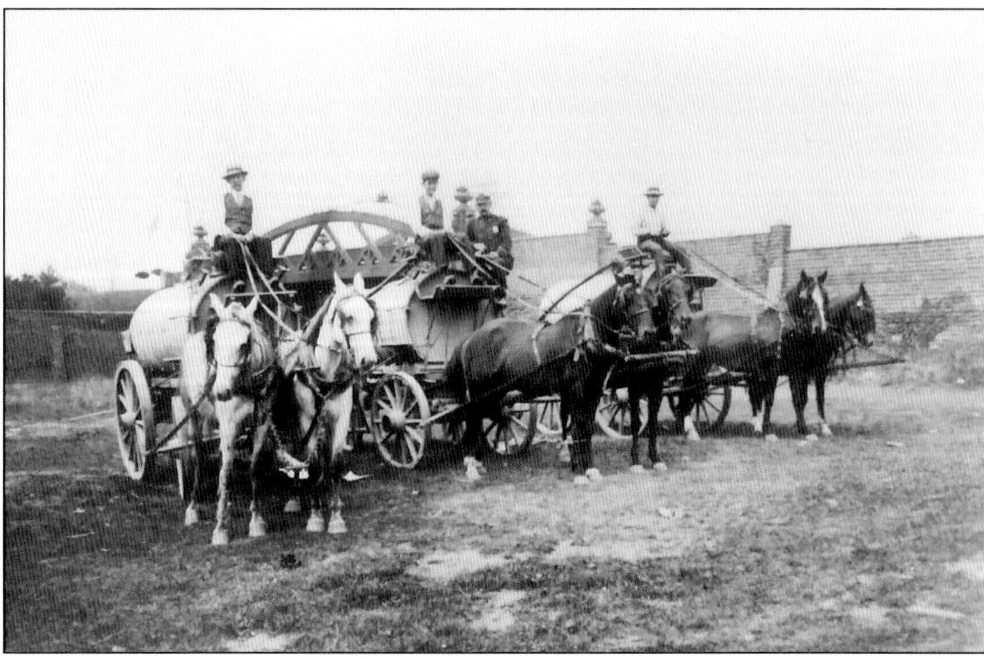

The Deal Harbor Estates water sprinkler wagons are seen on Atlantic Avenue, east of the railroad tracks, looking west. Police Chief Frank Rogers is on the center wagon. (Collection of Robert W. Speck.)

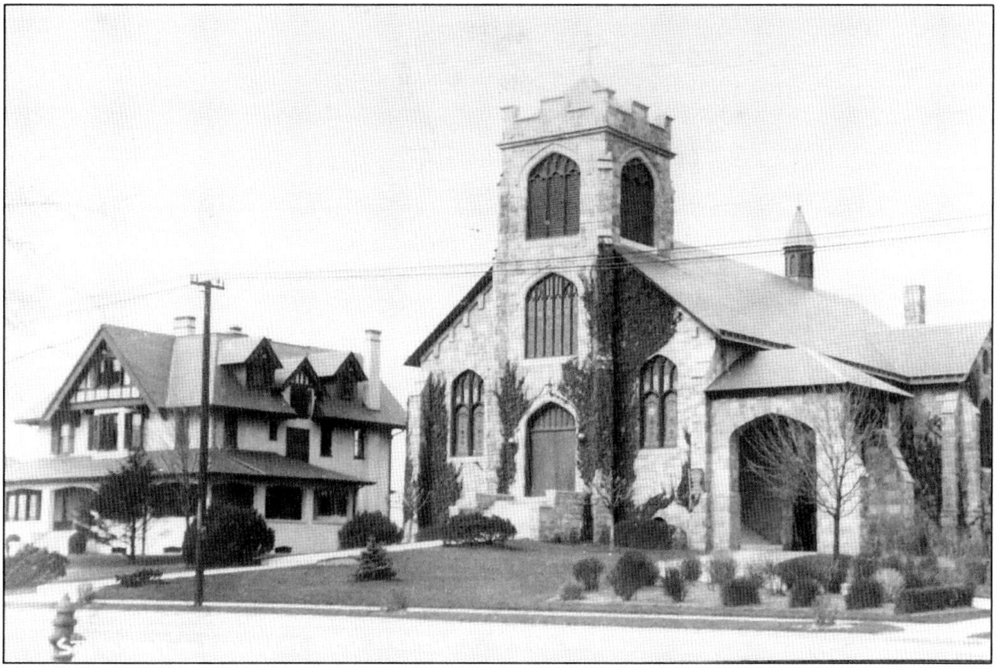

St. Mary of the Assumption Roman Catholic Church, 46 Richmond Avenue, Deal, was built in 1905 following years of worship under a tent. The Gothic Revival edifice is little changed; a statue of Mary was installed on the southern section of the front lawn. (Collection of John Rhody.)

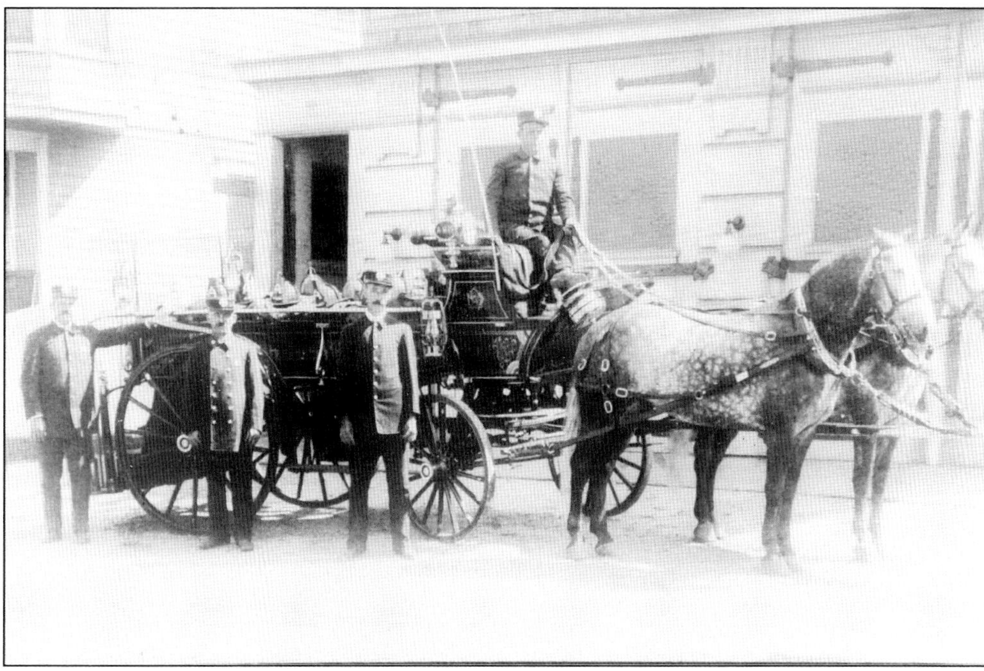

Four firemen in dress uniform and the horse-drawn apparatus of the Allenhurst Fire Company are seen in 1907. The company, founded in 1898, replacing protection afforded by the Asbury Park Fire Department, is celebrating its centennial this year.(Collection of John Rhody.)

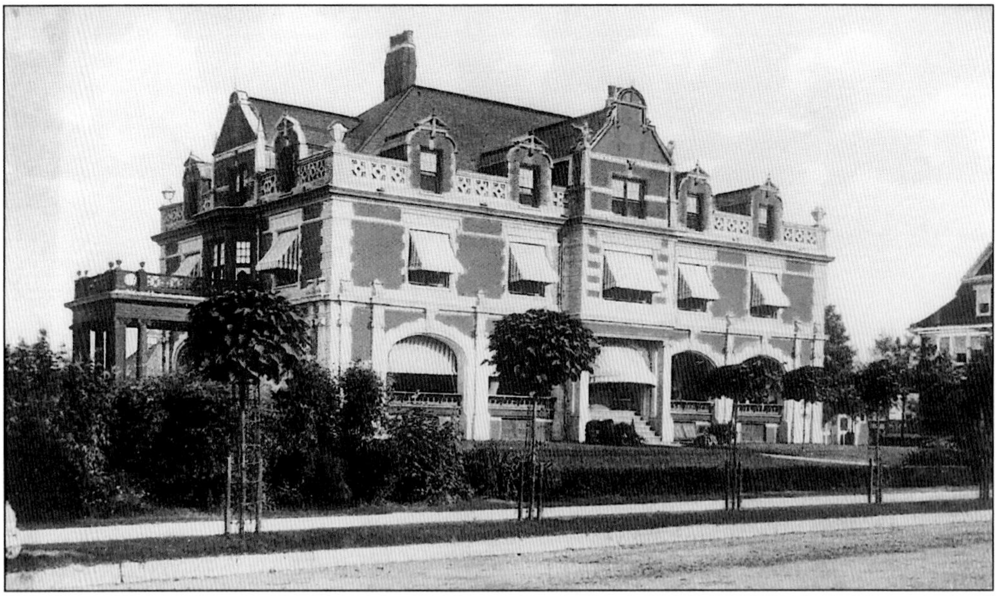

The Beaux Arts Peter Fisher house in Allenhurst, built *c.* 1902 at the southeast corner of Norwood and Allen Avenues, was designed by George K. Thompson. The owner was a principal of the well-known Sayre & Fisher brick works. The building was used by the Signal Corps during World War II, but was demolished *c.* 1950s. This image is *c.* 1906. (Collection of Robert W. Speck.)

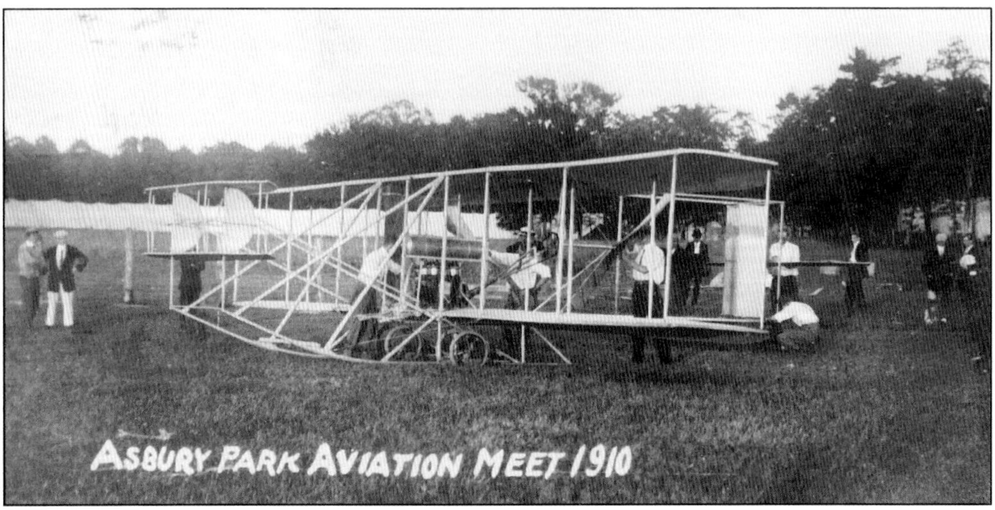

The "Asbury Park" air meet, held in a temporary field, part of which is now parkland in Interlaken, was an event of national significance in aviation's early days. The Wright Brothers' company was in charge of flying activities. Large crowds paid what was then substantial admission to fund major prizes. A canvas fence stretched around the field to shield events from the eyes of the unpaying curious. The sender of this card was inside the event, writing, "I saw this one knock over a fence yesterday." (Collection of John Rhody.)

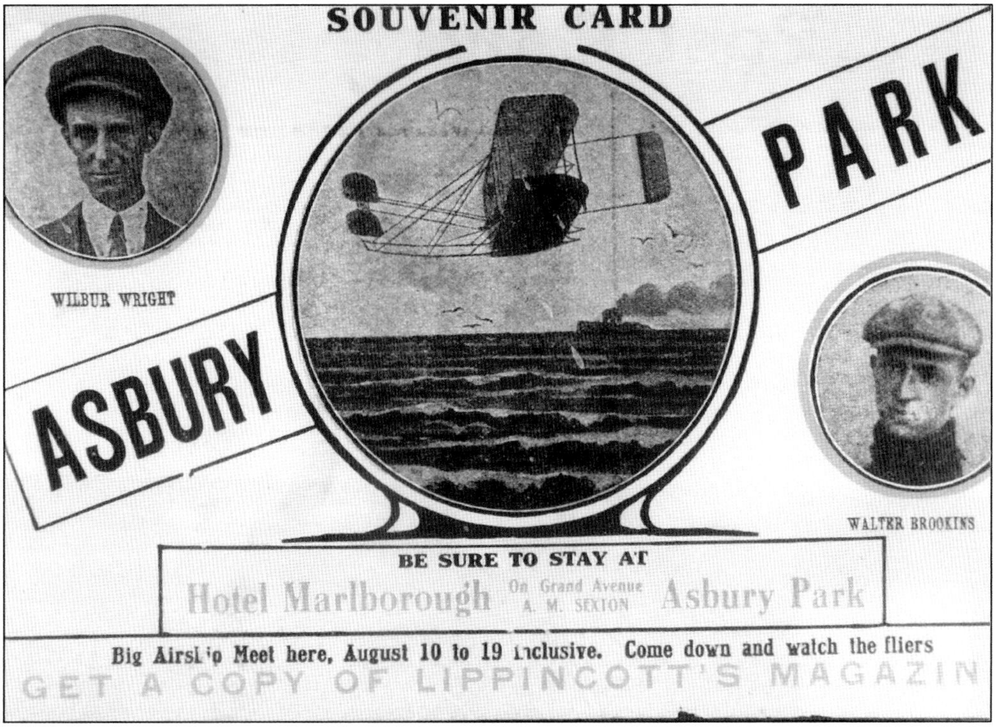

The Wrights did not fly, but had five noted pilots (before aviators were called that) under contract, including Walter Brookings, the first to take off on August 10, 1910. He crashed, injuring himself and 11 spectators. Not all participants were as fortunate. Benny Prinz, a parachutist, was killed. Poor weather extended the meet to August 27, and presumably hotel registrations, proving it is an ill wind, indeed, that doesn't blow someone some good. (Collection of John Rhody.)

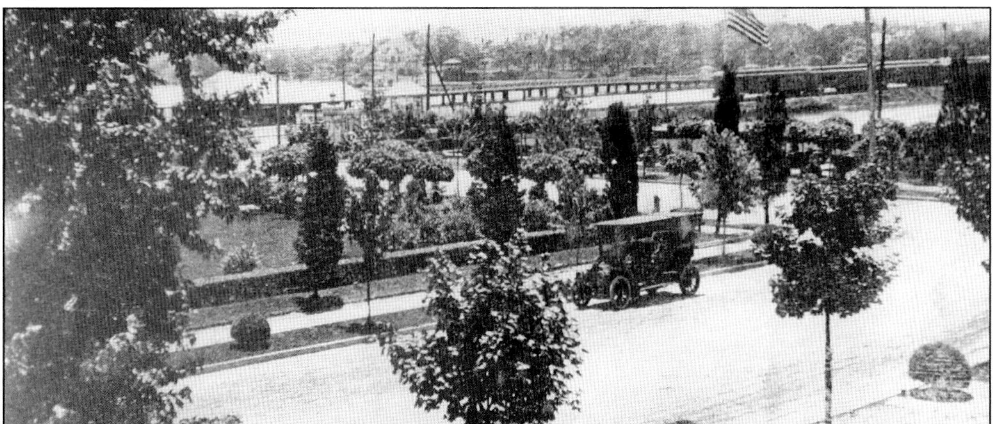

Dr. and Mrs. Francis Wells of Boston purchased 364 acres around Deal Lake in 1888, calling their estate Interlaken Farm in fond recollection of Interlaken, Switzerland, a small town they enjoyed that was also surrounded by water. Their plans to make a restricted summer home colony were in time controlled by a real estate developer; the property in 1922 was incorporated into the Borough of Interlaken. The back of this card indicated special inducements to purchase lots during the aviation meet would be made. (Collection of Glenn Vogel.)

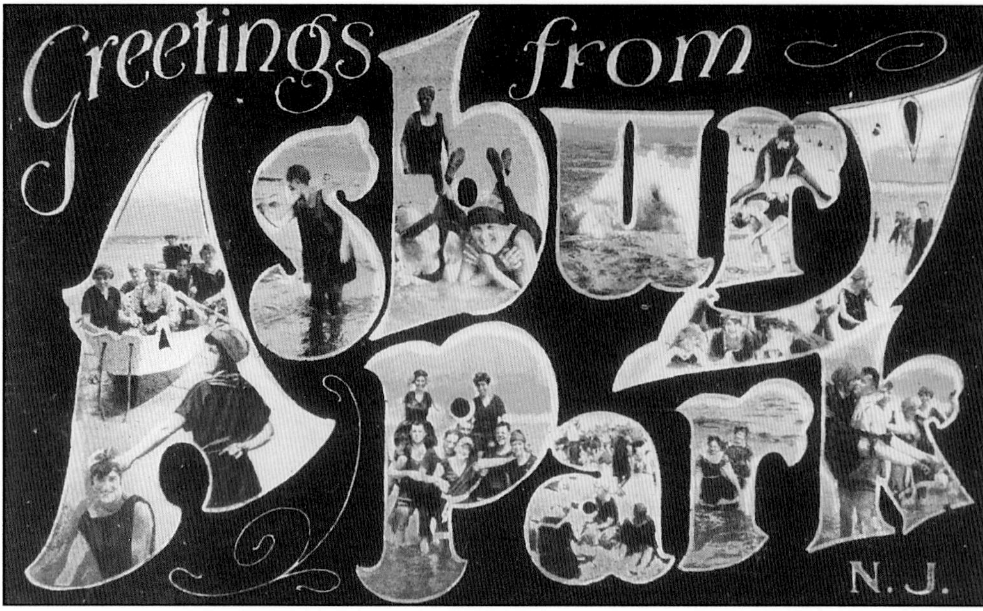

This "large letter"-type card is an early example of a genre that attained peak circulation during the linen era. The images within these letters are prosaic beach views, while later large letter cards typically showed scenes from the subject place within the letters. A later Asbury Park large letter example attained wide-spread circulation on the Bruce Springsteen record album jacket *Greetings from Asbury Park* and was sold as a postcard into the early 1980s.

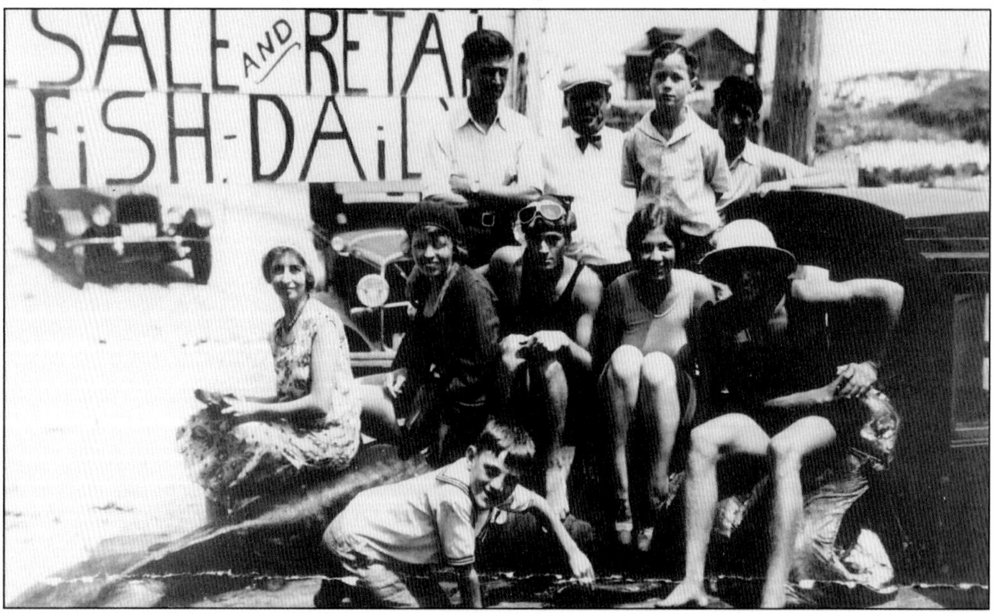

The site is somewhere on the New Jersey coast, while the subjects sure are having a good time, albeit in an unconventional way. The sign indicates they are in fish country, but why are they sitting on what appears to be a shark? By the time the card had been placed in the mail with the message "We set-up our own camp," the sender had reached Farmingdale, but the image reflects an instant and personalized greeting-souvenir from presumably the Monmouth coast. (Photo courtesy of Glenn Vogel.)

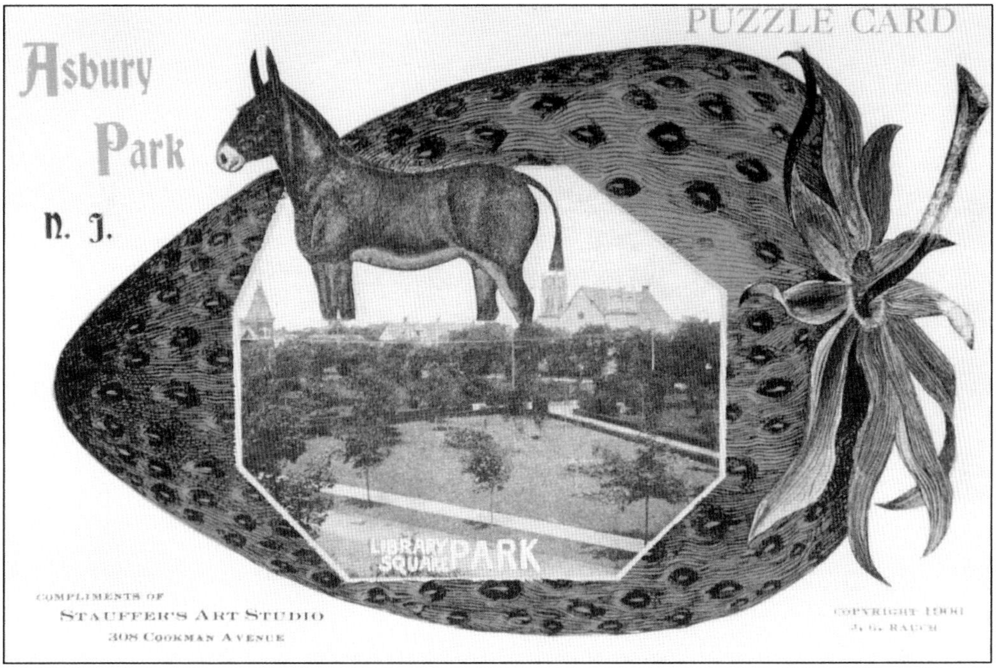

"What jackass made this card?", queried Barbara, the author's wife, on being shown the last card to be selected for the book, adding, "I don't get it." The card is clearly marked a puzzle, but there appears no connection with an Asbury Park street scene, a donkey, and a strawberry. Learned postcard observers did not get it either. Perhaps the publisher, James G. Rauch of Slatington, PA, intended timeless speculation. One wonders if the same puzzle appeared elsewhere. The author invites answers; his address is on p. 8. (Photo courtesy of Glenn Vogel.)

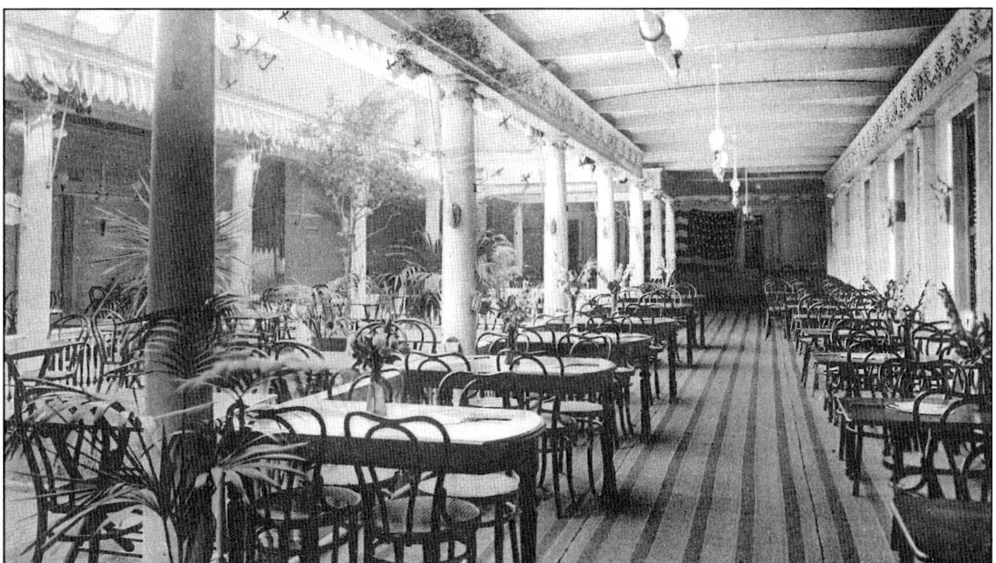

This c. 1907 Rotograph card of Day's Ice Cream Garden is described as Asbury Park, a no-longer extant store. However, a near-replica exists at 47 Olin Street, Ocean Grove, still looking like this ancient image. A singular, old-style shop possesses charm not found in the standardized chains, adding cachet to a refreshment stop there following any Ocean Grove event.

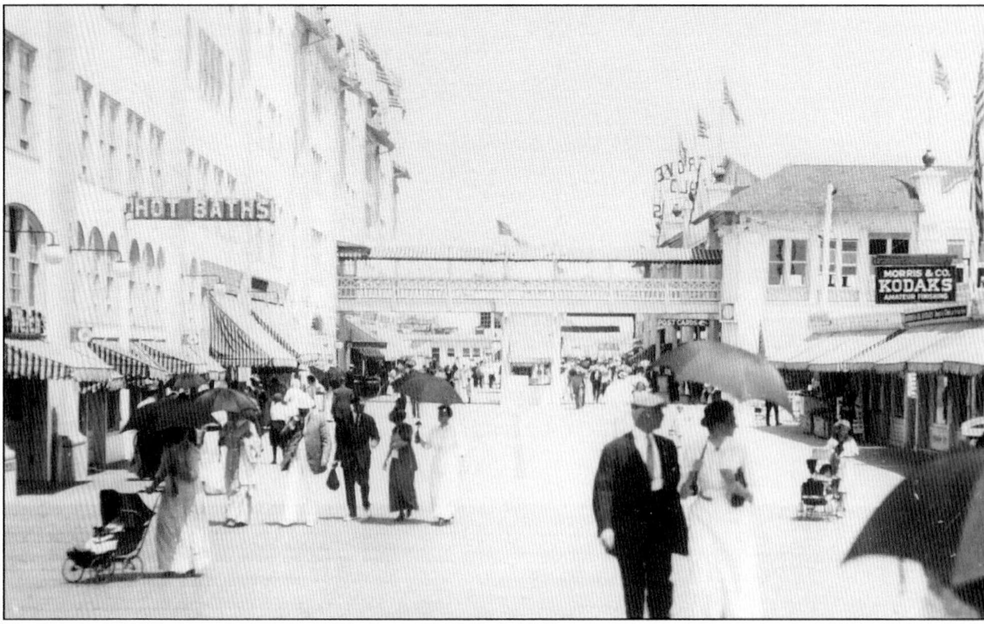

The North End Hotel marked Ocean Grove's boardwalk separation from Asbury Park; Wesley Lake provides the physical separation. The interior of the hotel was burned-out in 1924, while the five-story stucco-clad building was destroyed by a 1938 blaze. A rebuilt hotel occupied the spot until demolished in 1978. This card is *c.* 1915. (Collection of John Rhody.)

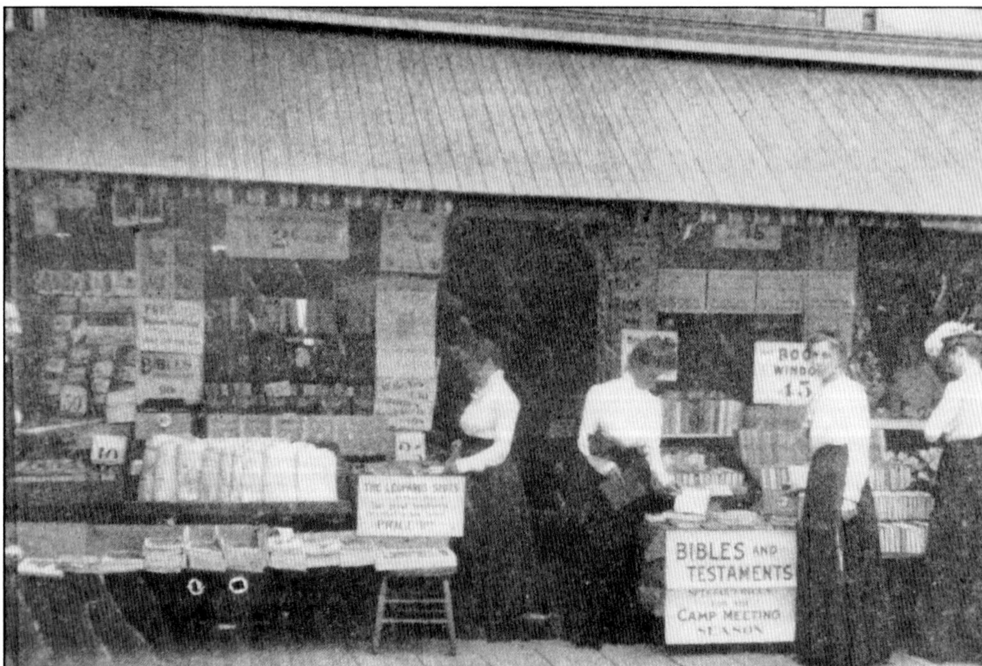

Ross' was part of the North End Pavilion; their sign reflects the main flow of the printed word in Ocean Grove—spiritual texts and tracts. Ross' is long-gone, but the current Ocean Grove seller of new books remains a religious shop. This example was postmarked 1904. (Collection of John Rhody.)

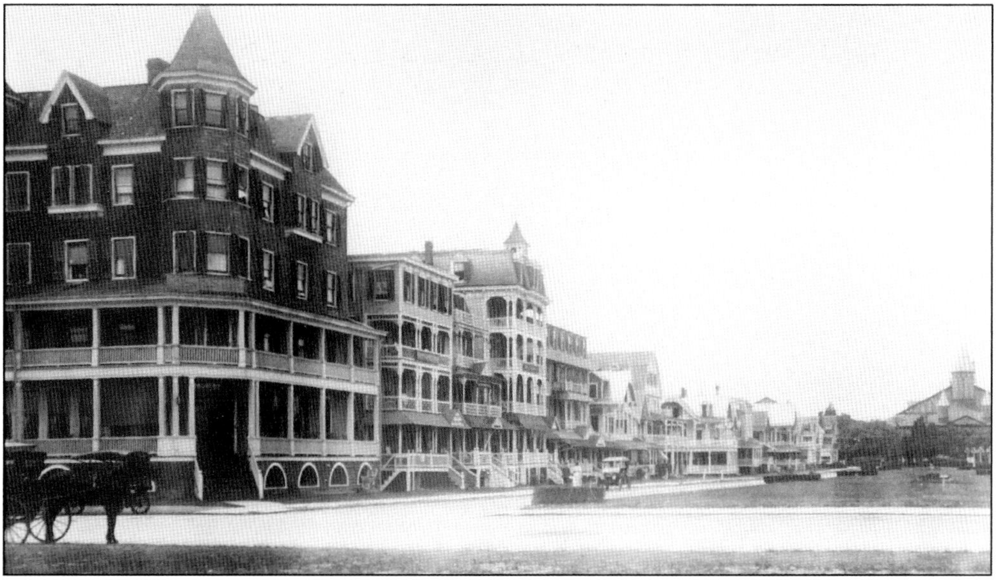

This c. 1910 image looks west on Ocean Pathway toward Ocean Grove's architectural gem, the 1894 auditorium, the largest frame building in Monmouth County. The block at left, east of number 14, the front-gabled building, was leveled by fire in the recent past; replacement structures are stylistically consistent with Ocean Grove's 1870–90 period. The gambrel-roofed building is number 18, the Ocean Plaza, restored in 1994. The wide lawn remains a popular space for fair-type events. (Collection of John Rhody.)

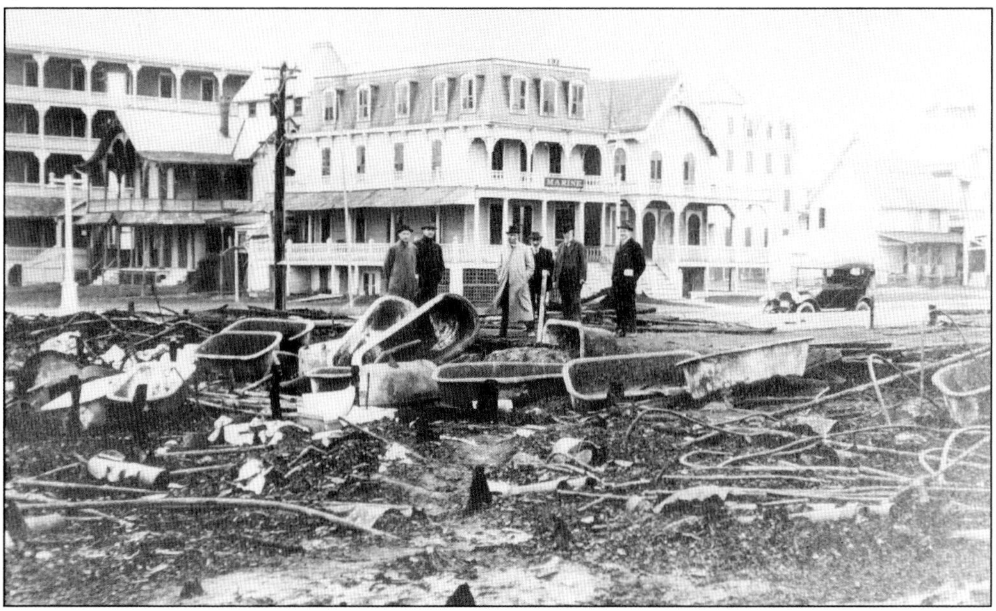

The Marine, the Mansard-roofed 60-person hotel once located at 28 Ocean Avenue, at its northwest corner with Pilgrim Pathway, is the key to viewing this c. 1915 scene today. The fire is unknown and the lot of the tall building at left is now vacant. The rest of the Marine's block is intact; number 27, to its right, and number 26, are readily identifiable. Most of the block is multiple dwellings. Construction was not planned for the east side of Ocean Avenue, accounting for odd and even numbers on the west side. (Collection of John Rhody.)

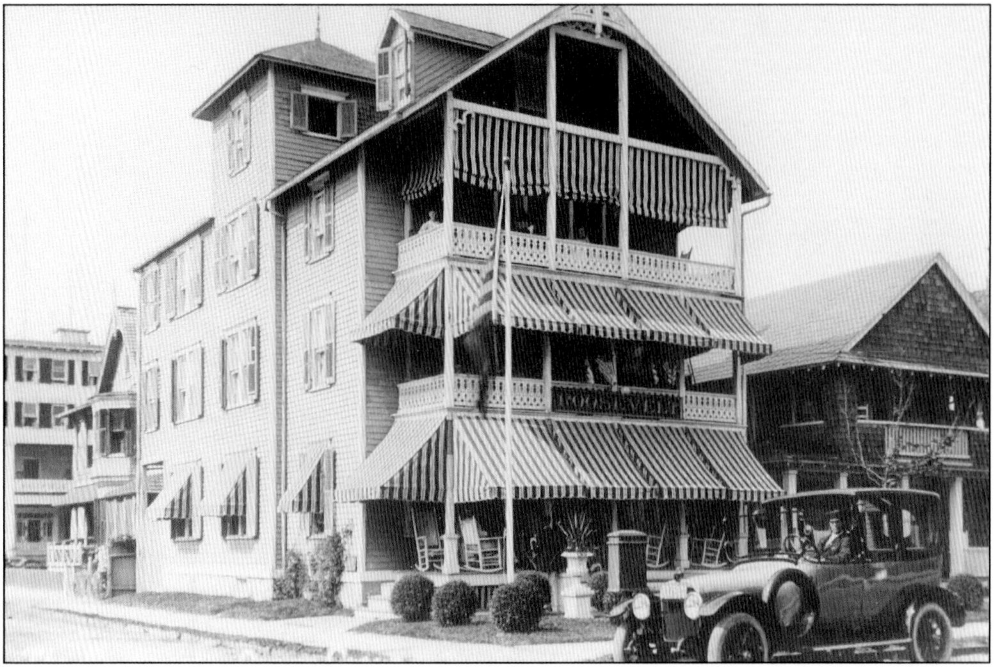

The Roosevelt, a 40-person hotel at 18 Atlantic Avenue, at its southwest corner with Beach Avenue, reflects the lasting appeal of Theodore Roosevelt, who visited Ocean Grove twice. The building, now the Beau-Rivage condominiums, retains its integrity, although clad in siding. The surroundings of this early 1920s scene are also recognizable. (Collection of John Rhody.)

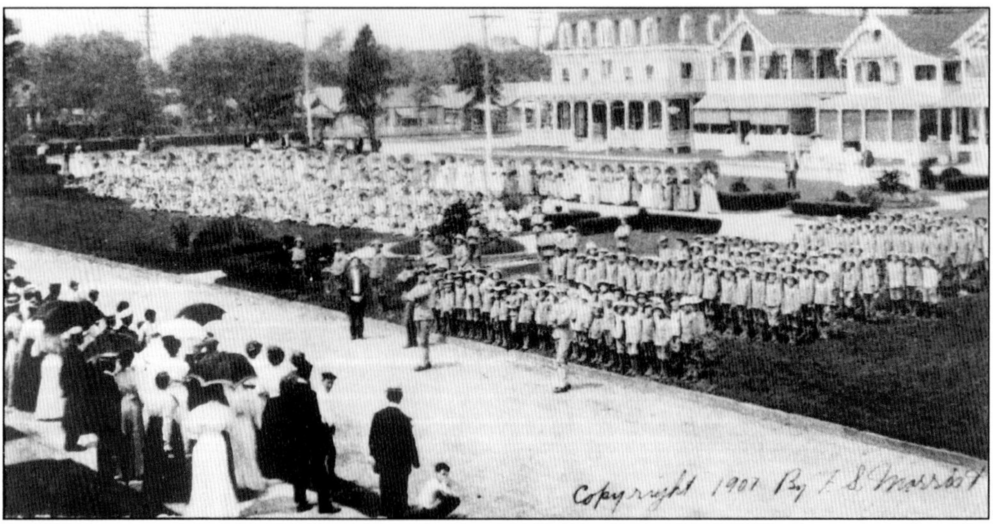

Theodore Roosevelt, during his first Ocean Grove visit on August 3, 1899, when governor of New York, filled the auditorium with a lecture entitled "Practical Politics and Decent Politics." He returned as president on July 7, 1905, to address the National Educational Association. Youthful admirers dressed as Rough Riders. Although this image is not labeled, the group may be the troop organized by Tali Esen Morgan as part of the Children's Festival Chorus, which ended the event by singing the Hallelujah chorus from Handel's *Messiah*. (Photo courtesy of Glenn Vogel.)

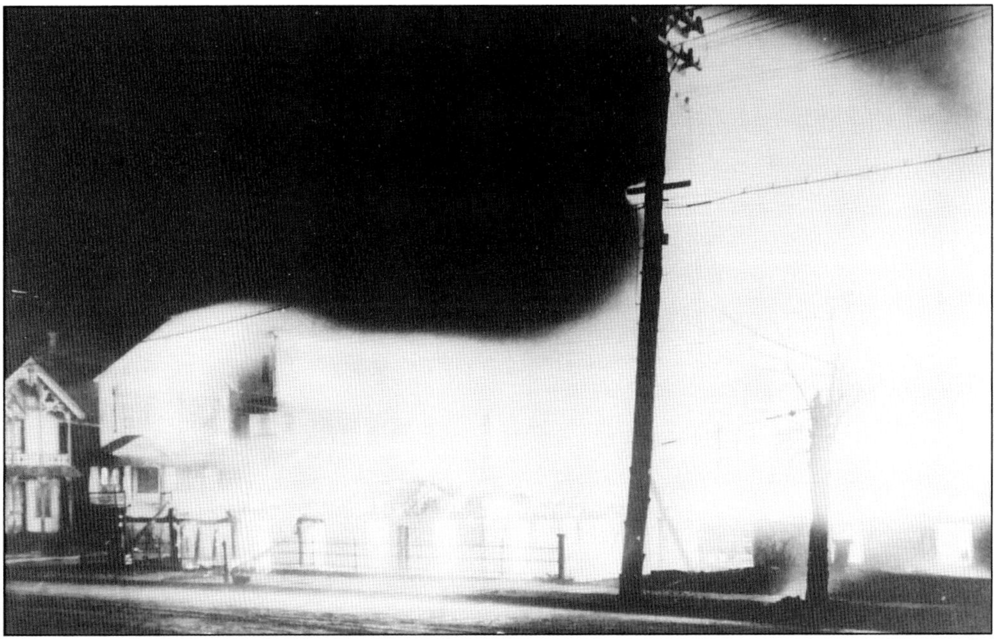

A fire early Sunday morning on February 17, 1918, destroyed the Fountain House, originally known as The Sheldon, and caused major damage to the adjoining Surf Avenue House, while threatening much of the Ocean Grove hotel community. Poor water pressure hampered firemen's early efforts, but they had the blaze under control after three hours. This was the building's third fire. (Collection of John Rhody.)

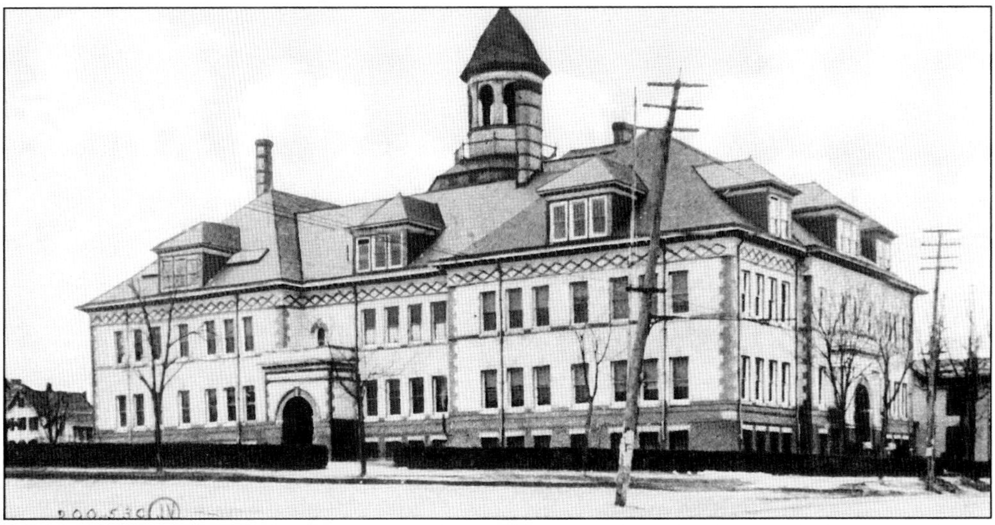

The original Neptune High School stands on the east side of Highway 71, facing the Main Avenue entrance to Ocean Grove. It was built in 1898 to a design by Brouse and Arend, an early work of Ernest Arend, a later Allenhurst resident, whose diverse output included several area schools, including Asbury Park High School. The Neptune School building served as a middle school after the present high school opened c. 1960, but has been vacant since 1979. The attractive building, built with light and dark patterned brick, retains its eye-appeal, although the cupola and dormers were removed. Plans to remodel the building for an educational and performing arts center are underway. The image is c. 1906.

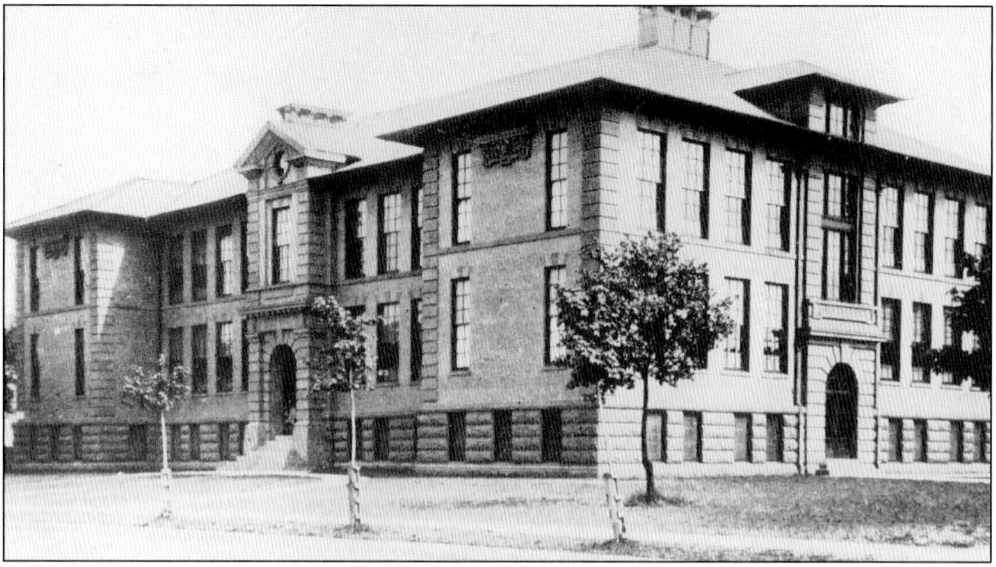

The Bradley Beach Elementary School, at the southeast corner of Brinley and Hammond Avenues, was possibly the most handsome school in the county when built in 1911. New York architect Clarence Wilson Brazer combined Romanesque and Colonial Revival elements. The rugged stone at the basement level and two-colored bricks still make a strong visual impact. A wing, indistinguishable from the building's apparent eight-room origin, was added on the west, to the right on this *c.* 1912 image; other additions followed in the rear. (Collection of John Rhody.)

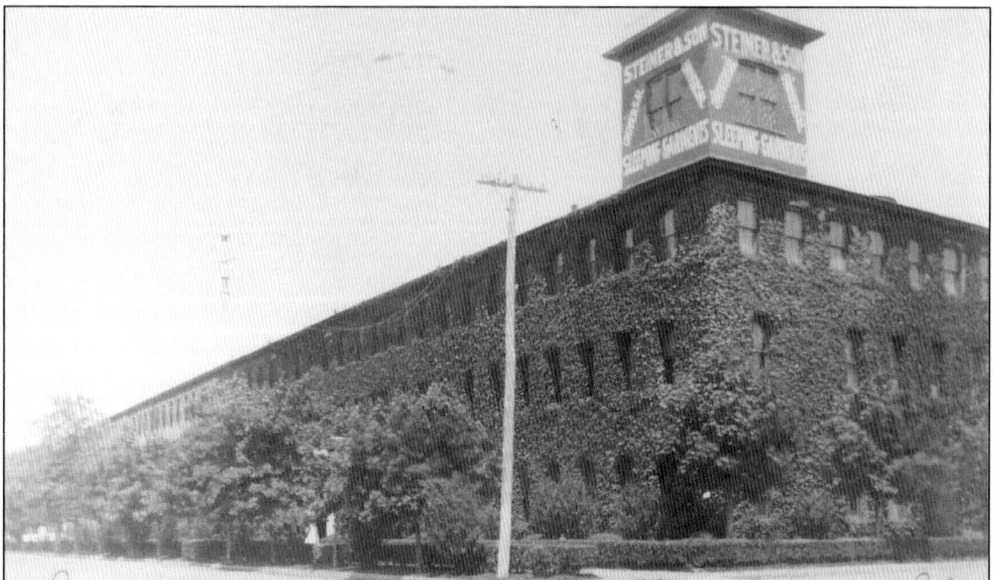

The Steiner Building at the northwest corner of Memorial Parkway and Fourth Avenue, in Neptune City, designed by C.S. Rogers, originated in 1891 as a James A. Bradley-inspired clothing factory. It was expanded later. The "Universal" around their water tower referred to their specialty, sleepwear called "Universal Night Shirts." The plant made military clothing in World War II. The needle trades waned and after a variety of other uses, the building became vacant in 1975. The structure stands today as an empty shell. (Photo courtesy of Glenn Vogel.)

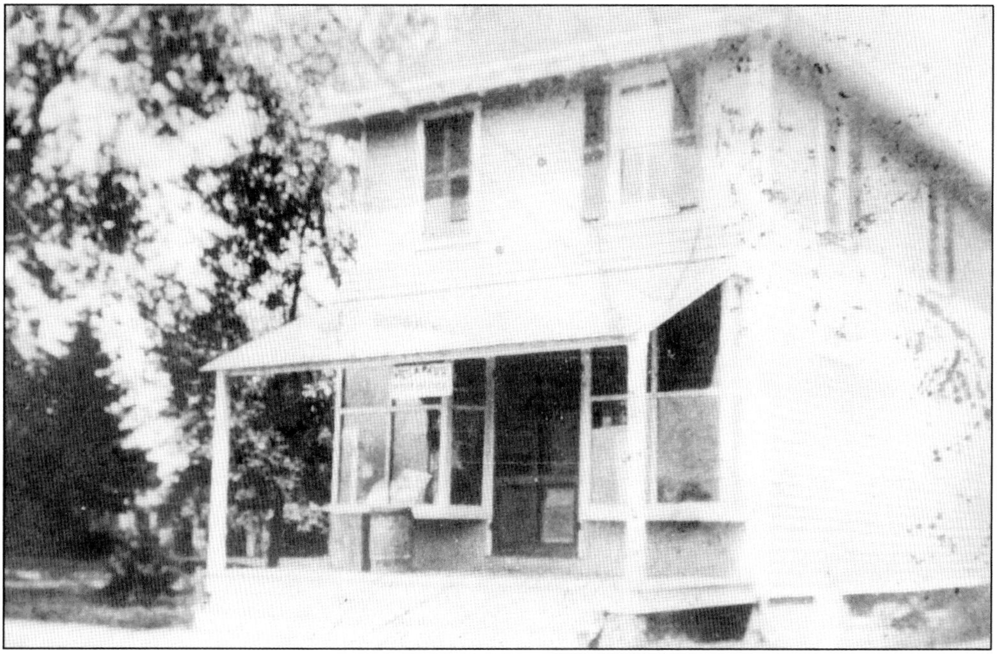

The Villa Park Post Office (two words) was founded in 1892. It was officially changed to one word between 1895 and 1910, a technicality that was overlooked on their sign in this c. 1905 photo card. The office was maintained until 1940, when it was serviced by a Spring Lake office founded in 1931. The post office occupied a store, typical of early mail facilities. (Collection of John Rhody.)

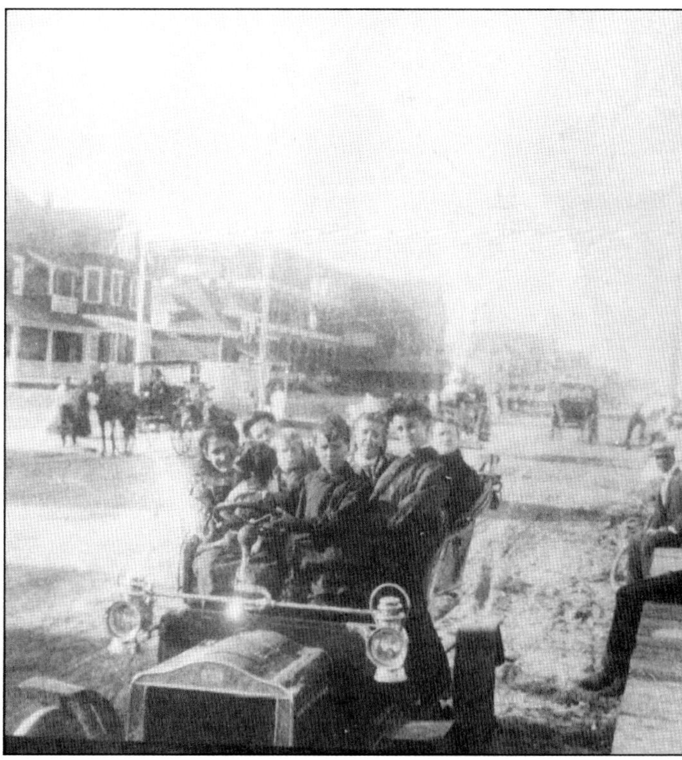

This cyanotype was processed on postcard stock with the penciled notation "summer of 1905 Belmar NJ" and mailed from Salem, NJ. The image captures the good time enjoyed by the crowded car's occupants in the manner a personal photo can, but which a postcard photographer would likely miss. The scene appears to be Ocean Avenue. (Collection of John Rhody.)

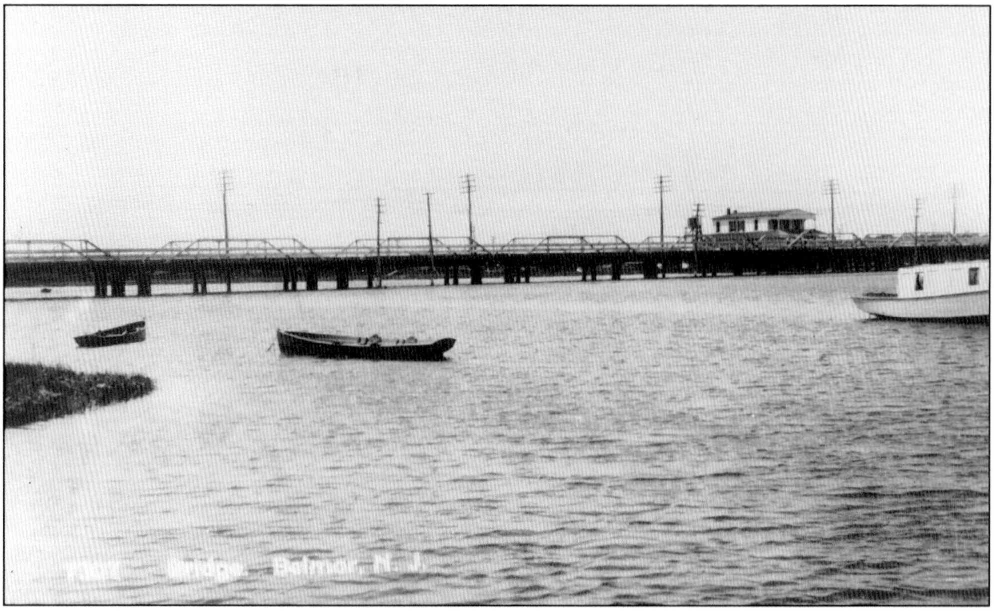

The Shark River is viewed *c.* 1911 on a Garraway card, with the highway bridge in the background, one now replaced by a higher structure. Belmar is on the right and Avon on the left. (Collection of John Rhody.)

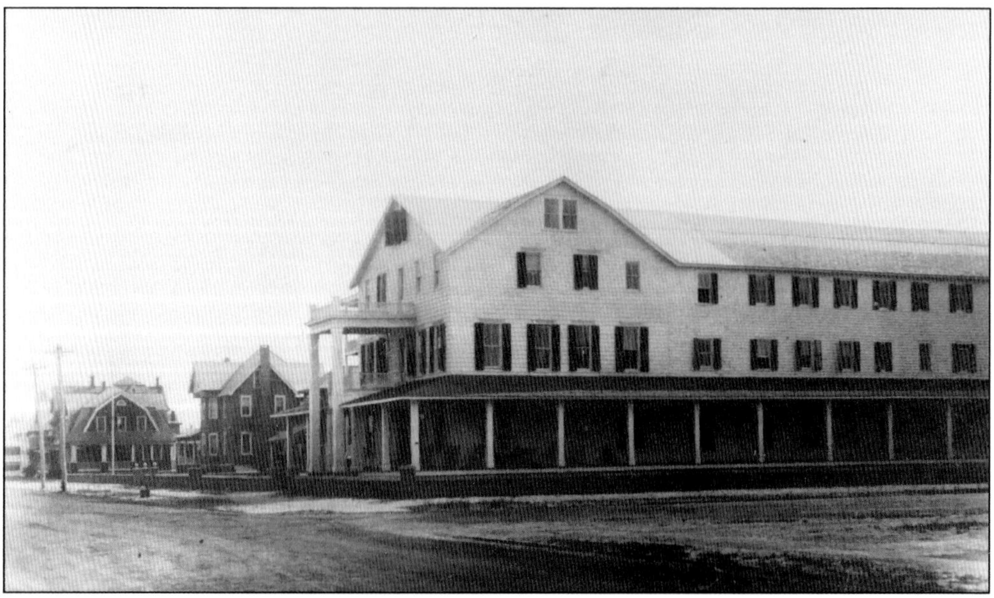

The *c.* 1910 Garraway image of the 300-person Melrose Inn at 1000 Ocean Avenue, its southwest corner with 10th Avenue, Belmar, is recognizable today, the building's stucco and siding cladding notwithstanding. An ad in 1920 by then-owners Weiss and Wunderman offered artesian drinking water, up-to-date Hungarian cuisine (with dietary laws observed), and their own dance floor. The place is now the Mayfair Hotel. The gambrel-roofed structure at left is La Belle Mer at 1100 Ocean Avenue. (Collection of John Rhody.)

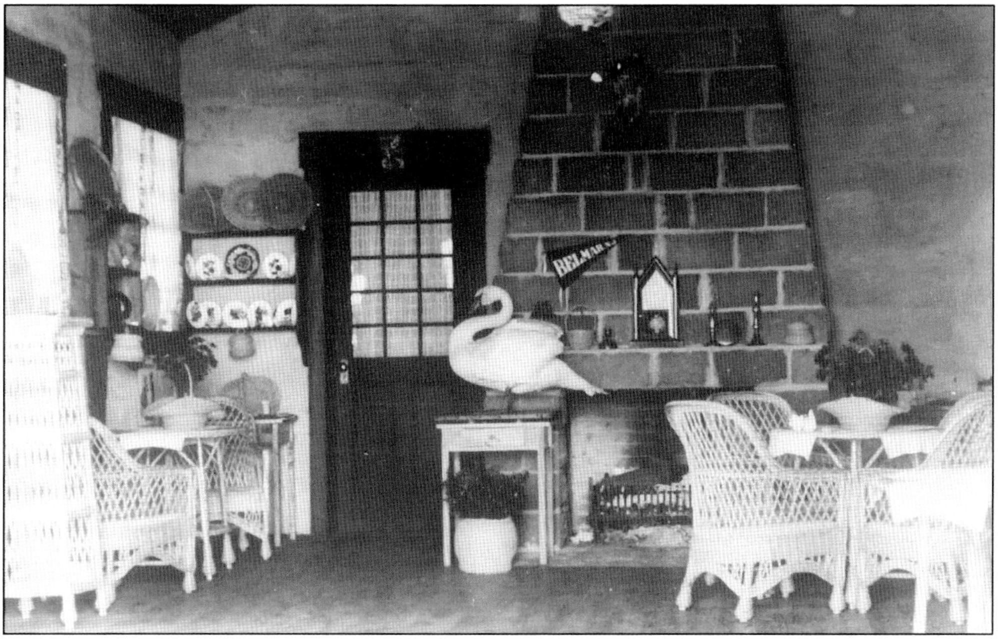

The *c.* 1915 image of The White Swan Tea Room presents an appearance of a genteel establishment, perhaps appealing to early family shore travelers. Its location in Belmar has not been found. The town became famed for a flock of swans, cared for by a borough caretaker and housed for the winter on an island in the middle of Silver Lake. (Collection of John Rhody.)

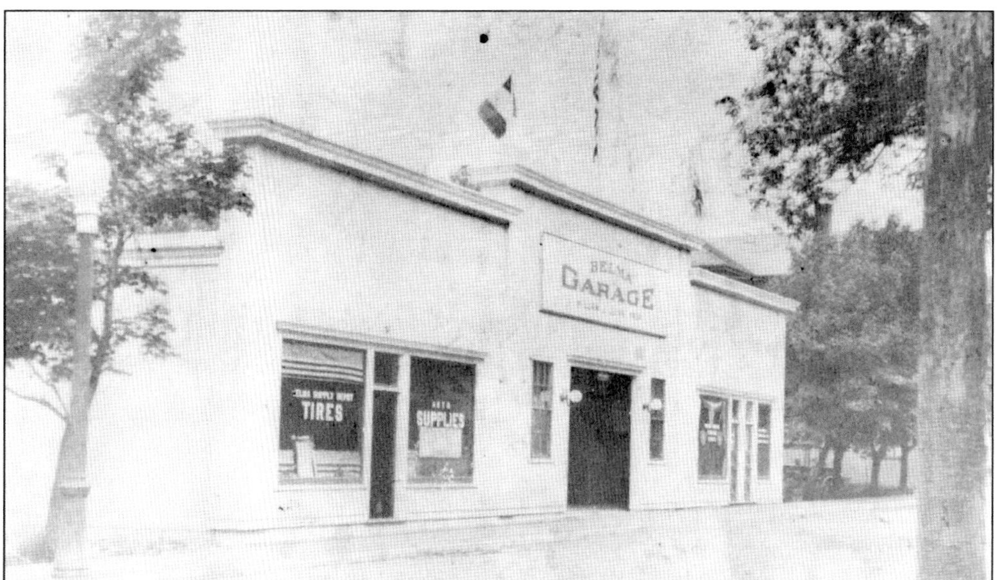

The Belmar Garage was located at F Street and Tenth Avenue, built there at a time of lower traffic levels, when garages could be located in the heart of town. (Collection of John Rhody.)

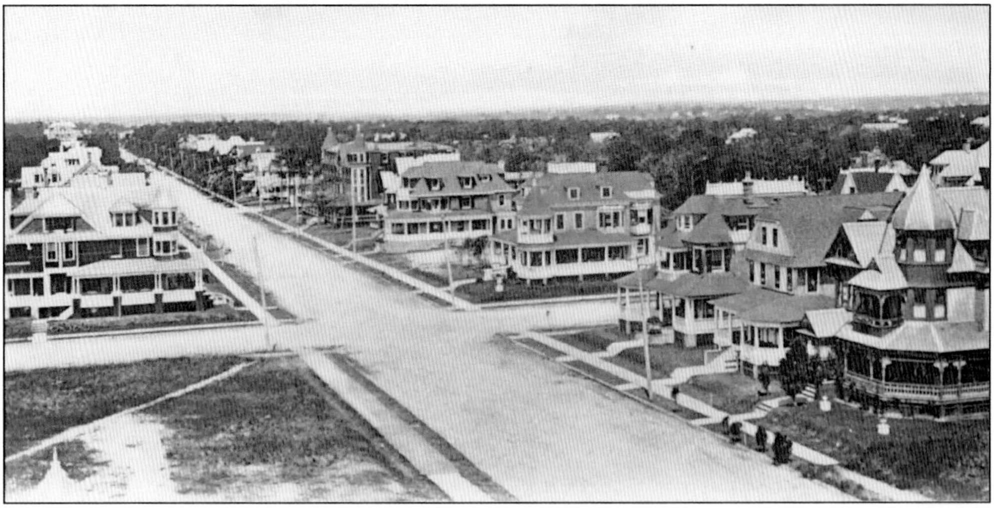

Sylvania Avenue, Avon, is seen looking west, with First Avenue crossing the card, in a virtual aerial *c.* 1905. The building at right, number 101, is now a bed and breakfast newly renamed Inn-to-the-Sea, which the pun-loving author thinks is a dandy choice. The dome on the building at right is gone, but the place, number 38, is readily recognizable, the building now sided with part of its porch enclosed. Number 42 next to it is little changed, as is 46 on the near corner; get a closer look at it on the bottom of the opposite page. The three large houses across the corner are recognizable, but the large place with the twin towers, The Buckingham, was demolished *c.* 1980s. Its lot remains empty.

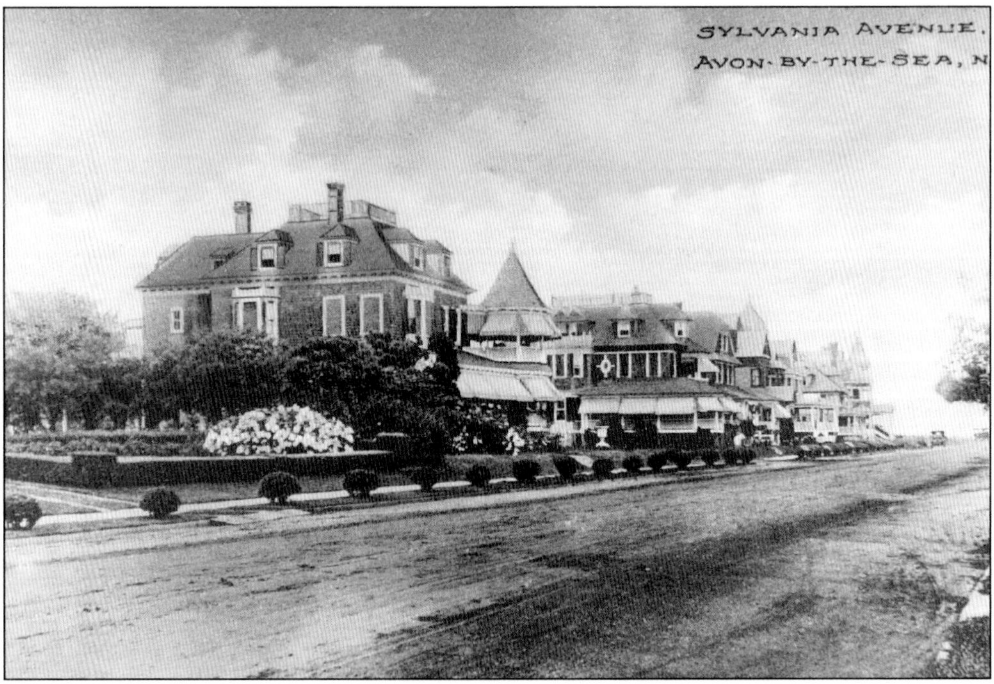

Sylvania Avenue from street level is seen *c.* 1910 looking east. The house at left, number 106, lacks only the roof balusters today. The domed place is 102, at First Avenue's northwest corner. Number 46, on the northeast corner, is seen close-up on the opposite page. (Collection of Michael Steinhorn.)

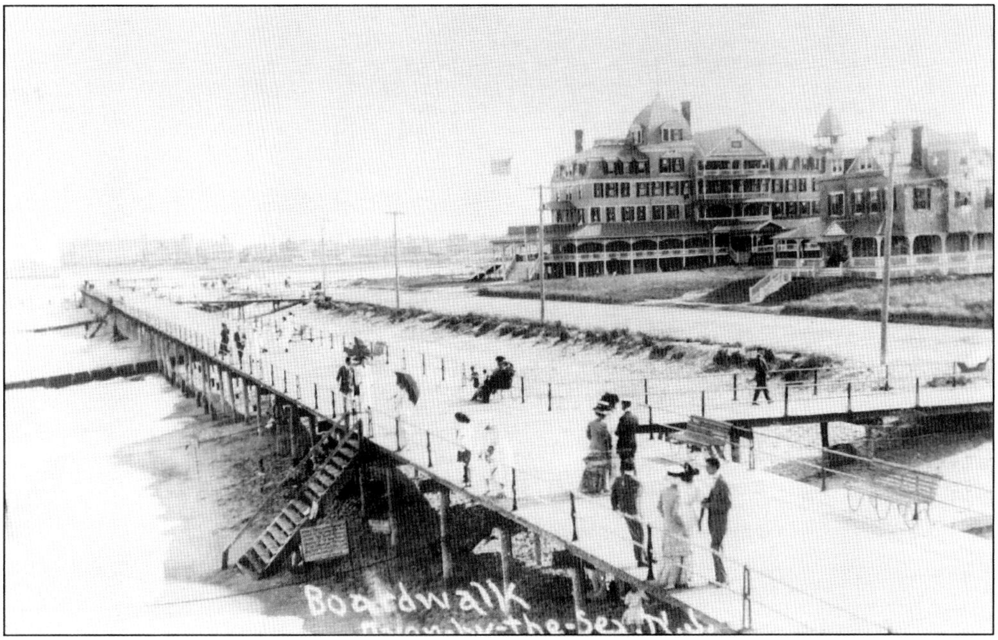

This *c.* 1910 view from the Avon boardwalk depicts the closeness of the beach to Ocean Avenue. The massive building is the 250-person Avon Inn, the likely vantage for the photograph on the opposite page. It was destroyed by fire in July 1978; its site is now occupied by four private houses. (Collection of John Rhody.)

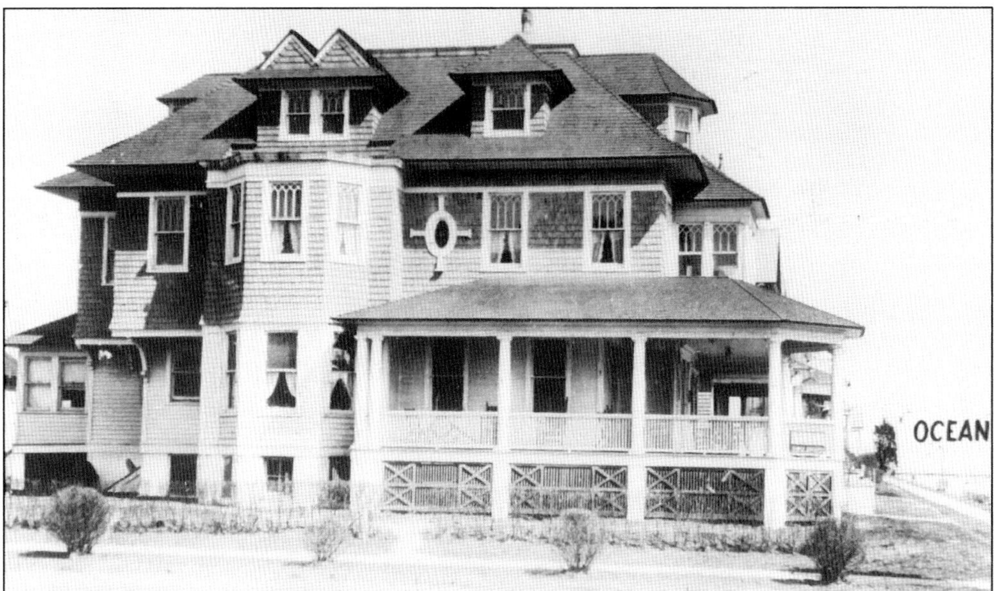

The Avalon guest house at 46 Sylvania Avenue, at the northeast corner with First Avenue, is now a private residence showing little change; part of the porch is enclosed. The owner had no reluctance to specify that only Christians were wanted. Belmar to the south was largely Jewish. (Collection of John Rhody.)

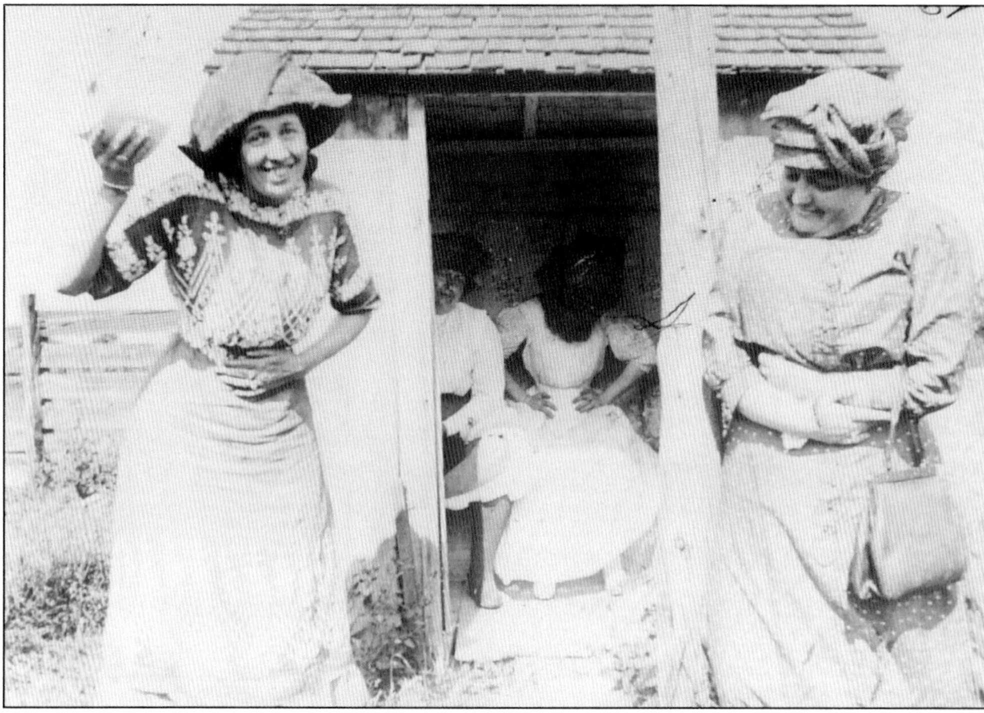

Roadside amenities were neither frequent nor fancy in the early days of motoring, but the subjects on this photo card hand-labeled "near Avon July 11, 1911, 9:30AM," appear cheerful, resilient, and willing to take advantage of available facilities. (Collection of John Rhody.)

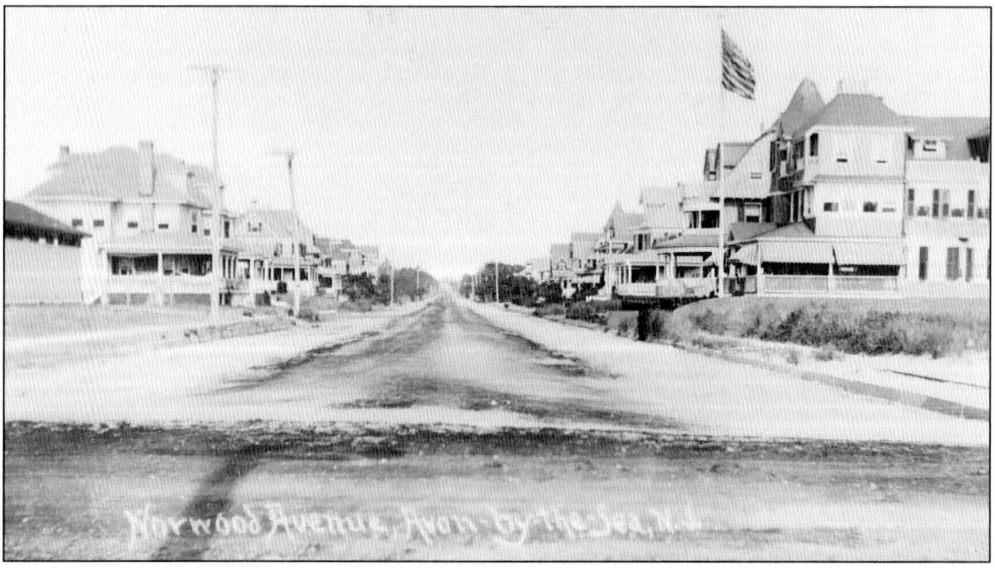

The intact condition of Sylvania Avenue deepened the disappointment of failing to find now this Norwood Avenue, Avon scene. First impression is a westward view from Ocean Avenue, but telephone poles now on the north side of Norwood dispel that reasoning. Norwood has incurred considerable change on the streets near the shore, this view's possible locale. (Collection of John Rhody.)

The sender of this photo card postmarked 1913 inscribed it, "our first house, Washington (no.500) and Fifth (Avenues), Avon." The vernacular house, probably c.1910 recalls varied styles, including a flared roof as pronounced as any c.1700 Monmouth County Dutch example. The tower seems leaning closer to Tudor Revival, than the by-then faded Queen Anne. The house is unchanged, other than the addition of a garage in the rear and the removal of the tower balustrade. (Collection of John Rhody.)

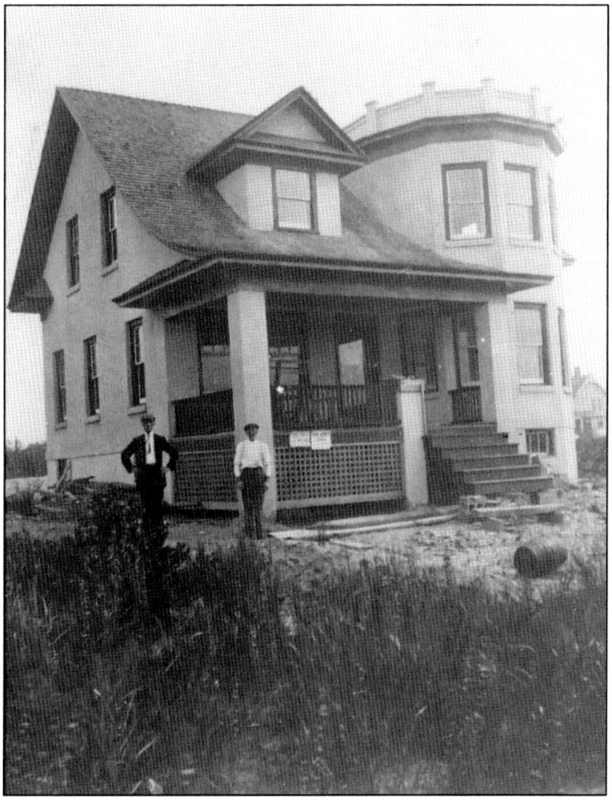

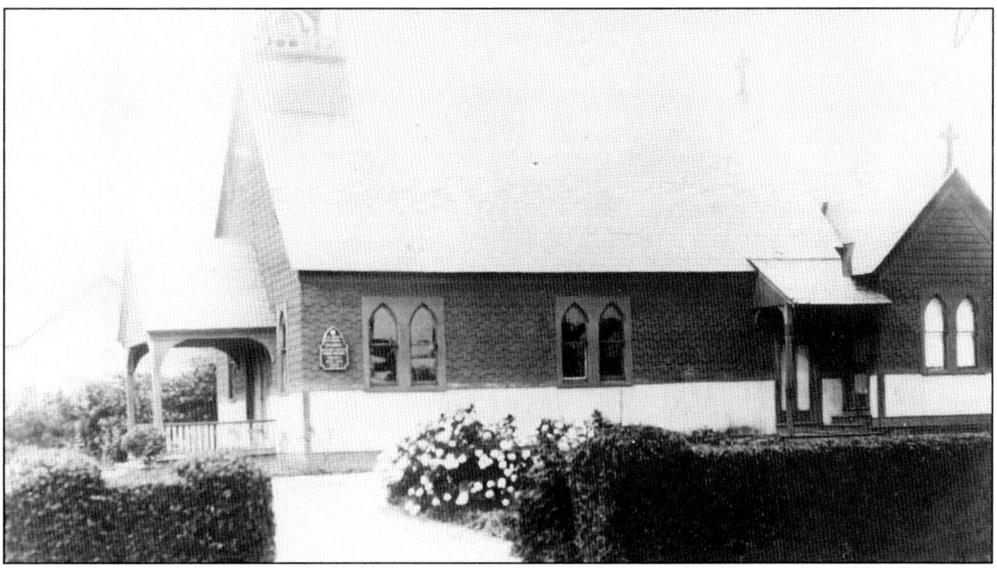

St.John's P.E. Church, 110 Woodland Avenue, at its northwest corner with First Avenue, Avon, was founded in 1883. Its frame, Vernacular Victorian edifice appears to date from that period. Its cruciform shape has been altered by the construction of a square tower in place of the transept at right. The bell tower at front has been removed, but the church is otherwise readily recognizable today. (Collection of John Rhody.)

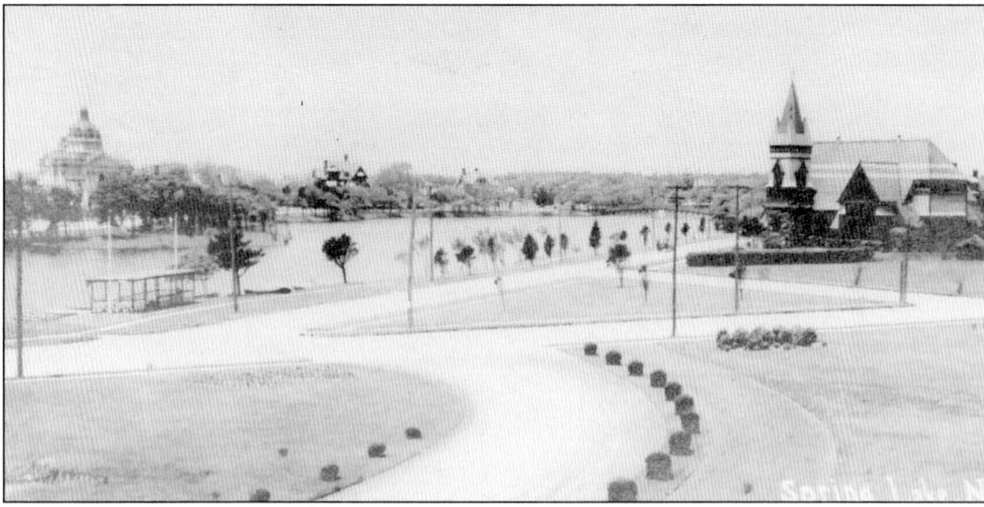

The c. 1911 view northwest from the west side of the block-long Monmouth Hotel embraced two churches on the shores of Spring Lake. The Spring Lake Presbyterian Church at right, designed by Benjamin Linfoot and built in 1882, was destroyed by fire in 1974. Two private houses at 100 and 110 East Lake Avenue are on the site now. St. Catherine's Roman Catholic Church, at left, is Monmouth County's 20th-century ecclesiastical gem (see p. 80). (Collection of John Rhody.)

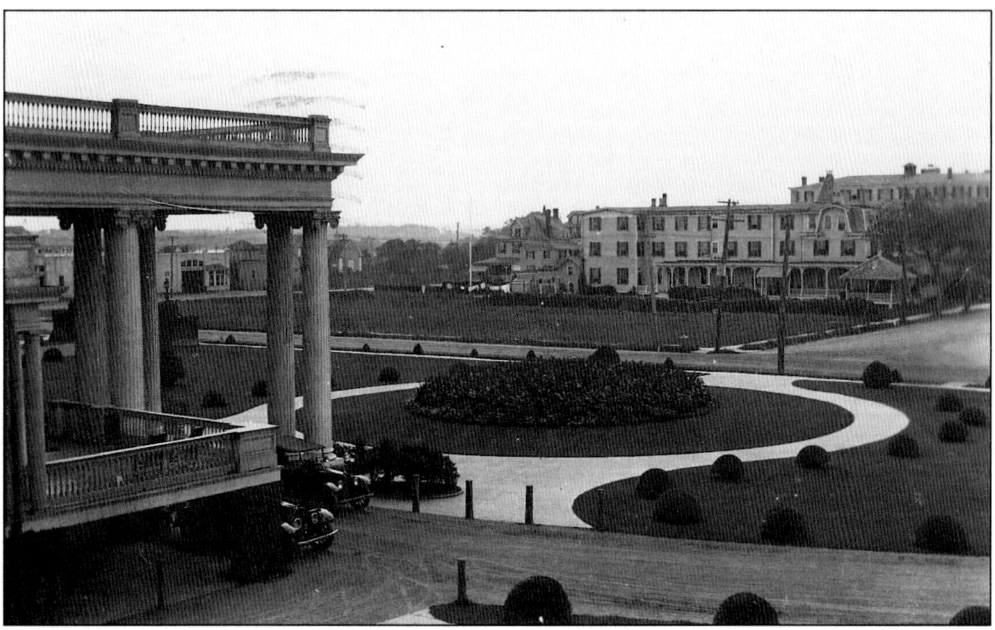

Neither the Monmouth Hotel, demolished in 1975, nor much of the view looking southwest from its rear, or west side, remain in Spring Lake. Two hotels dominate the background. The taller one, the Shoreham, was demolished in 1997; the shorter one, the Lakeview, earlier known as the Palmer House, was demolished c. 1970s. The house, 112 Atlantic Avenue, to the left of the Lakeview, stands and is the home of Patricia Colrick, author of Arcadia's *Spring Lake*.

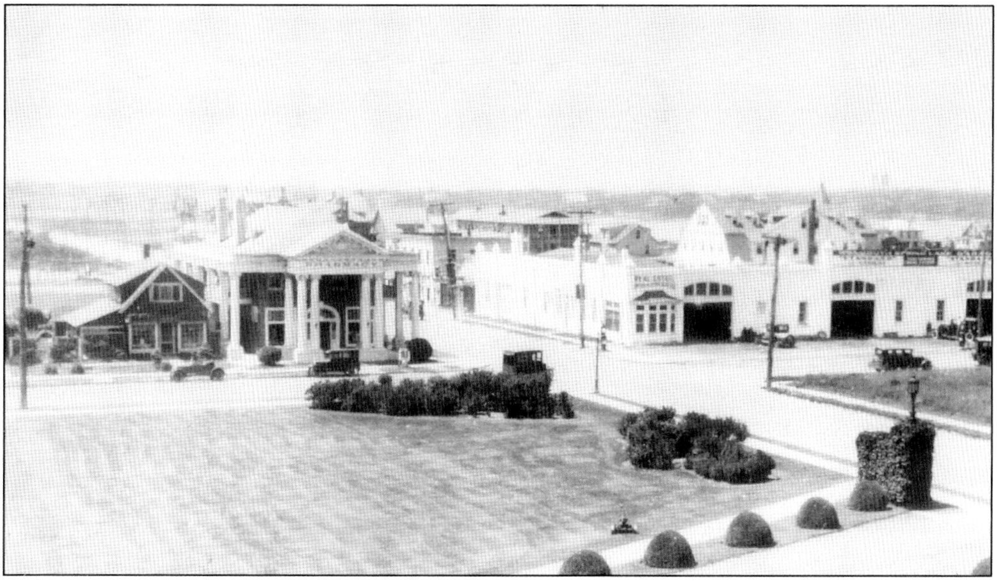

The *c*. 1925 view southwest from the rear of the Monmouth Hotel embraces First Avenue, at lower right, and Atlantic Avenue, at left. The pharmacy apparently a residence enveloped by a large classical porch and balconies, is now a seasonal ice cream store, the *Sundae Times*, and residences. The one-story section of the house at left was built-up, while the hotel's garages at right are gone. The two-story gambrel-roofed building at right can be seen at bottom. This and the bottom of p. 78 pierce the chapter's time line, but possess the character of the postcard era. (Collection of John Rhody.)

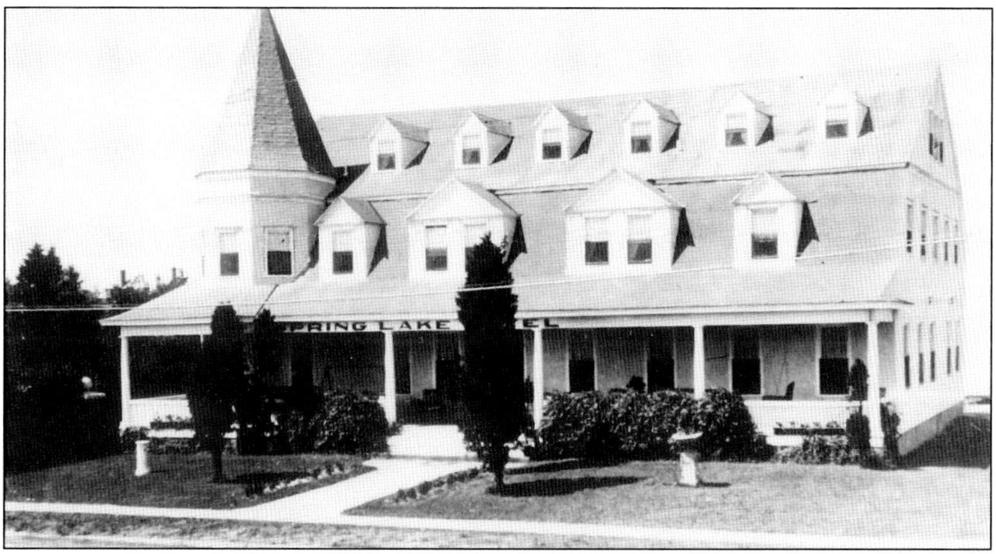

The Spring Lake Hotel at 104 Salem Avenue appears to be a *c*. 1890s structure, a meeting of the Colonial Revival and Queen Anne styles. The building was reportedly built on the south side of Atlantic Avenue, near First, and moved twice. It originated as Timothy Hurley's Grand View Stables—presumably the upper stories were rooms for horse and carriage men—and was later operated as the Hurley House Hotel. The card is undated, but the place's present appearance is little changed. A second story door and fire escape are present on the east elevation at right, while the present name is the Spring Lake Inn. (Collection of John Rhody.)

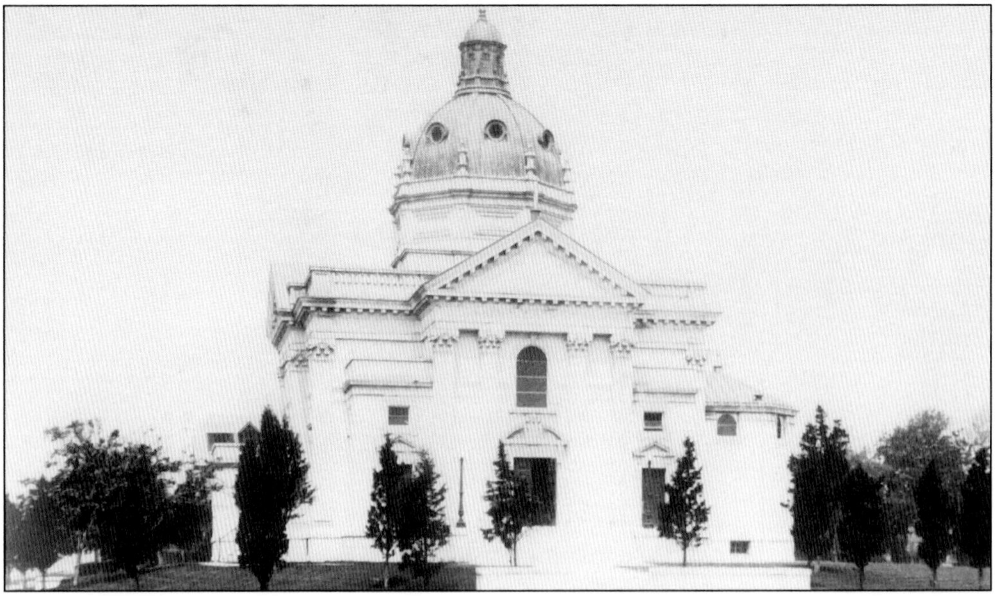

St. Catharine's Roman Catholic church at the corner of West Lake and Third Avenues was designed by Horace Trumbauer in the Classical Revival style and built in 1901–1902. The church was donated by Martin Maloney, a utilities magnate, who was designated a papal marquis and papal chamberlain for his generous benefactions to Catholic causes, and built as a memorial to his daughter Catharine, who died in 1900 at the age of 17. She and her parents are entombed in the family crypt beneath the chapel to the east. (Collection of John Rhody.)

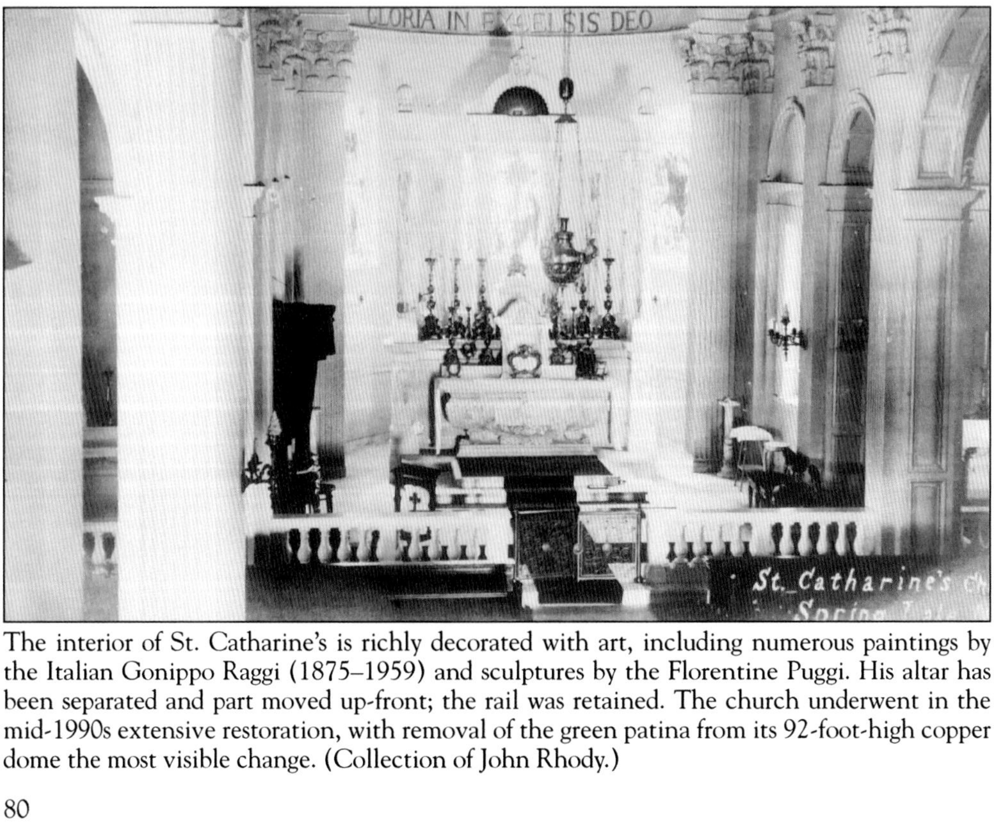

The interior of St. Catharine's is richly decorated with art, including numerous paintings by the Italian Gonippo Raggi (1875–1959) and sculptures by the Florentine Puggi. His altar has been separated and part moved up-front; the rail was retained. The church underwent in the mid-1990s extensive restoration, with removal of the green patina from its 92-foot-high copper dome the most visible change. (Collection of John Rhody.)

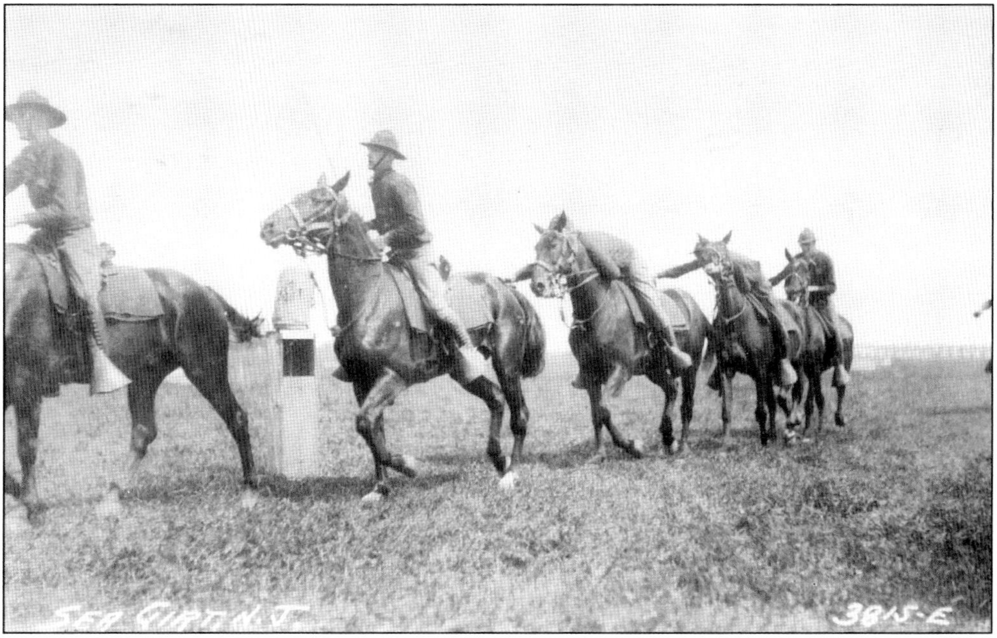

The State of New Jersey bought in 1887 a 120-acre tract for $51,000, bordered by the Atlantic Ocean, Sea Girt Avenue (north), the railroad, and Stockton Lake (south) for establishment of a National Guard summer camp. The state also moved here the New Jersey pavilion from the 1904 St. Louis World's Fair for use by the governor as a summer capital. Horsemen are seen in an undated photo card on an unidentified exercise.

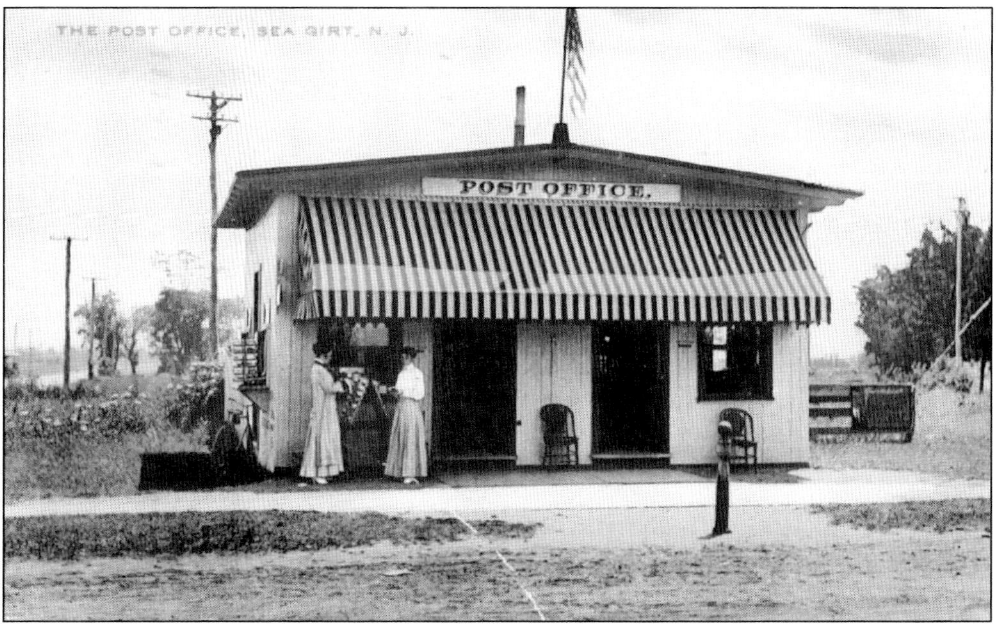

The Sea Girt Post Office opened in 1899, located at Sea Girt Avenue and Washington Blvd. Its first postmistress, Mary A. Blakey, held the office for 14 years, presumably keeping it at that spot for when this c. 1910 card was published. Note the two postcard racks. No, the original is not sharp enough to identify the cards through enlargement.

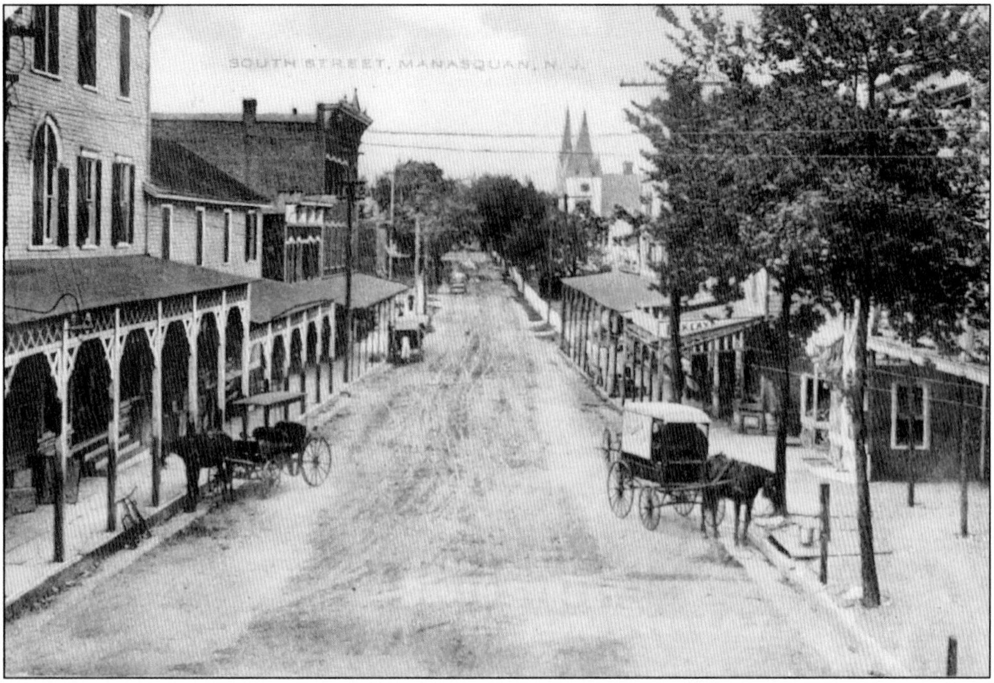

The divided back means the card is obviously 1907 or later, but the view of South Street appears older, with not a motorized vehicle in sight. The canopied sidewalks are both charming and practicable, but hardly the amenity that could survive street widenings. The church at right is Manasquan Baptist. The four-story brick building at left housed Vogel's butcher and Red Men's Hall; it was demolished in 1964.

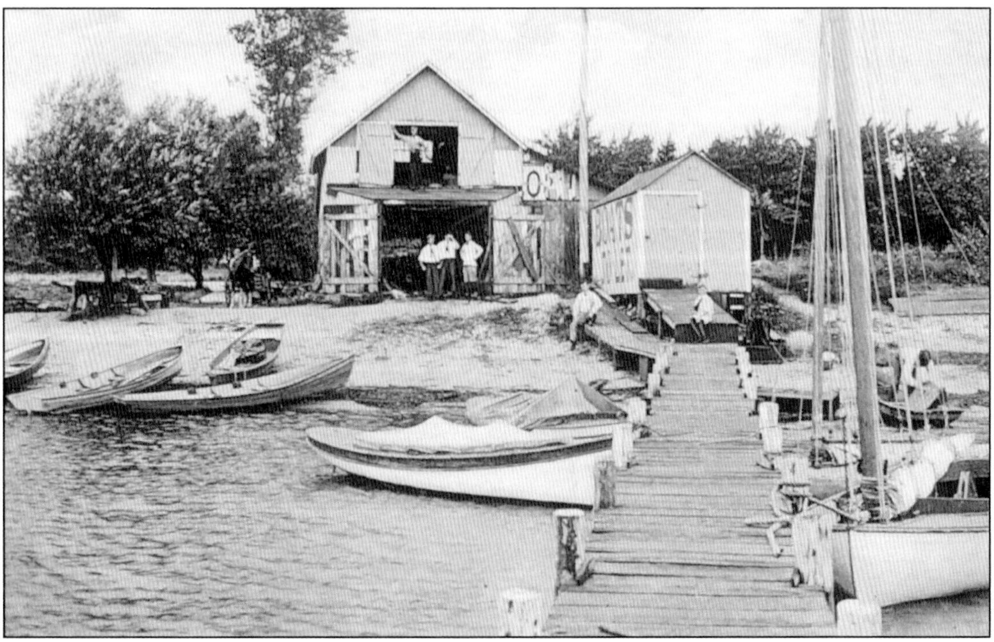

Pearce's Boathouse was on the Manasquan River, Brielle, near the railroad crossing. Appearing c. 1907 as a small business, the desirable boating site is now occupied by a larger marina.

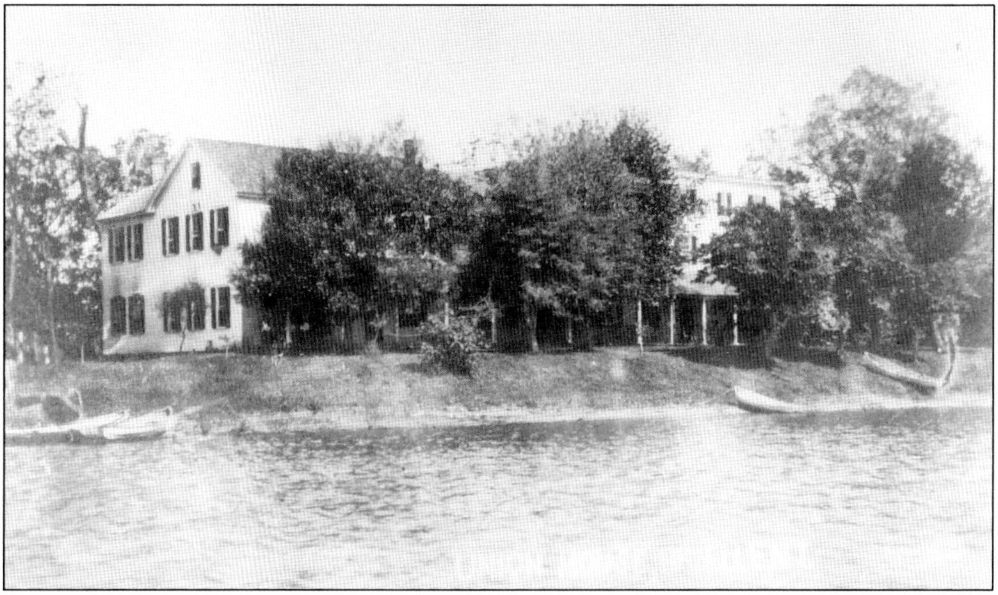

The Union House on the Manasquan River in Brielle, seen *c.* 1910, was a famed inn from the days that town was known as Union Landing. It was built by Capt. John Maxon, son of William Brown, a local boat builder. The place was filled with memorabilia of Robert Louis Stevenson, a famed visitor of the area, when it was destroyed by fire on February 15, 1914. (Collection of John Rhody.)

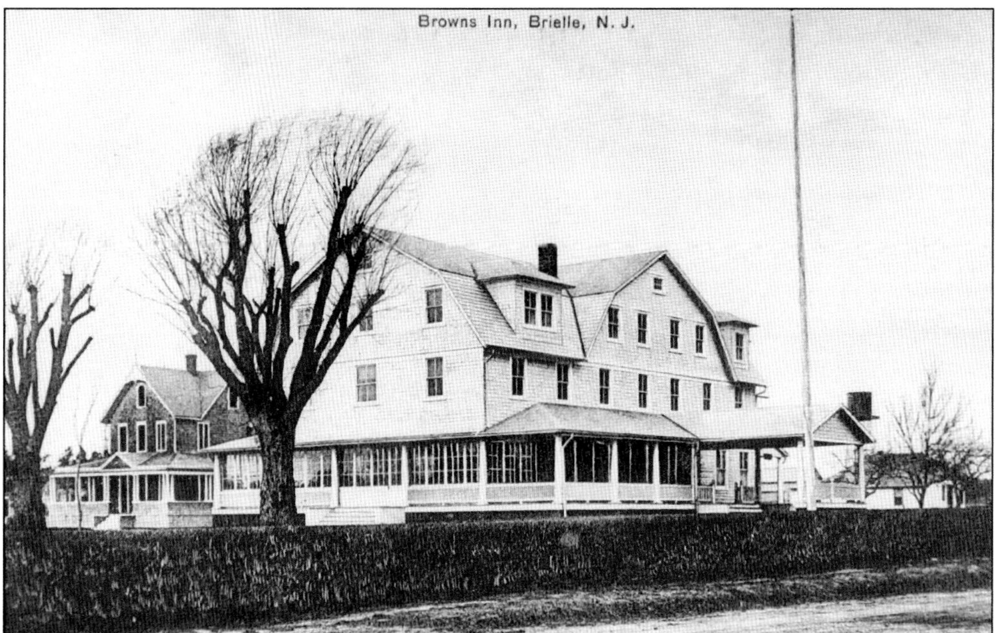

Browns Inn was built 1890 on the Manasquan River by Capt. Theodore S.P. "Dory" Brown. One wonders if this *c.* 1910 image reflects the hotel as it was first built, or a later expansion, as 1890 is early for gambrel-roofed intersecting gables. It, too, was destroyed by fire, *c.* 1989. (Collection of John Rhody.)

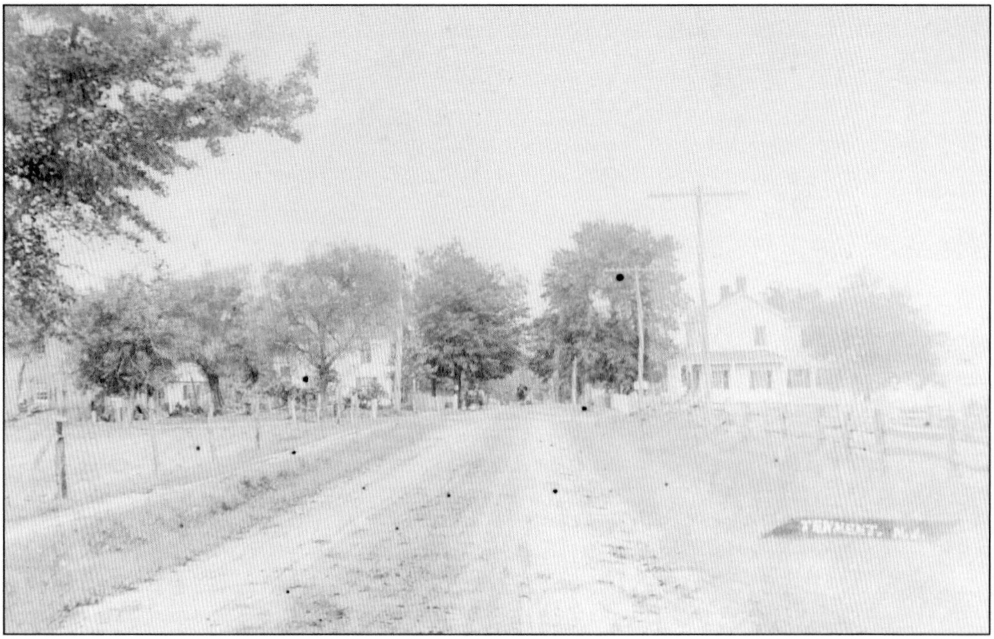

Tennent is the historic center of Manalapan Township, the site of the Old Tennent (Presbyterian) Church, which the legendary Rev. William Tennent served as pastor in for nearly 44 years. The Merriman image is apparently a stem of Tennent Road that has changed beyond recognition from his *c*. 1910 photo. (Collection of John Rhody.)

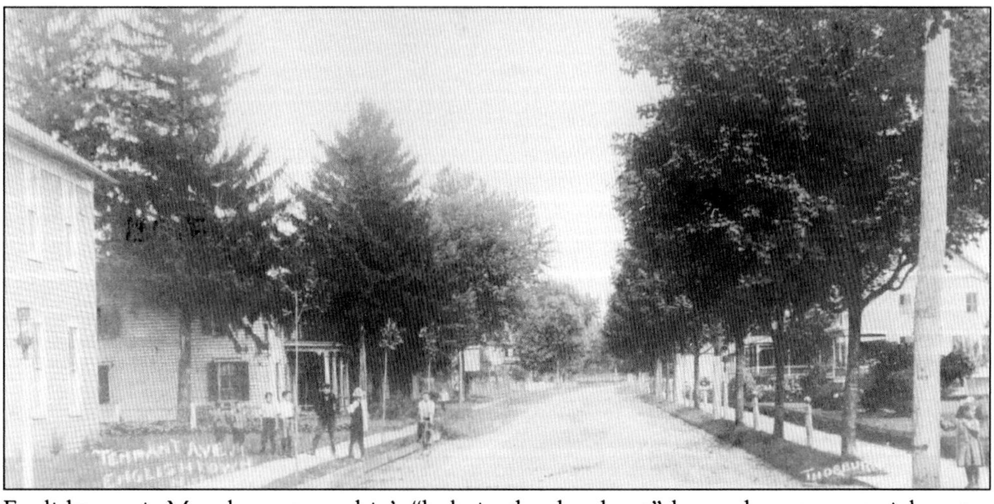

Englishtown is Manalapan township's "hole-in-the-doughnut" borough, a commercial center that separated from the latter in 1888. Tennent Avenue forms a "T" intersection at Main Street, the center of town, and runs east to Tennent, Manalapan's historic core. The house at left burned *c*. 1970; the corner today is unrecognizable from this *c*. 1905 photo card. A liquor-convenience store and a bank are now on the left and right, respectively.

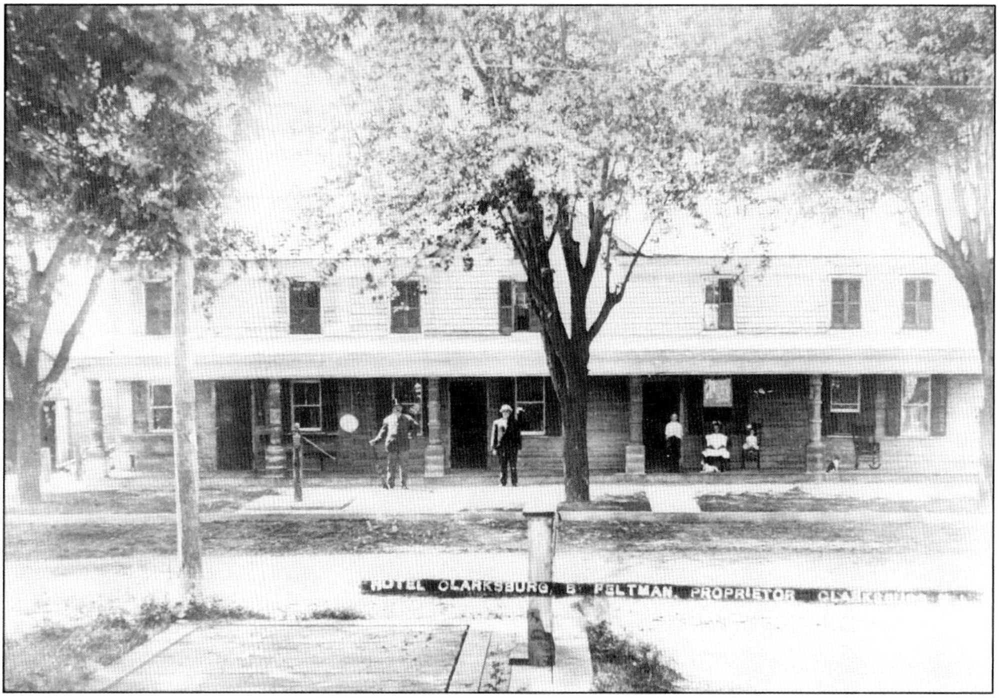

The western Millstone Township village of Clarksburg developed near tavern sites situated around a key old road juncture, today's County Highways 524 and 571. The Clarksburg Inn, identified as "hotel" in this c. 1910 Merriman photo, built in 1834, long served as town center for the small settlement. It still stands and is recognizable from this image. (Collection of John Rhody.)

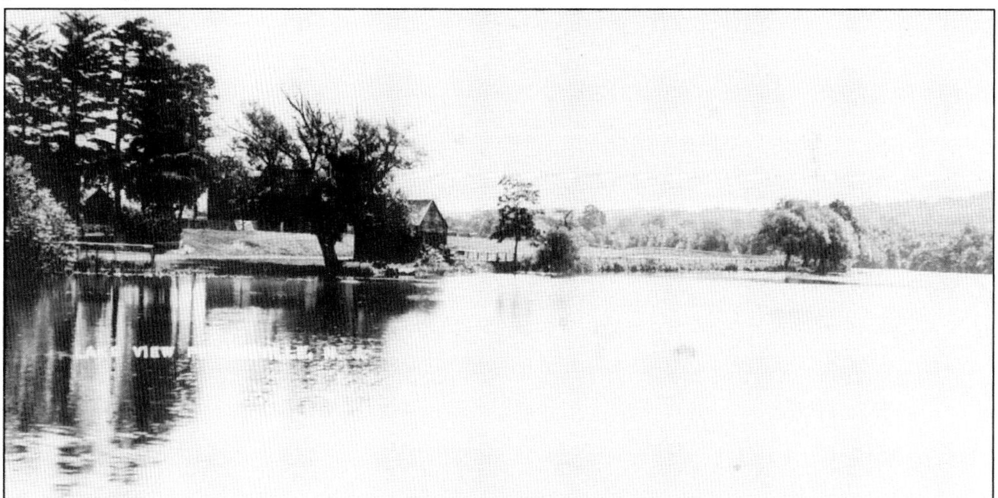

Early milling was a key factor in developing the Millstone Township section, Perrineville, with the damming of Rocky Brook forming a lake still of visual appeal today. Sweetmans Lane becomes Perrineville Road, the only thoroughfare through town; apparently, it is the one in the rear of Merriman's c. 1910 view. (Collection of John Rhody.)

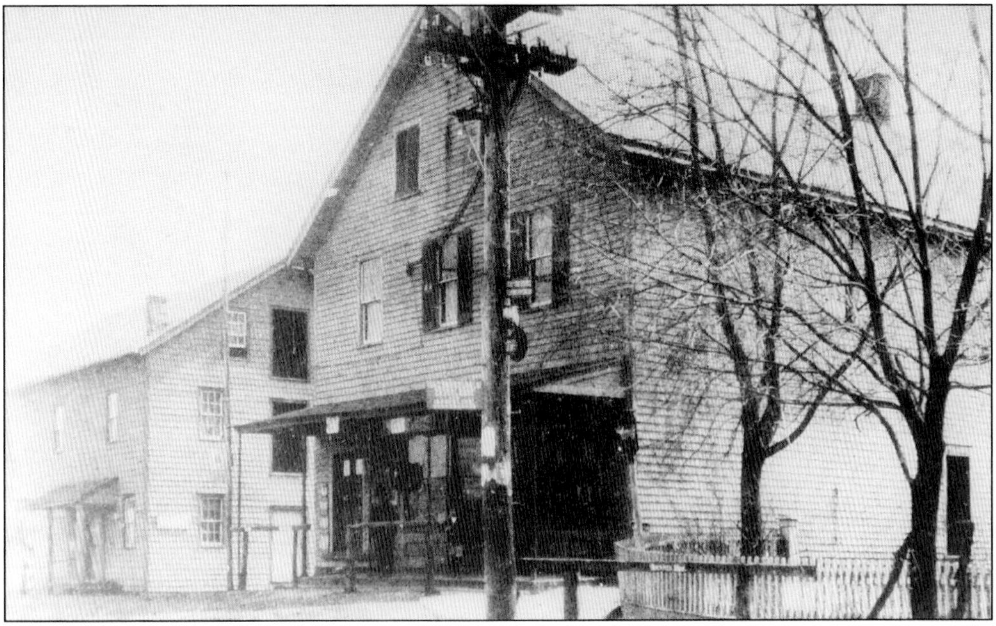

Imlaystown, founded in 1690, is popularly known for its short, crooked main street, about the length of a New York cross-town block, running south from County Highway 526. The village center is a square at the street's end, surrounded by structures that gave rural spots the character of a settlement. They included a hotel, township hall (vacant), and Salters Mill (at left), skillfully converted to offices by landscape architect Robert Zion, with minimal disruption of its mill character. The main subject of this *c.* 1912 image is the general store, now a four-family house. (Collection of Glenn Vogel.)

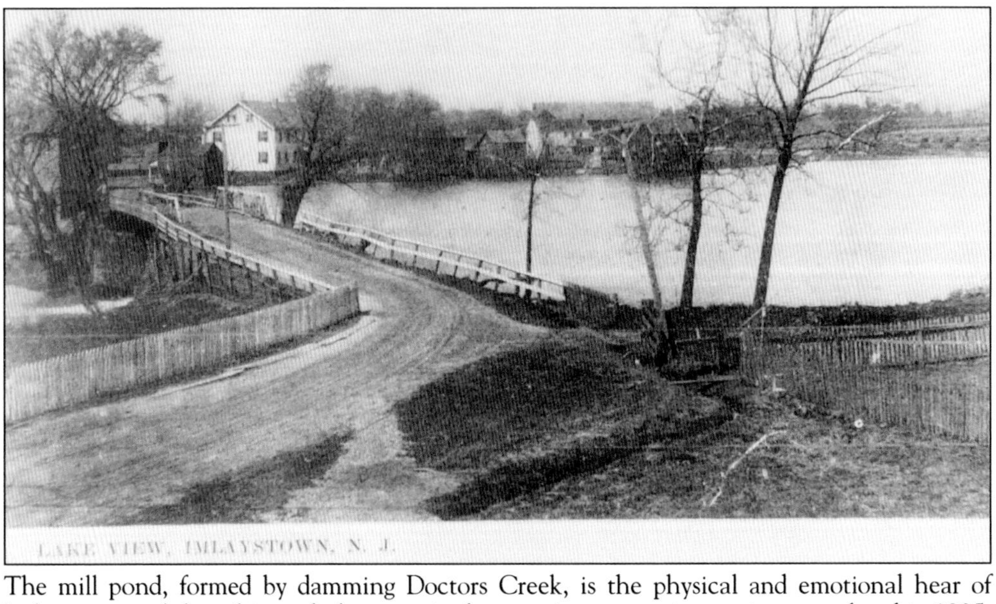

The mill pond, formed by damming Doctors Creek, is the physical and emotional hear of Imlaystown and the subject of a long-awaited, extensive restoration project completed in 1995. This view is north, with the former Lakeview Hotel at top; it is now the Happy Apple Inn. Imlaystown, exuding quaint charm, is well-worth a visit. Surely the reader must be curious how a block-long village can have a center and a square. (Collection of Glenn Vogel.)

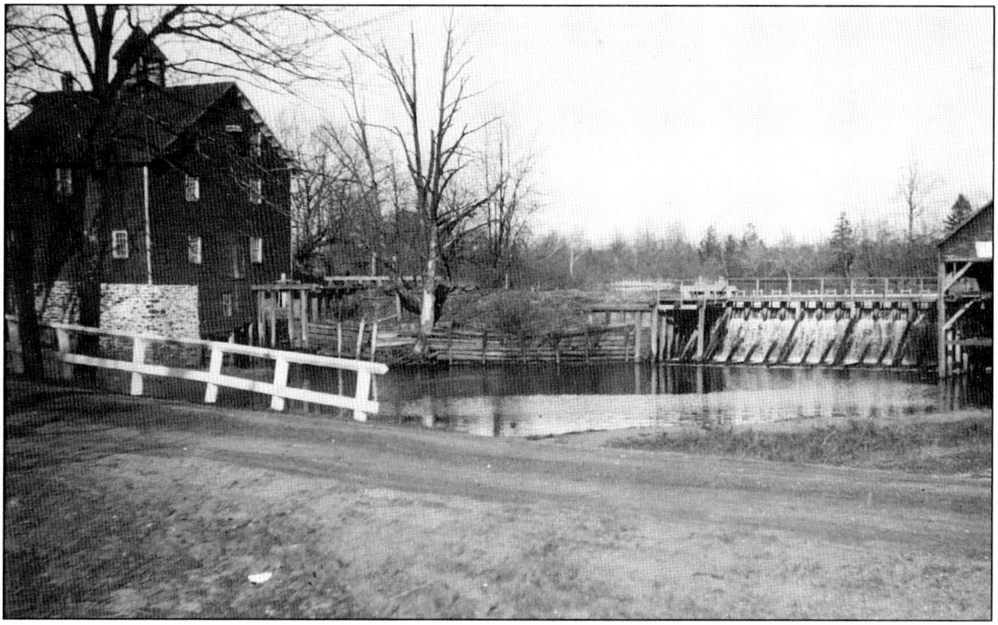

Hornerstown, a small village in southwestern Upper Freehold Township, had early mills established on Lahaway Creek. Ellis states Caleb Ivins built grist and sawmills prior to 1800; they were later known as Hutchinsons Mill. The building at left is a typical 3-story, front-gabled gristmill; the partially seen building at right is likely the sawmill. The view is c. 1910.

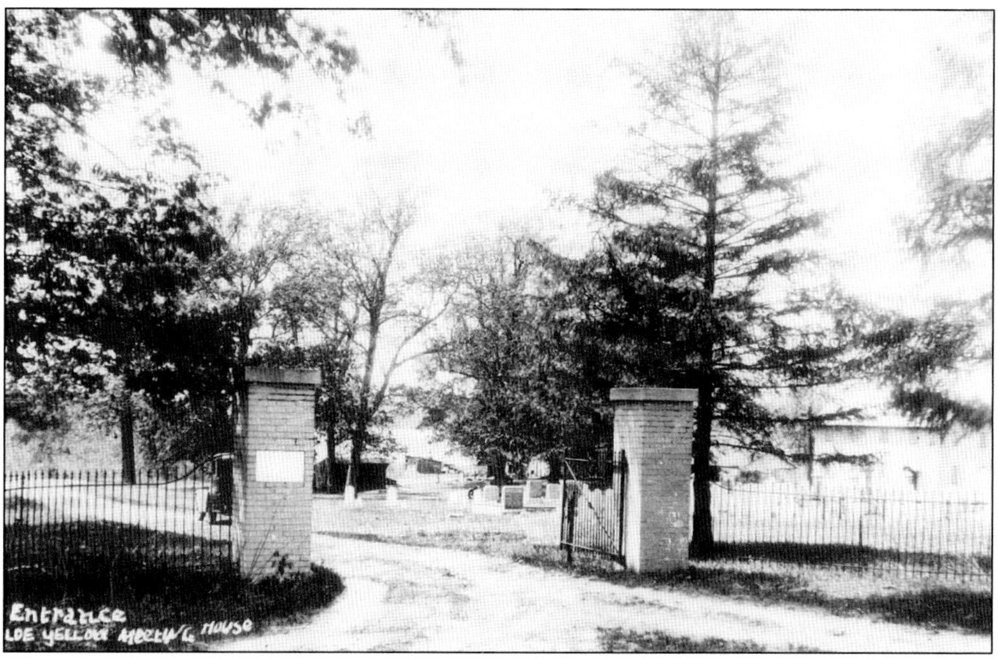

The Old Yellow Meeting House is the popular name for the Upper Freehold Baptist Meeting. The 18th-century church, located at Yellow Meeting House and Red Valley Roads, was listed on the National Register of Historic Places in 1975. This image of their entrance is c. 1905. (Collection of John Rhody.)

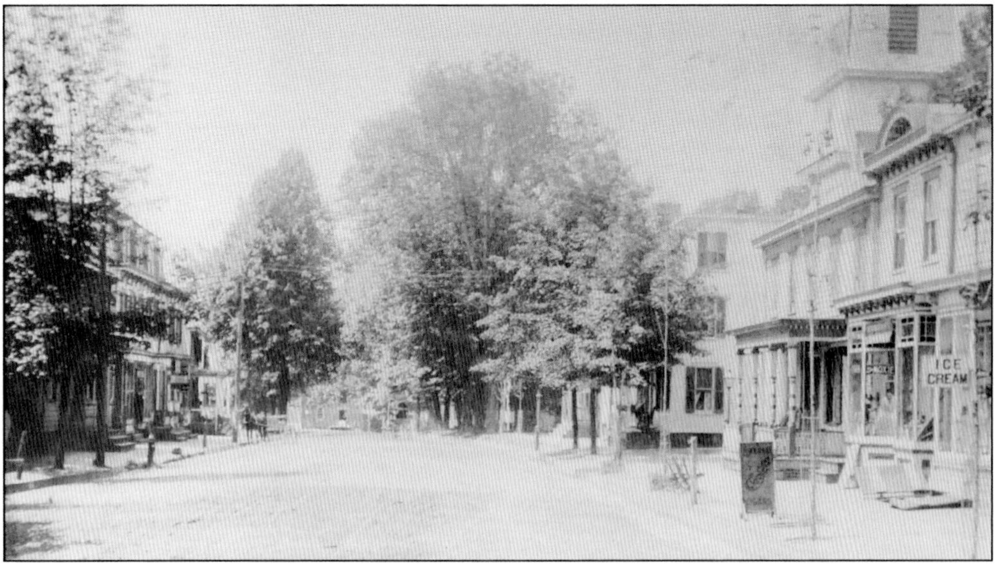

Main Street, Allentown, part of County Highway 539, has the atmosphere of an old country town; most of its early buildings are intact. This *c.* 1908 image looks west from just beyond Church Street. The five-bay store is now the post office. The tower of the First Baptist Church is visible behind it. The church, built in 1879, incurred significant fire damage in the early 1970s. It was purchased by the Allentown Library, located adjacent on the west, which succeeded magnificently in a 20-year campaign to remodel the interior for library use; its worth a visit! (Collection of Glenn Vogel.)

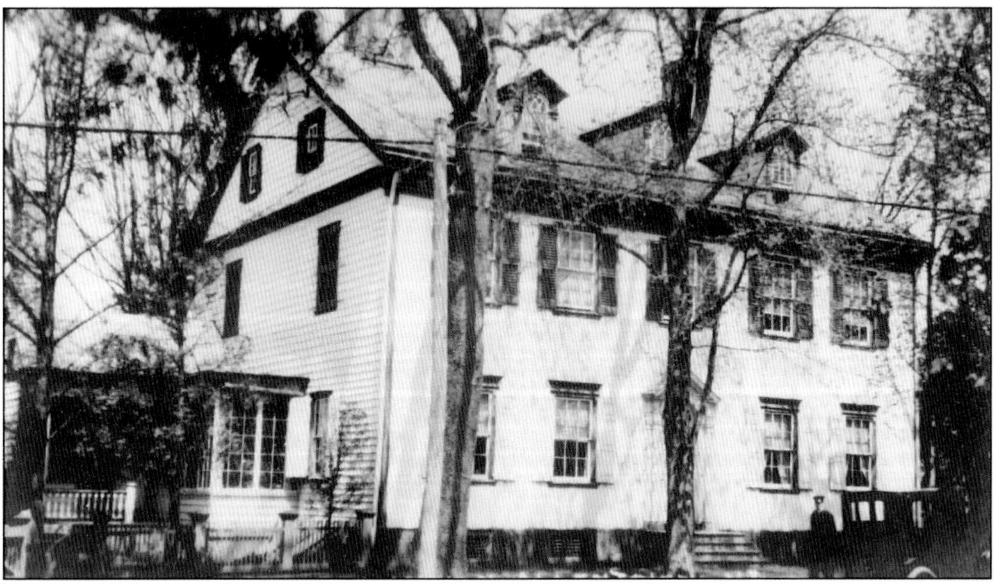

The frame residence John Imlay built in the early 1790s at 28 South Main Street, still known by his name, is one of Monmouth county's outstanding Georgian houses. Its interior plan is the expected center hall, with two rooms on each side. The exterior is well preserved; the interior is now occupied by shops, with a canopied entrance covering the fine door enframement. The house later served as Dr. Walter D. Farmer's hospital. This image is *c.* 1912. (Collection of John Rhody.)

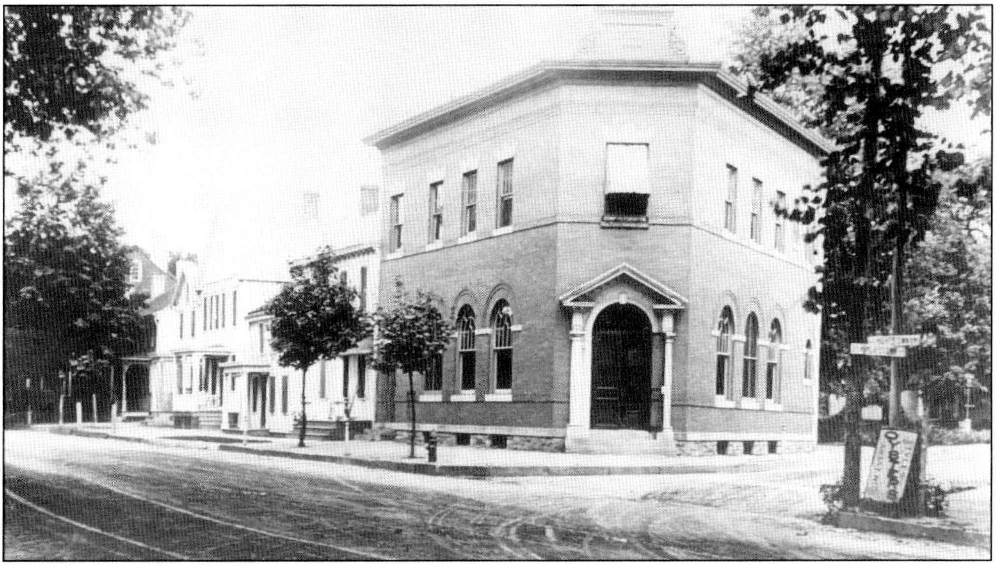

The Farmers National Bank, founded in 1886, was first located at 29 North Main Street, prior to the 1905–1906 erection of this building, designed by W.A. Poland, at the corner of North Main Street (left) and Walker Avenue. The bank grew and prospered while Allentown was a local commercial center for the surrounding farm country. Farmers merged into the Central Jersey Bank and Trust Company in 1963. The building is well preserved. The crest on the cornice is gone, but a bank clock, mounted on the Main Street facade after issuance of this c. 1910 photo card, is still in place. (Collection of John Rhody.)

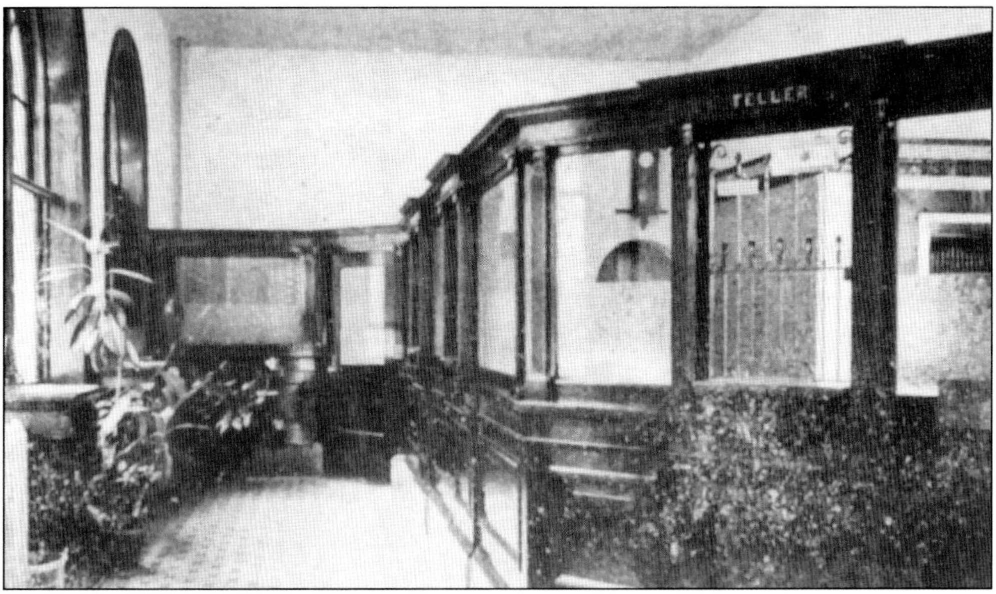

The interior is also well preserved, although banking fixtures are removed and a modern ceiling was installed. However, the oak table at left, and the vault at right are still in place, the latter used for storage. After years as shops, the place is now a marketing office for Mc Bee Systems, a manufacturer of specialty business forms. A large, portable safe on wheels unopened for years, occupies a corner which is not visible in this c. 1906 *Allentown Messenger* postcard. If any local reader remembers the combination (or can crack a safe), contact the friendly folks at Mc Bee.

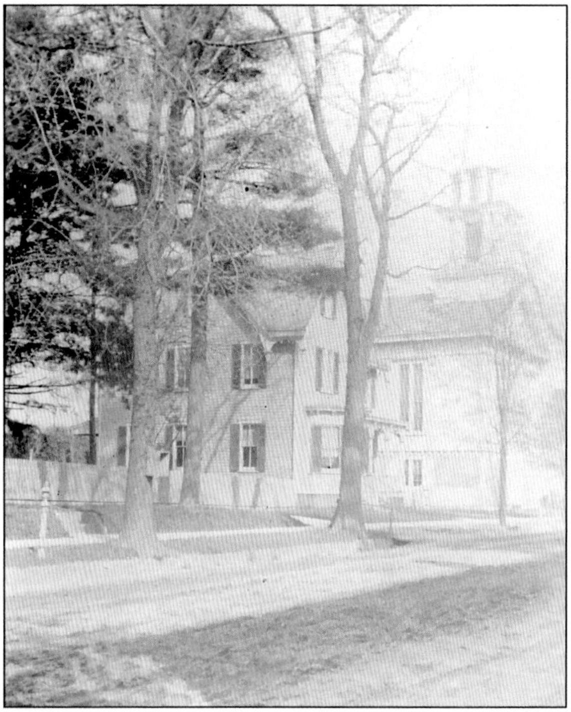

Early Methodism in Allentown is traced to *c.* 1795. The present Church Street edifice was built in 1859–60 and dedicated February 20, 1860. The church stands, little changed, but the steeple, long a safety concern, was removed in 1913. The house at number 23 is also well-preserved, but the place behind the stairs and hitching post is gone. The site is the entrance to the church parking lot. This divided back photo card is obviously pre-1913. (Collection of Glenn Vogel.)

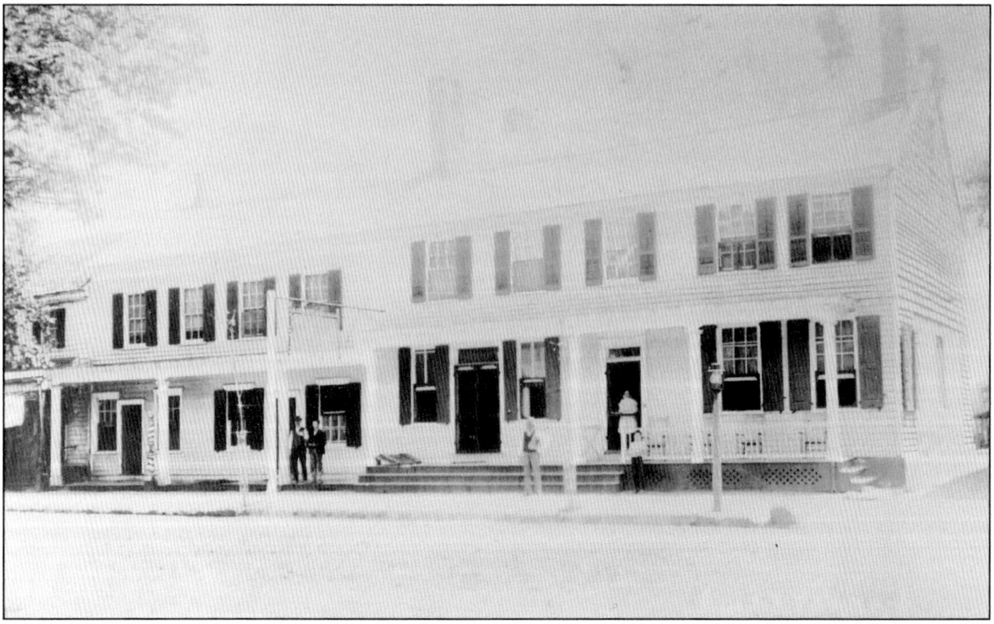

The Union Hotel, later known as the Allentown Hotel at 1 North Main Street, has 18th-century origins. It served as a stagecoach stop and for many years as a meeting place for various groups. This *c.* 1910 image links two buildings made more distinct today by separate occupancies. The shorter extension at left was removed for a gas station's lot, while the four-bay section to its right is the Allentown Wine & Liquor Store. The part at right is Di Mattia's Restaurant. The upper story is readily recognizable, but the ground-floor windows and doors have been altered considerably. (Collection of Glenn Vogel.)

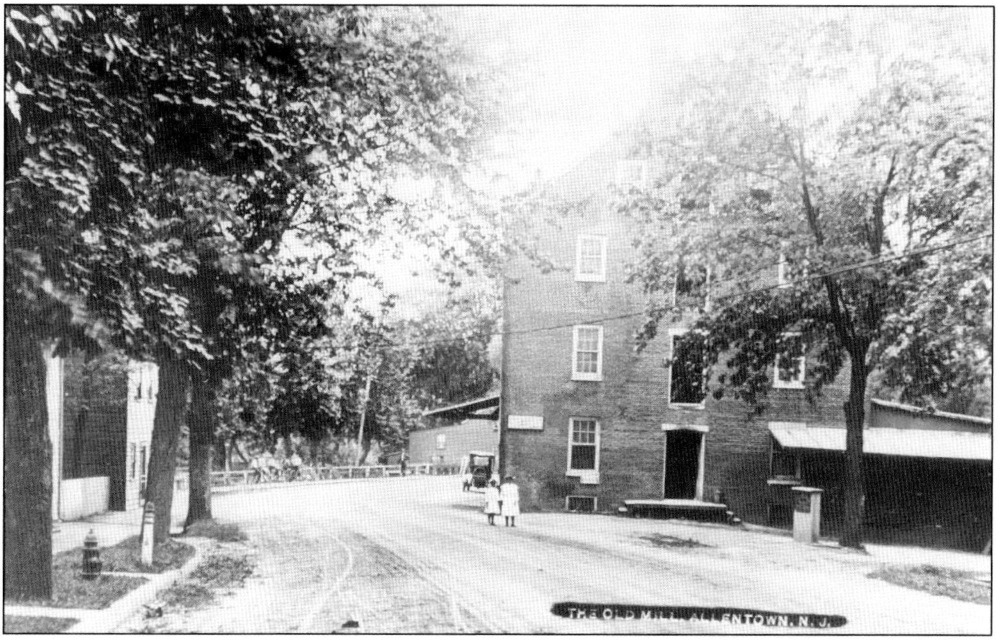

Nathan Allen purchased 110 acres on Doctors Creek in 1706 and built a gristmill that is the antecedent of this 1855 structure erected by Abel Cafferty, located south of the earlier structure, at 42 South Main Street. Its bricks were manufactured locally. A succession of owners operated the mill to 1963. This east elevation is readily recognizable today, although covered by paint. Shops and a restaurant occupy the building. Glenn Vogel, who lent several of the Allentown cards, is a descendant of Nathan Allen. (Collection of John Rhody.)

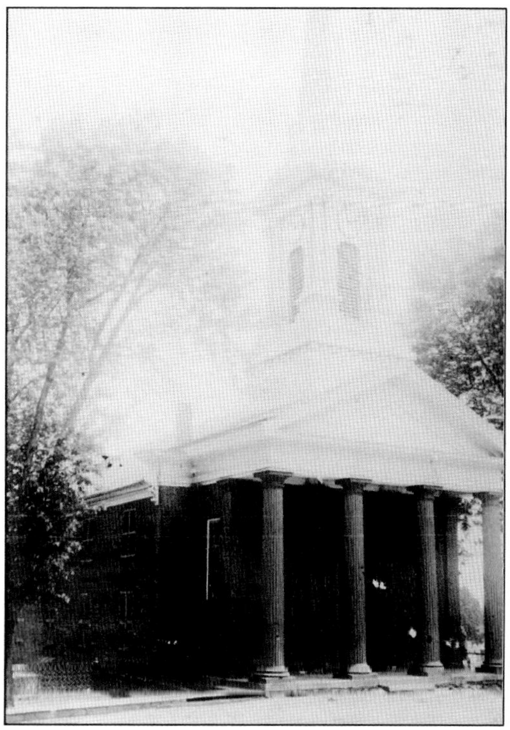

The Allentown Presbyterian Church was founded by 1756 according to a date stone on the facade, but their local history dates even earlier. This fine Greek Revival edifice was built in 1837 on High Street making extensive use of material from an older church. The steeple and portico were added in 1856. The church stands little changed from this c. 1907 image, other than the fence. (Collection of Glenn Vogel.)

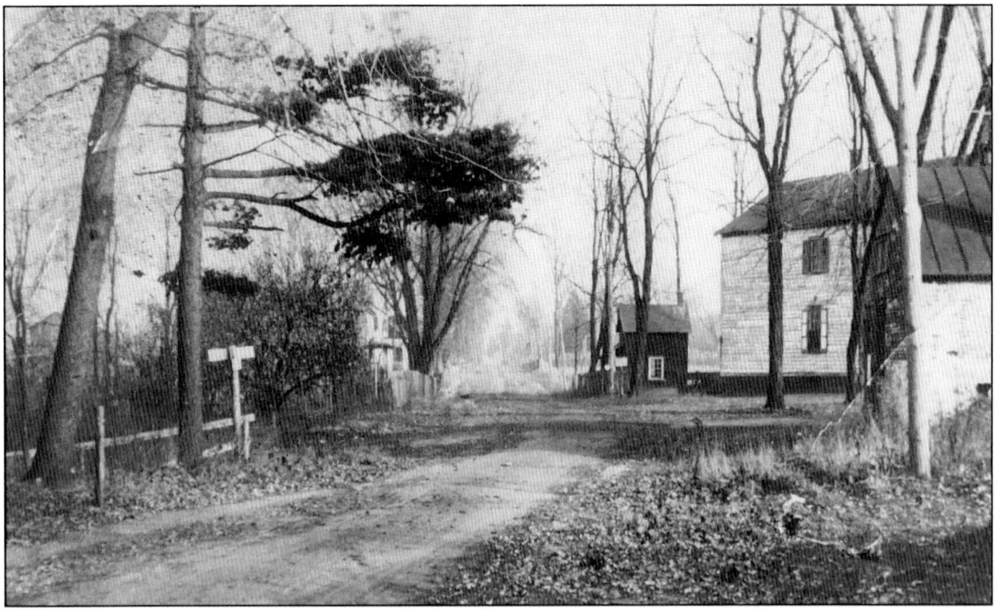

Ellisdale is a tiny hamlet on the Monmouth-Burlington border; Ellisdale Road runs east to Walnford, a settlement that developed around the country estate bought by Philadelphian Richard Waln in 1772. Commercial activity centered around a gristmill; its present *c.* 1873 structure is newly restored by the Monmouth County Parks System, the focal point of Crosswicks Creek Park. This image is a *c.* 1910 Underwood card. (Collection of John Rhody.)

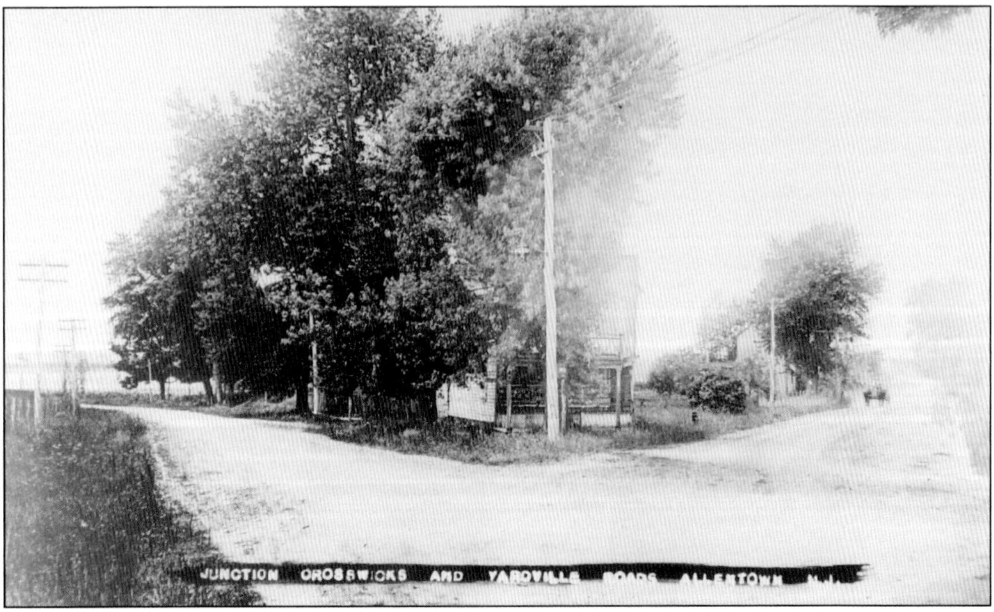

The juncture of County Highways 34 and 524, to the left and right respectively, was long a key separation in the road west of Allentown, a reminder of the town's crucial location. Crosswicks and Burlington are to the left, while Yardville and Trenton are reached via the road at right. The card also points out that western Monmouth County is much closer to Trenton than to the shore. A gas station-convenience store is at the intersection now. The Merriman photo was taken *c.* 1910. (Collection of Glenn Vogel.)

Three

The White Border Era

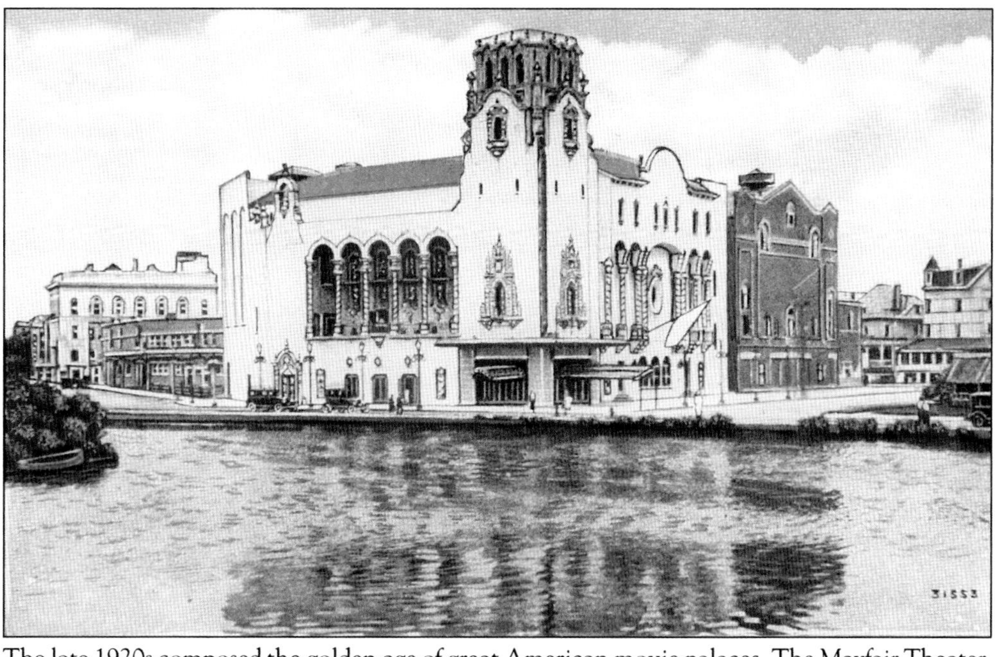

The late 1920s composed the golden age of great American movie palaces. The Mayfair Theater, on Lake Avenue, Asbury Park, arguably Monmouth County's finest, opened in August 1927. Changing demographics and movie exhibition practices, particularly smaller, multiple screens in one building, contributed to the Mayfair's demise. It was demolished in December 1974.

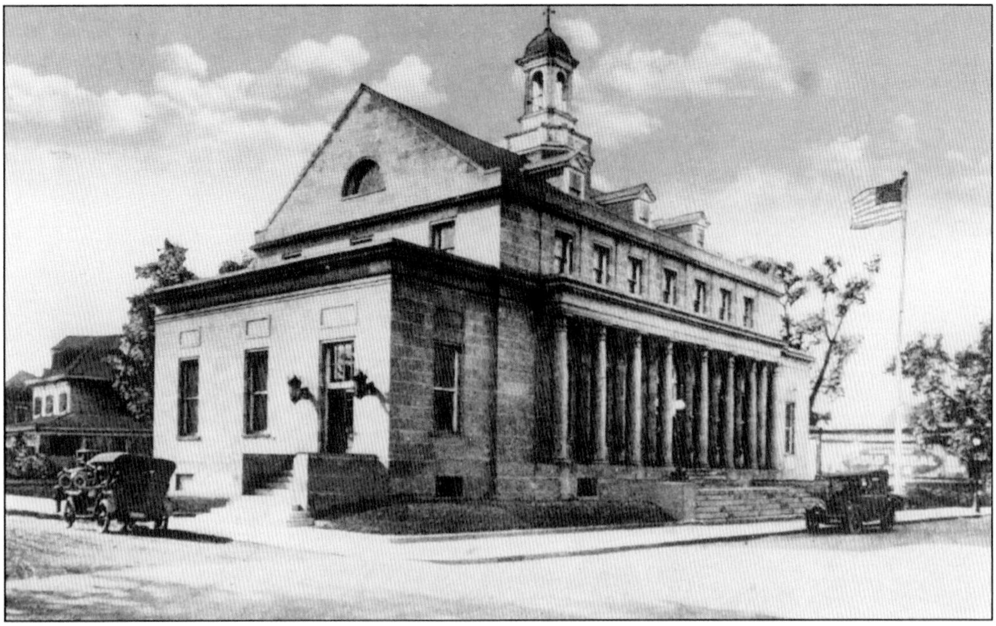

The post office at 60 Third Avenue, Long Branch, was designed by the government's architecture office and opened in 1915. The fine Colonial Revival design maintains today the appearance of this *c.* 1918 card. (Collection of John Rhody.)

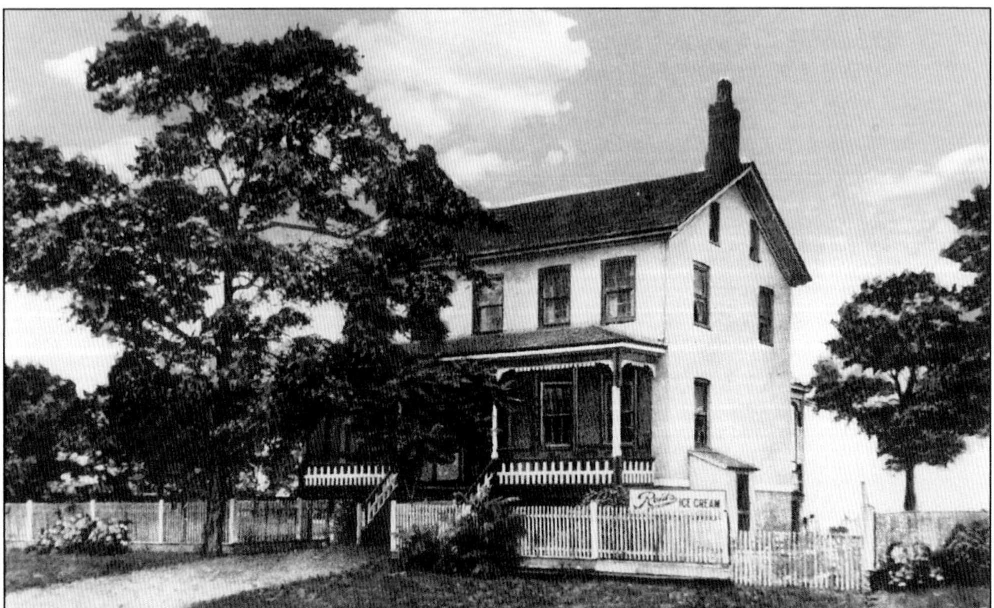

The varied career of the Lorraine Hotel, on Front Street overlooking the bay, has included other names and a past not usually discussed in genteel circles. It was long-ago converted to a private residence.

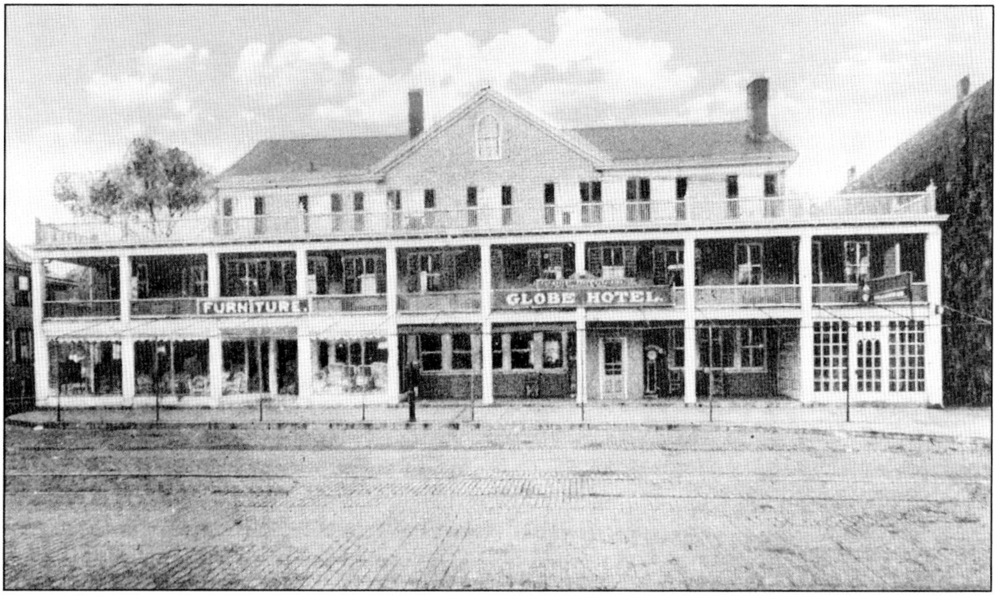

The Globe Hotel, on the south side of Front Street, a block east of Broad, had origins as a *c.* 1840 dwelling built by Robert Hunt. It was expanded for hotel use by Tobias Hendrickson, its 1844 buyer. The frequently illustrated place, long a major Red Bank gathering spot, shows change on this *c.* 1920s card; a third-floor balustrade was added and part of the ground floor was altered for a store. The hotel was destroyed by fire on December 19, 1936, with only the restaurant and bar left standing. (Collection of Keith Wells.)

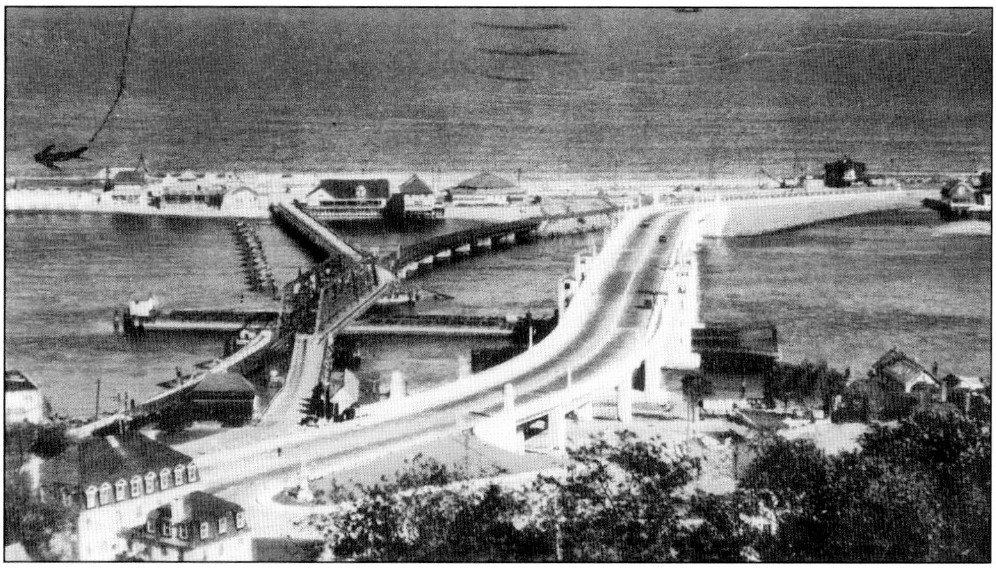

A new Highlands-Sea Bright highway bridge was built in 1932–33 and, having been opened earlier in the month, was dedicated on Saturday, September 30, 1933, with a parade and other festivities. The older bridge remained in service for rail operations, which were discontinued *c.* 1947. Note Sandlass' Pavilion in the left background, in Highland Beach, which is not and was not part of the borough of Highlands. This same view exists as a linen card, so the image may be said to bridge the two postcard eras in Monmouth County (pun intended). The bridge's replacement in being planned in 1998.

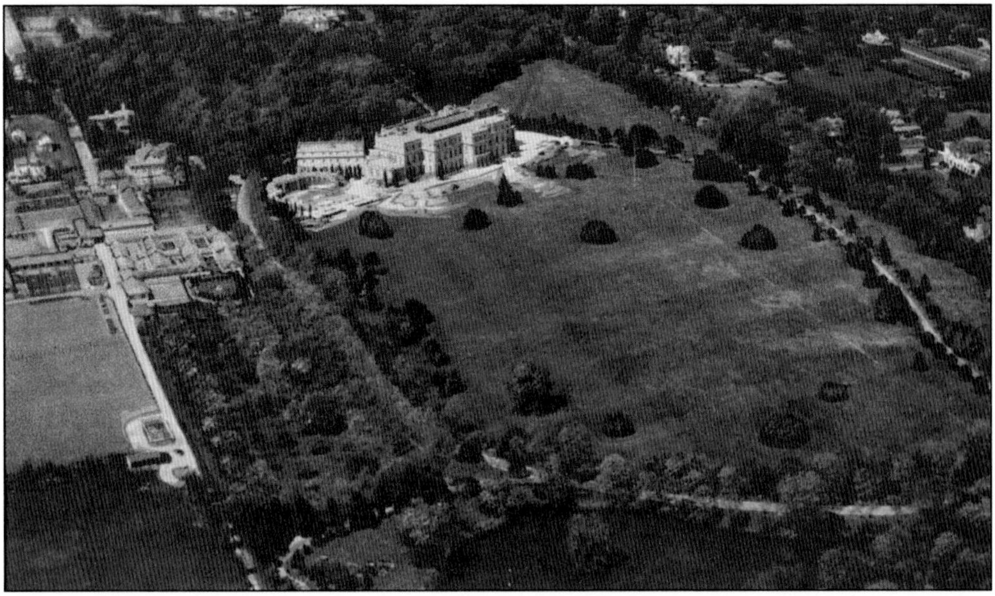

Hubert Templeton Parsons, a protégé of Frank W. Woolworth and president of the firm, commissioned Horace Trumbauer, a Philadelphia architect whose practice included some of the nation's finest country houses, to build a new Shadow Lawn (see p. 58). The Neo-Classical mansion, completed in 1930 and called the Versailles of America, is the costliest house ever built in Monmouth County. Parsons lost the house to foreclosure in 1938, unable to pay its estimated annual costs of $350,000 after losing his $650,000 salary following retirement in 1932 at Woolworth's mandatory age 60. The house is now the Woodrow Wilson Hall of Monmouth University.

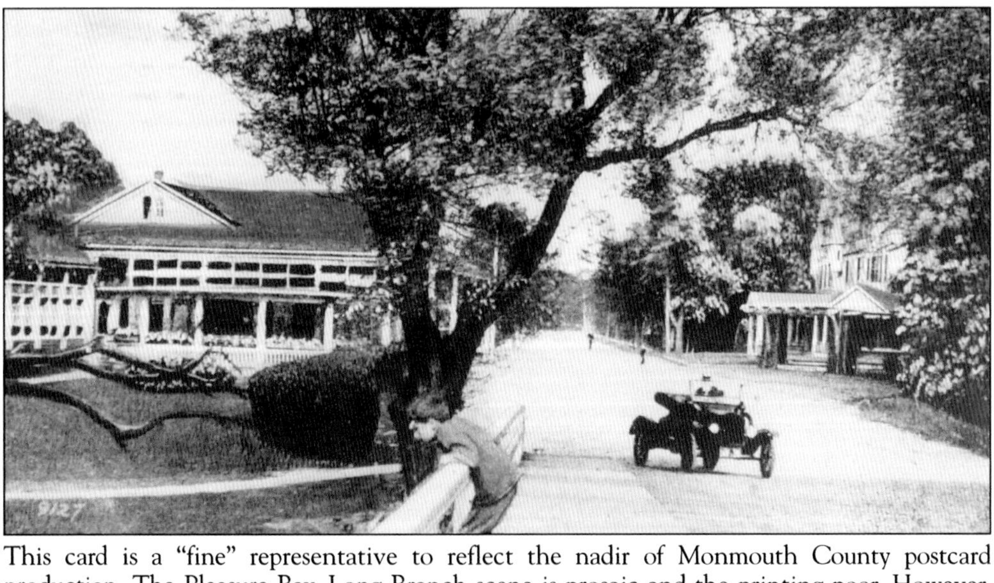

This card is a "fine" representative to reflect the nadir of Monmouth County postcard production. The Pleasure Bay, Long Branch scene is prosaic and the printing poor. However, it is the automobile, added by an artist in distorted size, that gives the card its deserved status. The linen era that followed was dismal graphically, but at least their coloration, at times outrageous, at others delicately subtle and sometimes what we now call "funky," stimulated the eye. (Collection of John Rhody.)

Four

The Linen Era

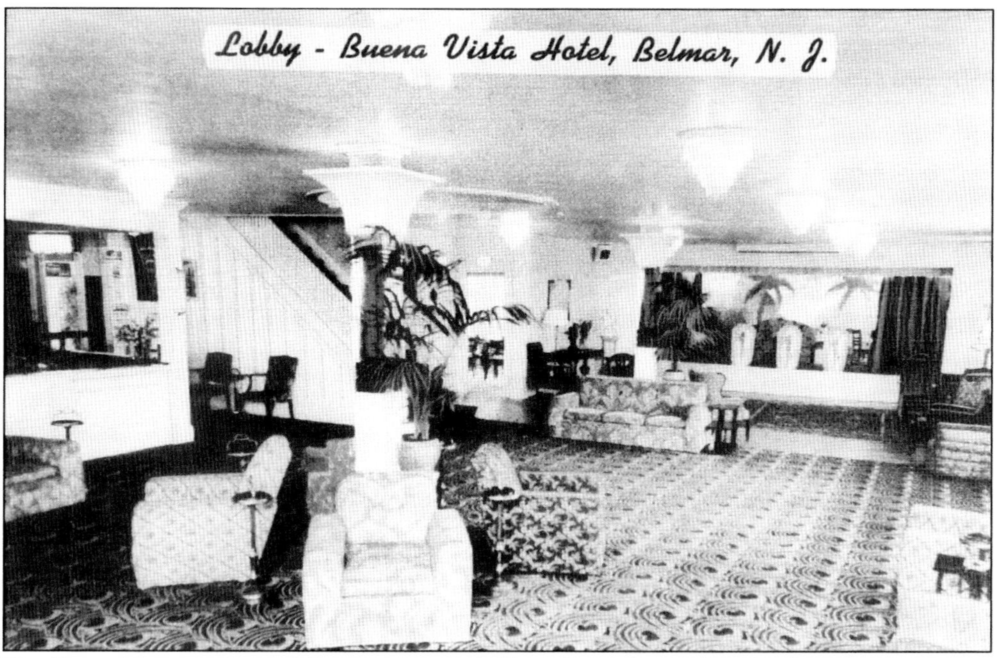

The Buena Vista, on Second Avenue, was probably Belmar's largest hotel judging by its capacity of 450 in a 1930s hotel guide, the period of this card. The warm pastel colors of the original linen created in inviting appeal for the place. The printed message advertised the proprietor's (M. Goldman in 1932) winter facility, the Hotel Jacobs in Lakewood, New Jersey. (Collection of John Rhody.)

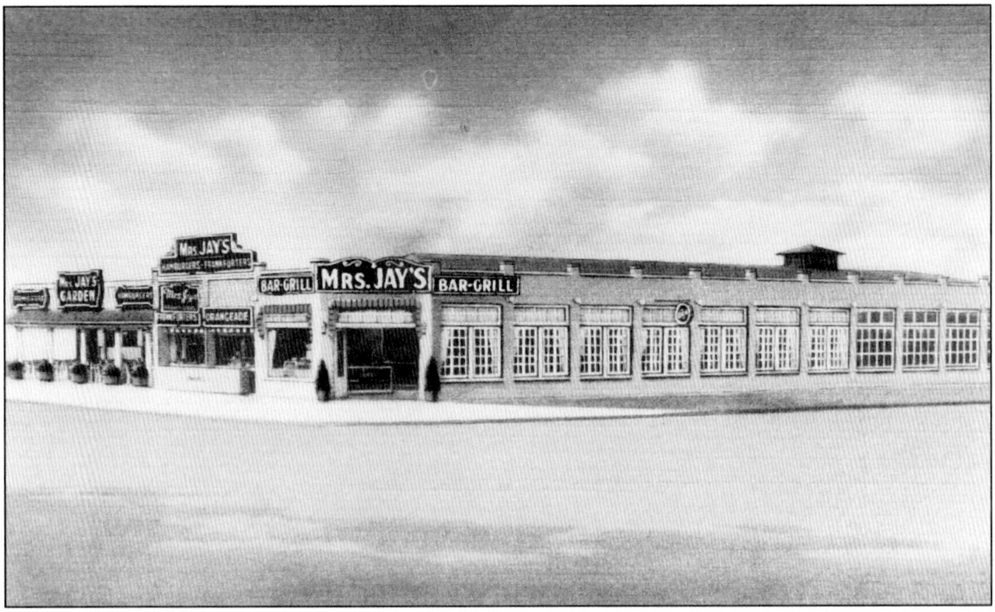

The original Mrs. Jay was Ida Jacobs, who began selling hot dogs on Ocean Avenue c. 1922. The seasonal restaurant was popular for its outdoor facilities. It survived into the 1980s, helped in its later years by proximity to the popular Stone Pony. Mrs. Jay's closed in December 1988; the building was demolished in 1990. (Collection of John Rhody.)

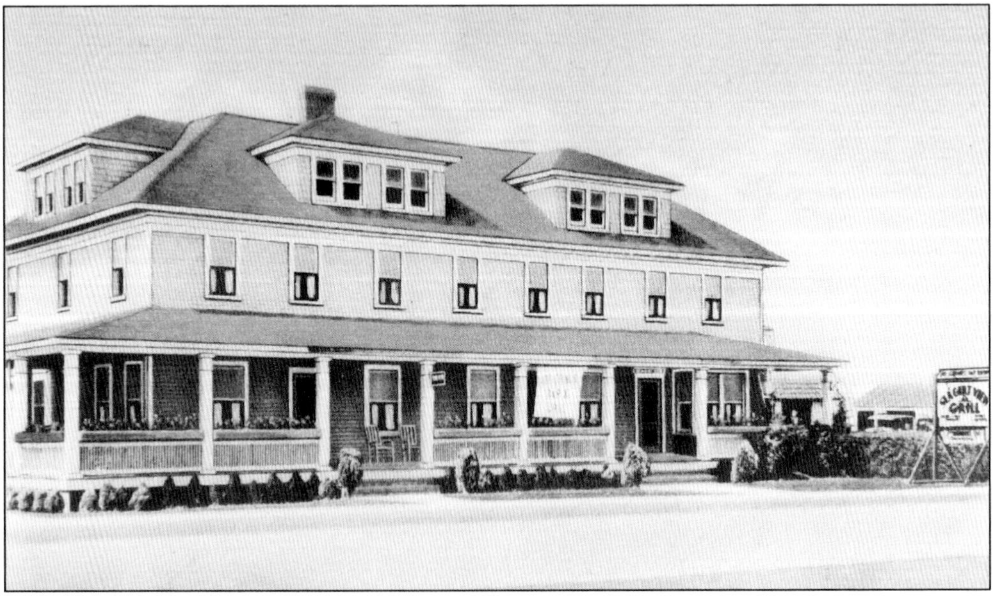

Joe Crine's Sea Girt View Hotel and Grill was located at Highway 71 and Sea Girt Avenue, facing the Sea Girt station. Its proximity to the National Guard Camp found the place a large military following in training season. (Collection of John Rhody.)

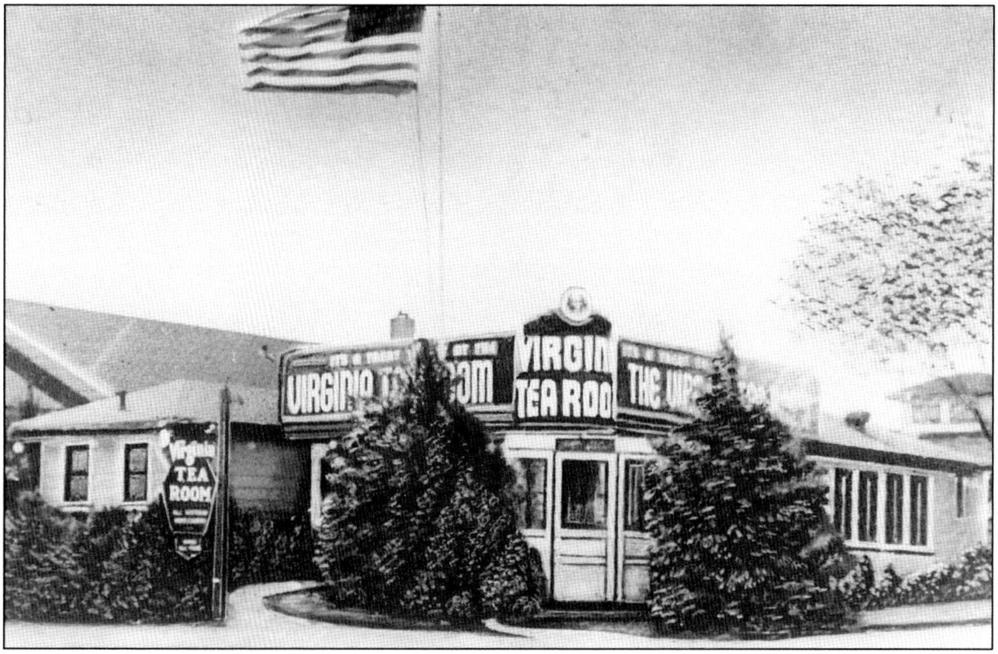

The Virginia Tea Room, a family eatery in the manner of the genre, located at the corner of Highway 35 and Munroe Avenue, is seen c. 1940 on a colorized Collotype Co. card. It was demolished in the late 1950s, unable to survive Highway 35's fall from stature as the shore's main road. Evelyn Stryker Lewis, curator of the Neptune Historical Museum, has fond memories of her childhood visits there. Her mother would inform the establishment that Evelyn's middle name was Virginia, a revelation that usually enhanced her dessert or afforded her a special attentiveness. (Collection of John Rhody.)

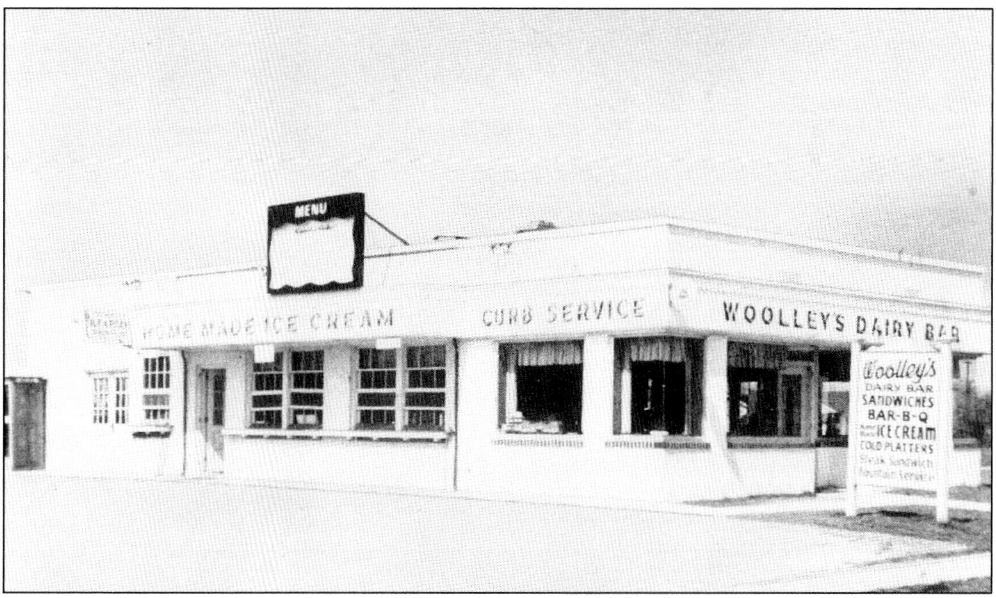

Woolley's was one of several Neptune dairies. Their highway drive-in was long-popular for good food and benefited from its proximity to Asbury Park. Woolley's became a casualty of changing roadside dining patterns at an unspecified date. (Collection of John Rhody.)

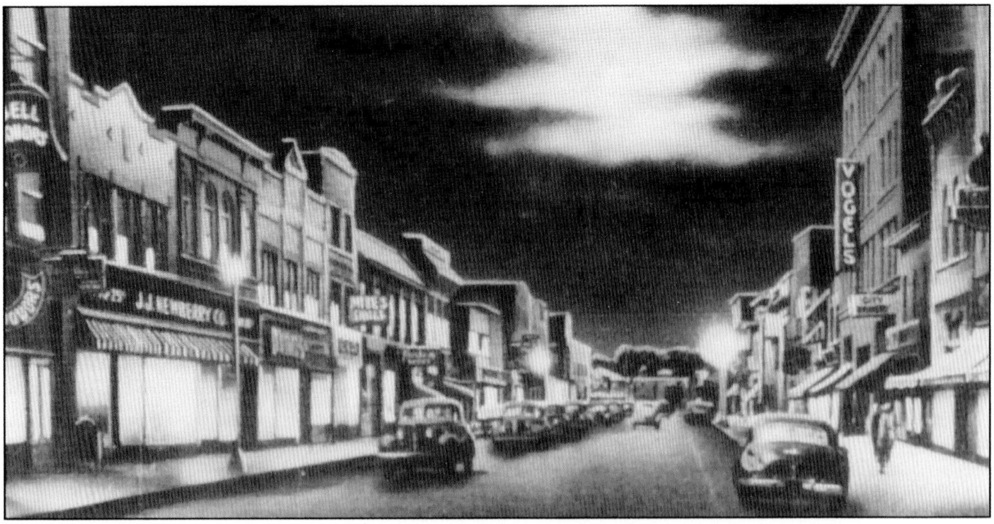

Broadway, Long Branch's main shopping street, is seen looking east, from east of Third Avenue in the 1940s, a time when that city was a major Monmouth County mercantile center. Five and dime variety stores, e.g. Newberry's, are becoming extinct, while Vogel's, located in the former Steinbach building, was destroyed by fire in 1978. The night colorization gave a dramatic ambiance to a mundane cityscape.

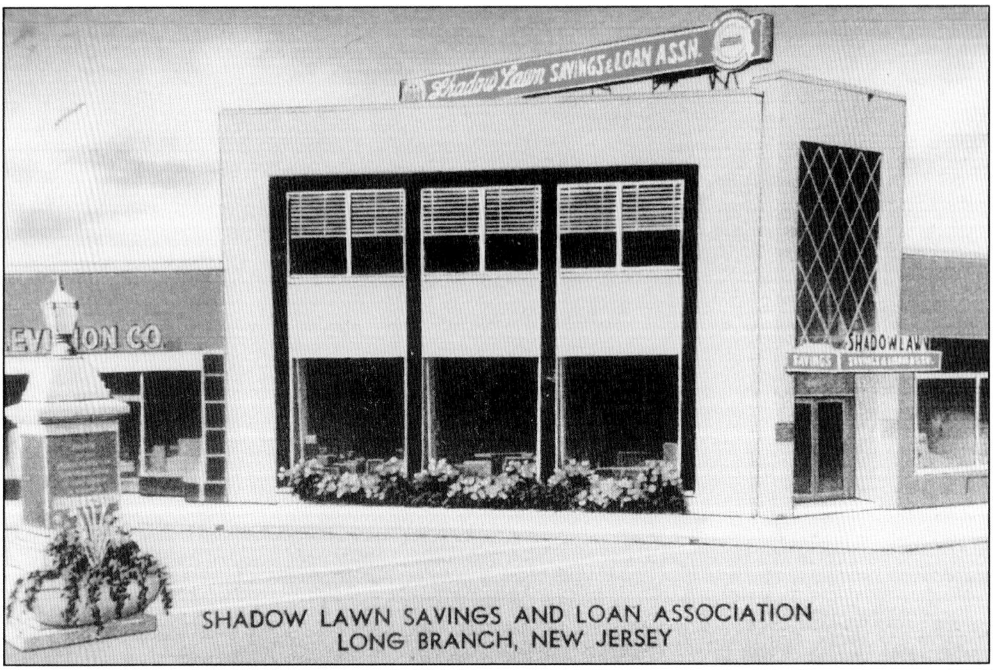

The Art Moderne headquarters of Shadow Lawn Savings & Loan Association added contemporary fashion to the old Long Branch upper Broadway business district when built c. 1930. Located at number 600, at Broadway's southwest corner with Norwood Avenue, Shadow Lawn claimed with a printed message on the back to be "The largest insured association in middle and southern New Jersey." Sovereign Bank occupies the place now, but the facade has lost its luster and the Chattle Monument at left was moved to the premises of the new city hall in 1978.

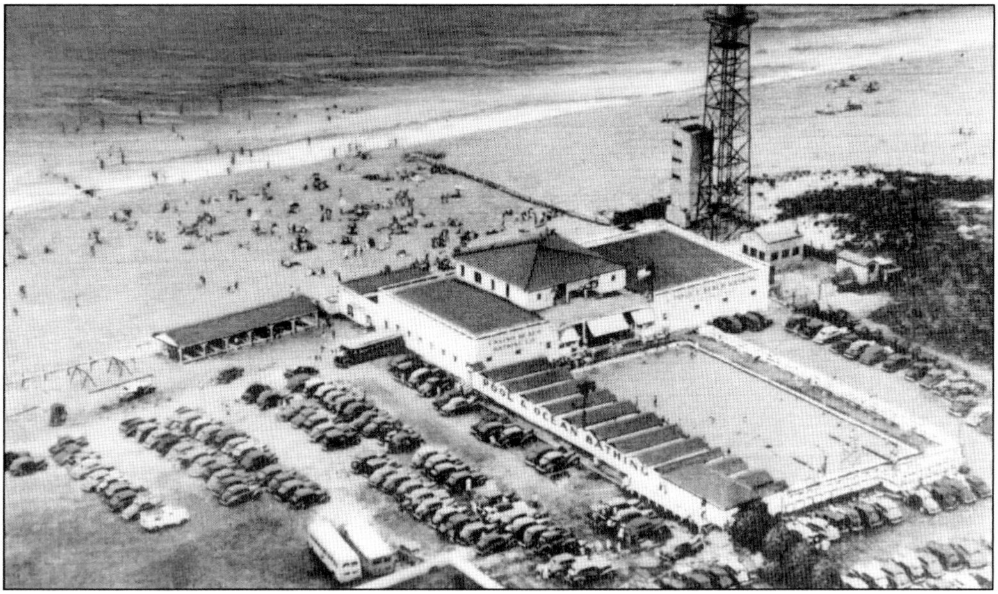

The Casino Beach and Pool at Avenel Boulevard in North Long Branch is believed to have opened in 1931 as the Villa Beach club. Later known as the White Sands, the place was sold to the City of Long Branch and destroyed by fire in 1978. (Collection of John Rhody.)

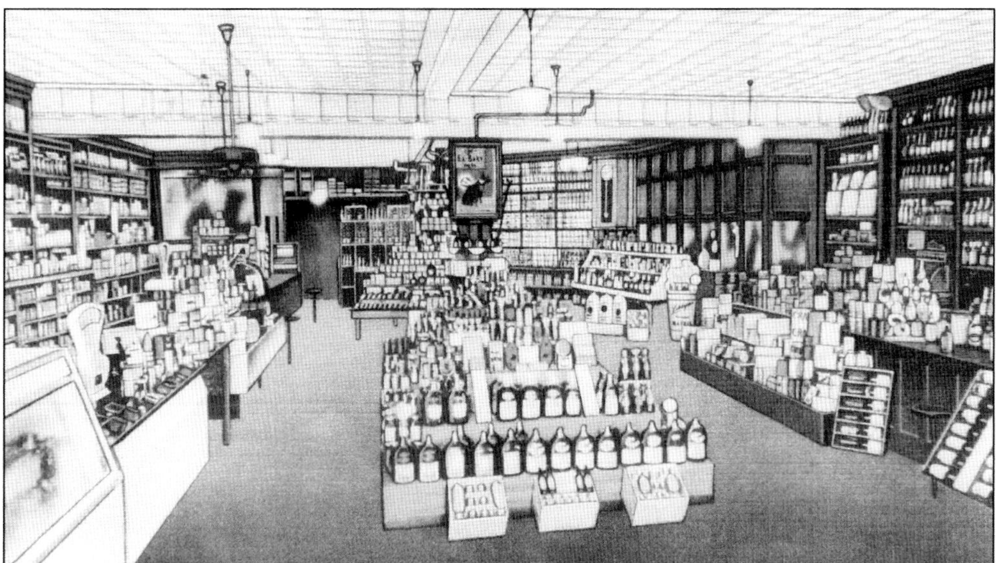

Linen store interiors are unusual. This Allenhurst Grocer card has a strong appeal, probably because it manages to depict considerable detail on a card medium not really suitable for same. This c. 1940s card must have been mailed by the store in quantity, as this example was franked with a printed bulk-rate indicium. (Collection of John Rhody.)

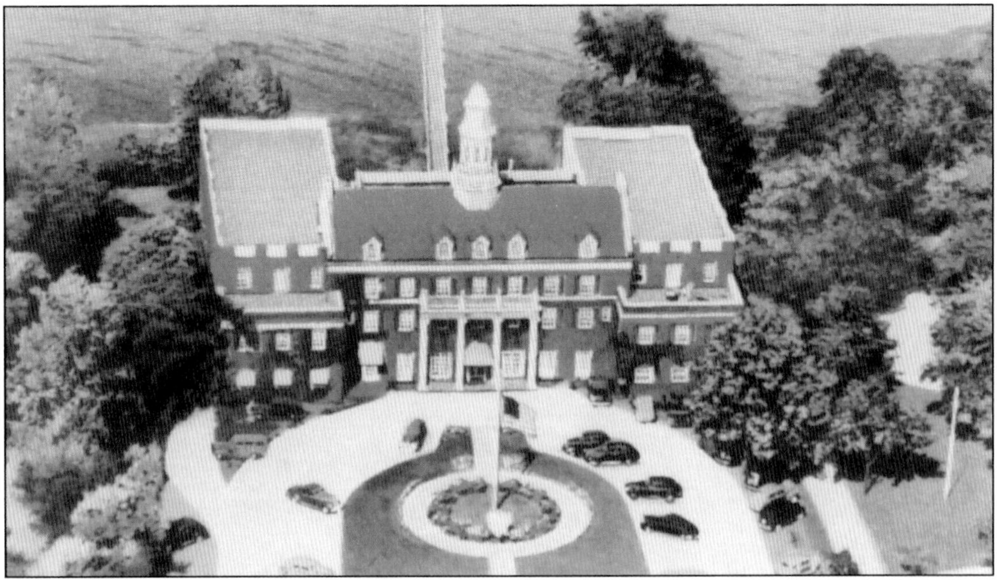

The Molly Pitcher Hotel, 88 Riverside Avenue, Red Bank, opened in 1929. Its architect was Nathan Harris and its Georgian Revival style reflected the influence the area's Revolutionary-era history had in design at the peak of the Colonial Revival, and even yet today. A few cars scattered around the semi-circular driveway suggests that the automobile was hardly the principal means of arrival in the 1930s. The facility thrives following extensive interior remodeling, is now known as the Molly Pitcher Inn, and has a large parking lot on the west, or left. Author's tip: their Sunday brunch buffet.

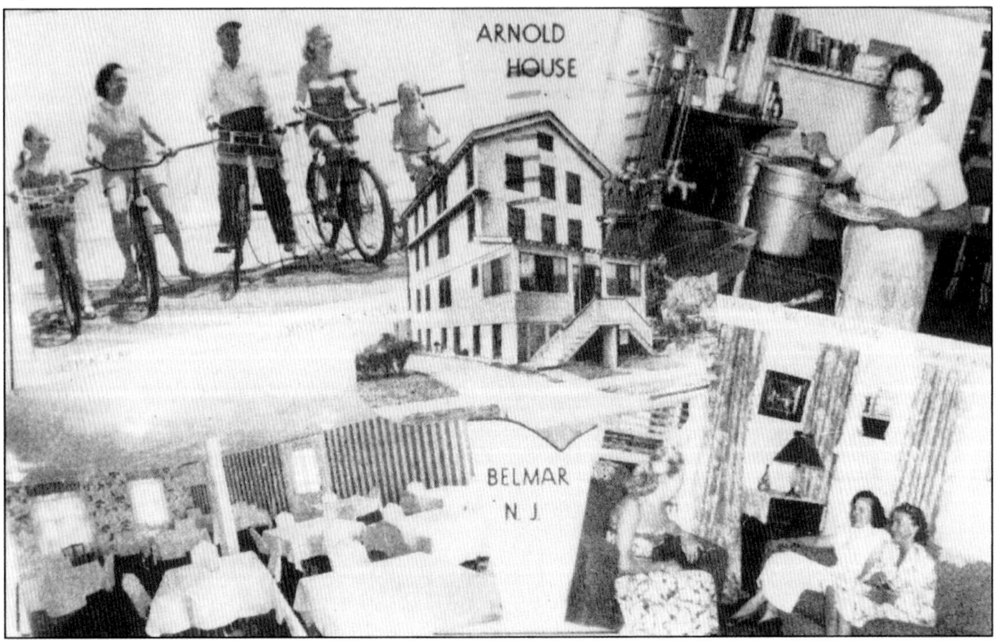

The Arnold House, 405 14th Avenue, makes maximum use of available space to convey the varied charm of this Belmar hotel *c.* 1950. It is a reminder of the disappearing free distribution of hotel postcards, once given by managements eager to broadcast their facility's appeal through the mail. (Collection of John Rhody.)

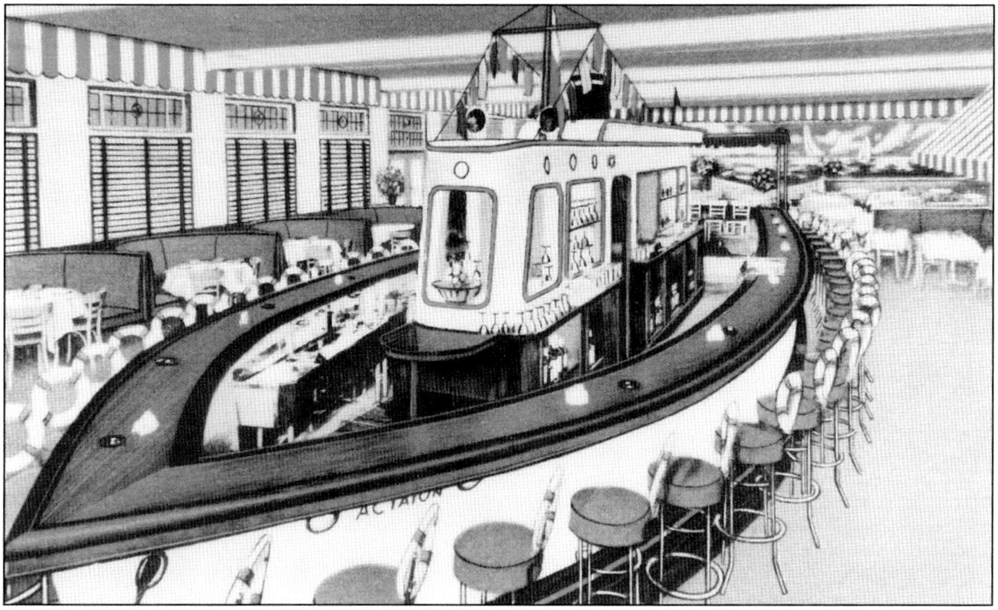

The *c.* 1930s card came with a preprinted message: "Hello. Just stopped in at the Actnion Yacht Bar and Grill and had my favorite cocktail and a delicious sea food dinner. Wish you were here to join me." This example was evidently sent by a teetotaler, who rubbed out the word "cocktail." John Rhody has seen the same view from a New York facility, making one wonder if either card is an error, or did the manufacturer of the bar provide the card suggestion. (Collection of John Rhody.)

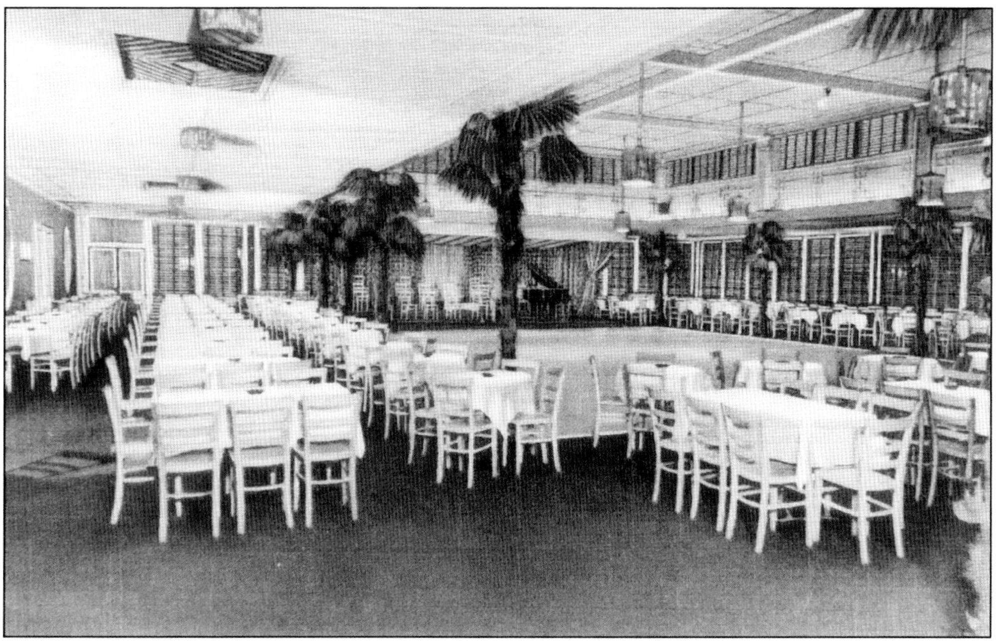

The enormous Sea Girt Inn on Route 71, viewed in the 1930s, was once a fashionable ballroom and wedding hall. The place was widely known as Jimmy Byrne's in the past generation, taking on later a new life around rock music entertainment. The facility deteriorated and a long-vacant, former highlight of shore life was demolished earlier in the 1990s.

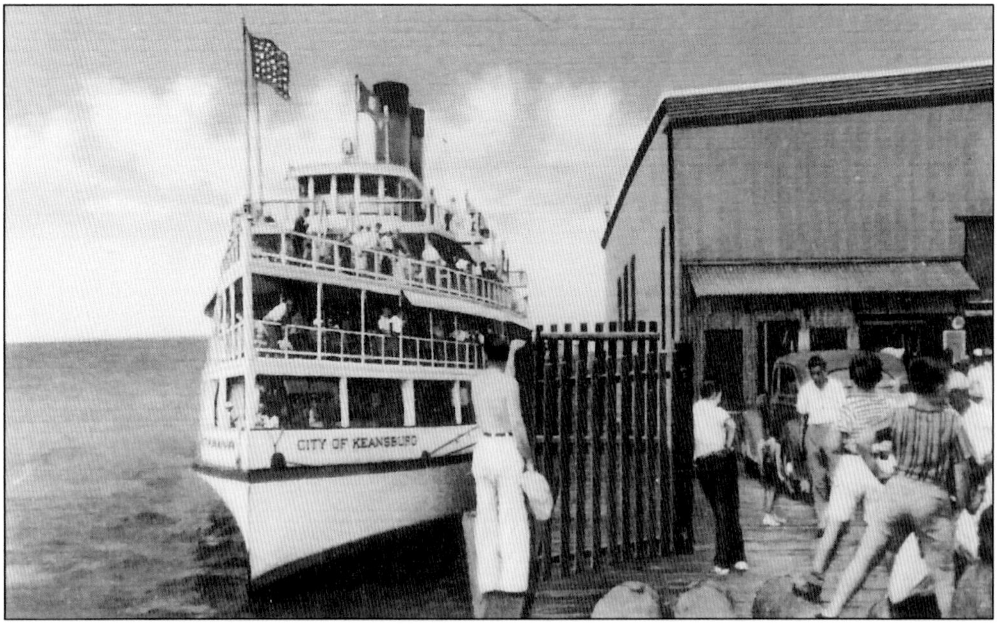

The *City of Keansburg*, built in 1926, replaced the *Keansburg*, destroyed by fire earlier that year. It was a 250-foot ship with two sets of 750-horsepower, 3-cylinder engines. It could carry 2,000 passengers and made three round-trips daily in season from New York City. The vessel ceased operations after the 1968 season, having attempted sightseeing trips and runs to Monmouth Park after its Keansburg pier burned in 1965. It now lies in a marine graveyard in Florida.

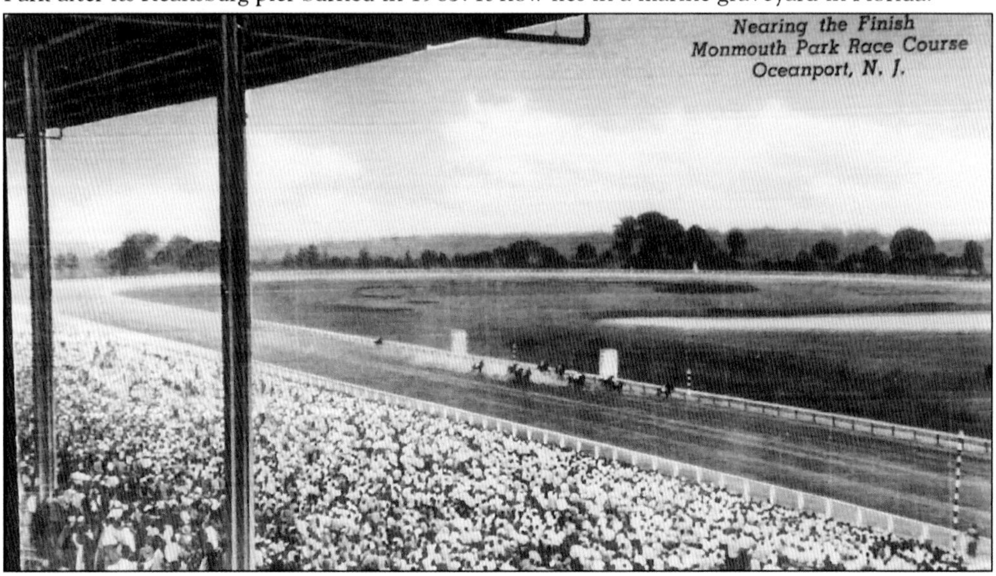

The present and pictured Monmouth Park at Highway 36, Oceanport, and Port au Peck Avenues, Oceanport, is the county's third track of that name. A not-yet-completed park opened in June 1946, following a long-campaign led by Amory L. Haskell to return the sport to New Jersey. Horse racing vanished following an 1893 ban on gambling. The clubhouse was completed in 1947, with numerous buildings added to the handsome facility over the years. Monmouth Park's most prominent race is the annual Haskell Invitational run in August and named for their modern founder.

Five

Mid-Century Miscellaneous

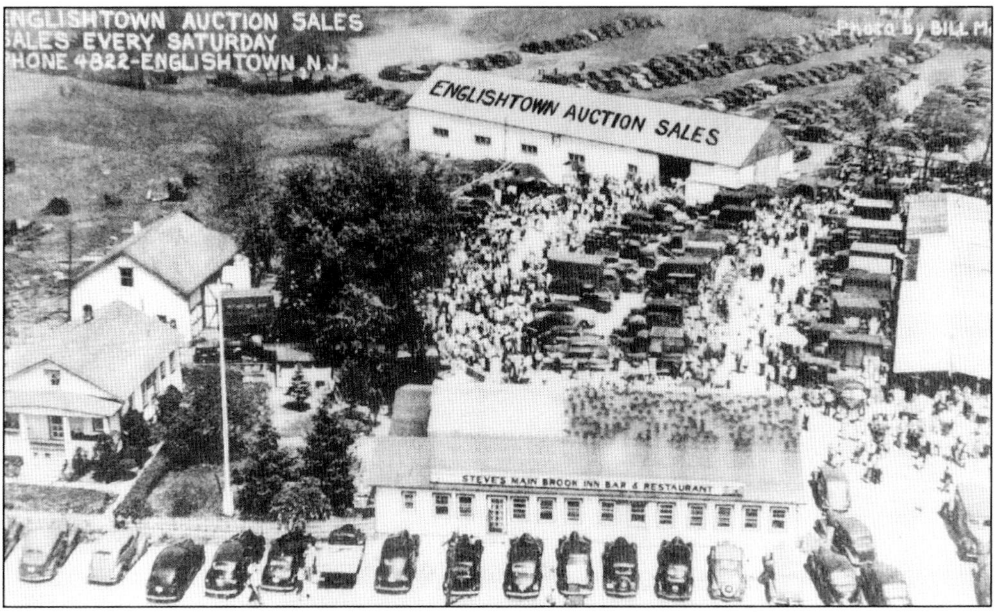

The 1929 origin of the Englishtown Flea Market, between County Highway 527 and Pension Road in Manalapan Township, was a farmers' auction. It took its exclusively flea market character over the past few decades. Although once dominated by used goods, new merchandise gained prominence over the past 10 years or so, much to the regret of those who liked the atmosphere of mystery surrounding estate sales and attic clearances. Nevertheless, Englishtown, as the place is known without further qualification, remains the state's largest and best-known outdoor market. This image from the late 1940s is unrecognizable. The old buildings were destroyed, notably by fire in December 1977; several steel buildings provide a sizable indoor section, too. (Collection of John Rhody.)

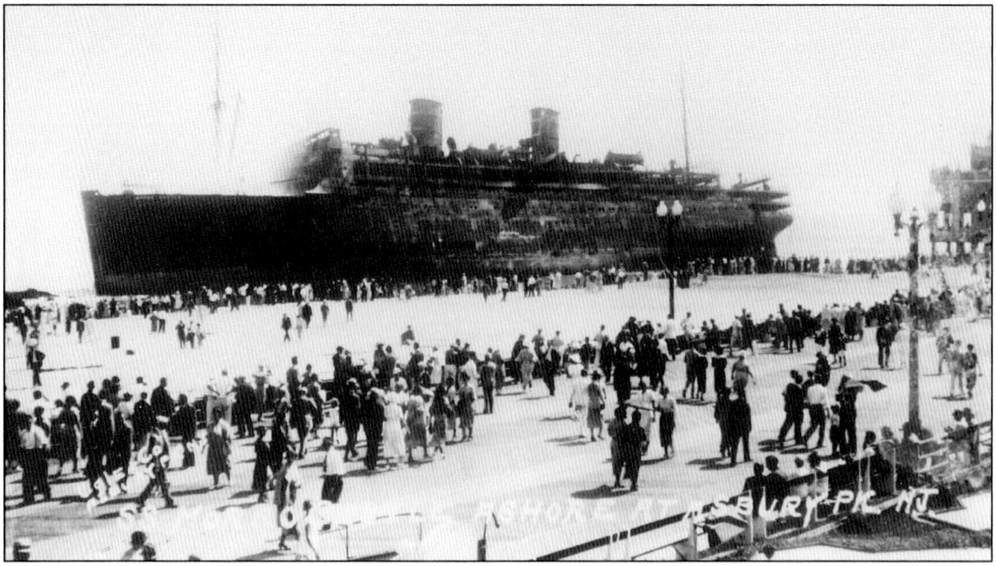

The American Ward Line cruise ship *Morro Castle* burned off Asbury Park on September 8, 1934, killing 86 passengers and 49 crew members. The ship's aground position a short distance from the Casino (right), attracted throngs of on-lookers, many with cameras, making the disaster one of the most photographed and published events of the 1930s. The ship was towed from the beach the next March and scrapped. The event still sparks debate on the judgment of the captain and behavior, and possible criminal culpability, of some of the crew.

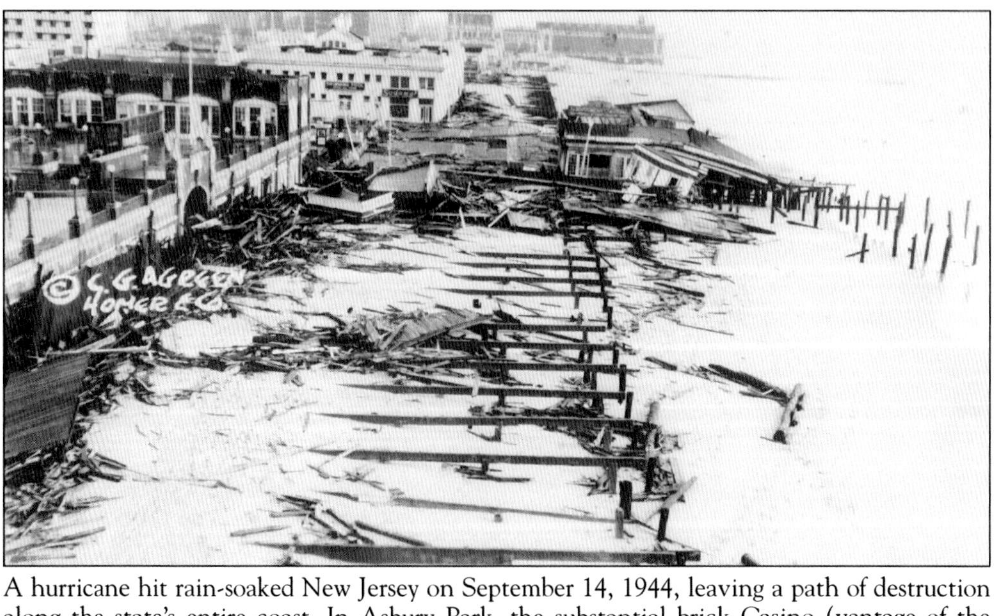

A hurricane hit rain-soaked New Jersey on September 14, 1944, leaving a path of destruction along the state's entire coast. In Asbury Park, the substantial brick Casino (vantage of the photographer) and the Convention Hall, seen in the distance, were spared, but the devastation of the boardwalk is evident, its assault including smashing by a reported 50-foot wave. (Collection of John Rhody.)

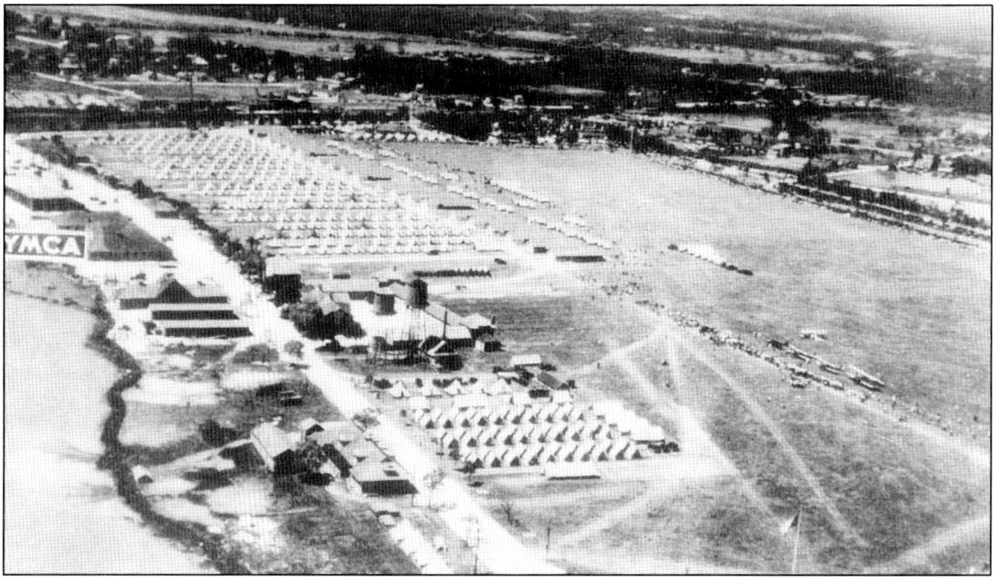

The National Guard Camp included an extensive camp ground for tents, a rifle range, equestrian facilities, and an air field. The camp name changed regularly to honor the sitting governor. One wonders from which of A. Harry Moore's three terms this Artvue aerial dates. The bi-planes may suggest 1926–28, but they may also have been in National Guard use later. Moore also served 1933–35 and 1938–40.

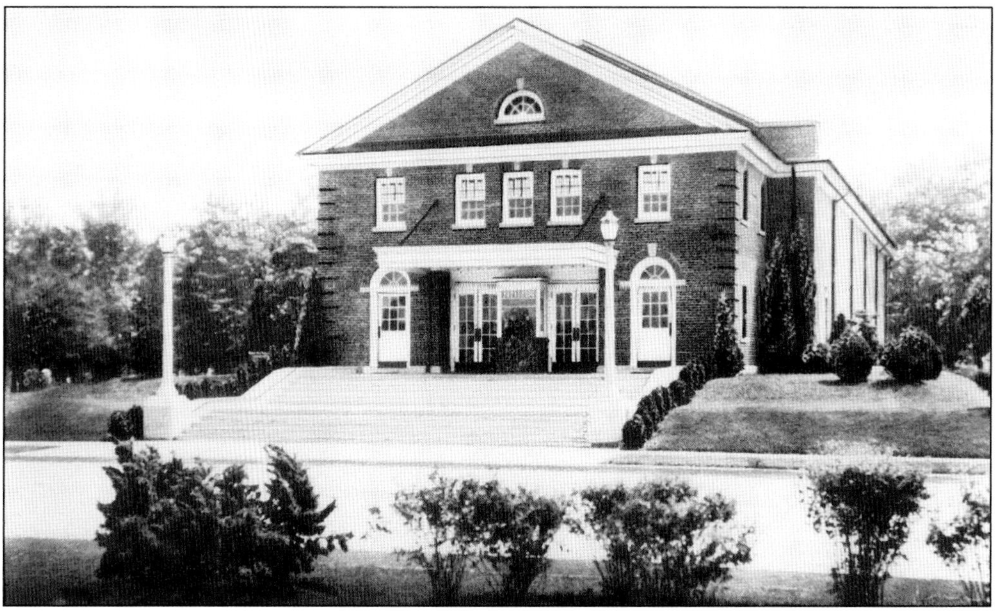

The 574-seat Colonial Revival-style Fort Monmouth Post Theater (architect unknown) opened in December 1933, its construction financed by Army Motion Picture funds. Building 275, initially called War Department Theater Number 1, was dedicated in December 1953 as Kaplan Hall in memory of Major Benjamin Kaplan, who served 25 years at Fort Monmouth in both military and civilian capacities. Today the building is the Fort Monmouth Communications Electronics Museum; its curator is Mindy Rosewitz. Exhibits tracing army communications history include the war hero carrier pigeon Cher Ami.

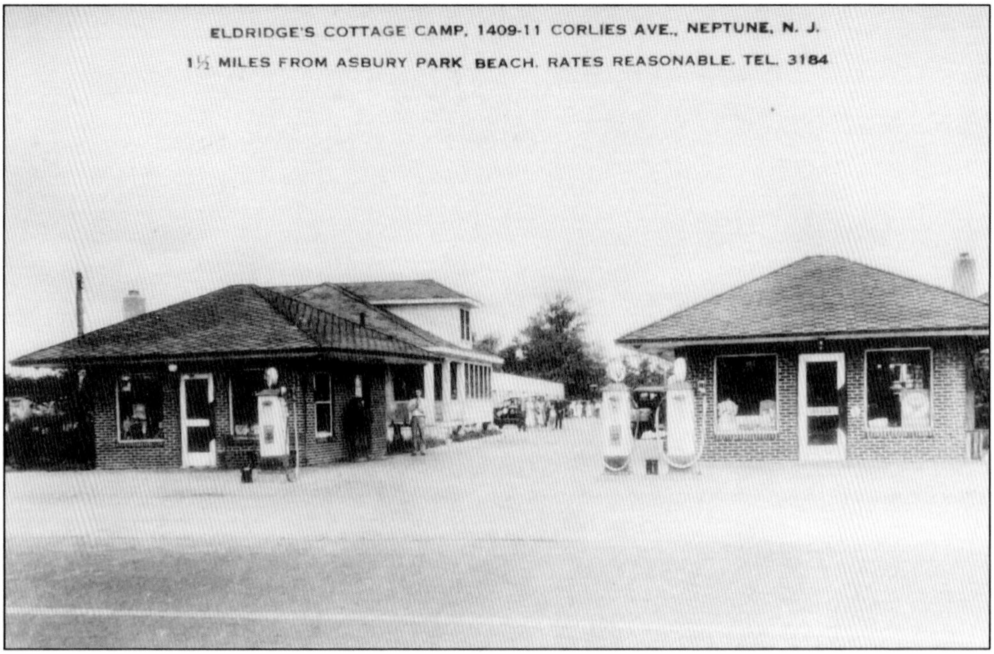

Eldridge's *c.* 1940 card advertised great amenities of the day—gas, electric, running water, and public hot and cold showers! There was a tent and trailer camp, with part of the latter still in existence. However, the north side of Highway 33 frontage is now filled by the leviathan of the highways, McDonald's. (Collection of John Rhody.)

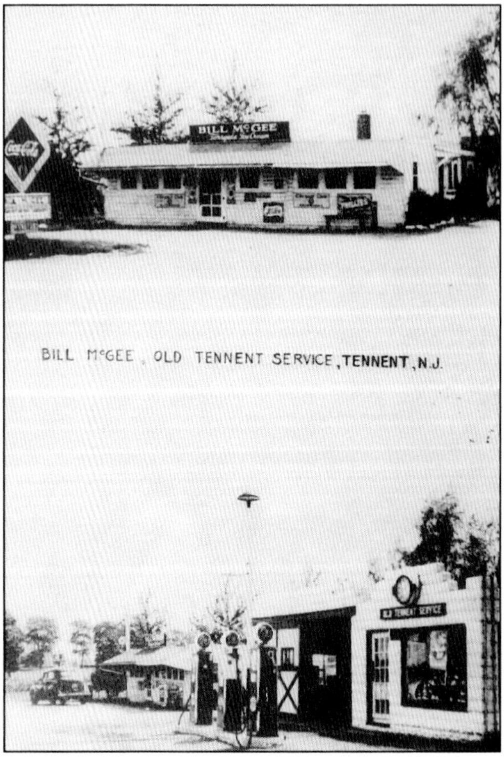

Bill McGee's rustic roadside eatery with window service was remodeled *c.* mid-1970s to a conventional store; its name, Battleground Deli, reflecting the historical influence of the nearby Revolutionary War Monmouth Battlefield. The former Gulf service station has been remodeled beyond recognition. It is behind a wood frame enclosure housing the Tennent post office. The vertical Collotype card is from the 1940s. (Collection of John Rhody.)

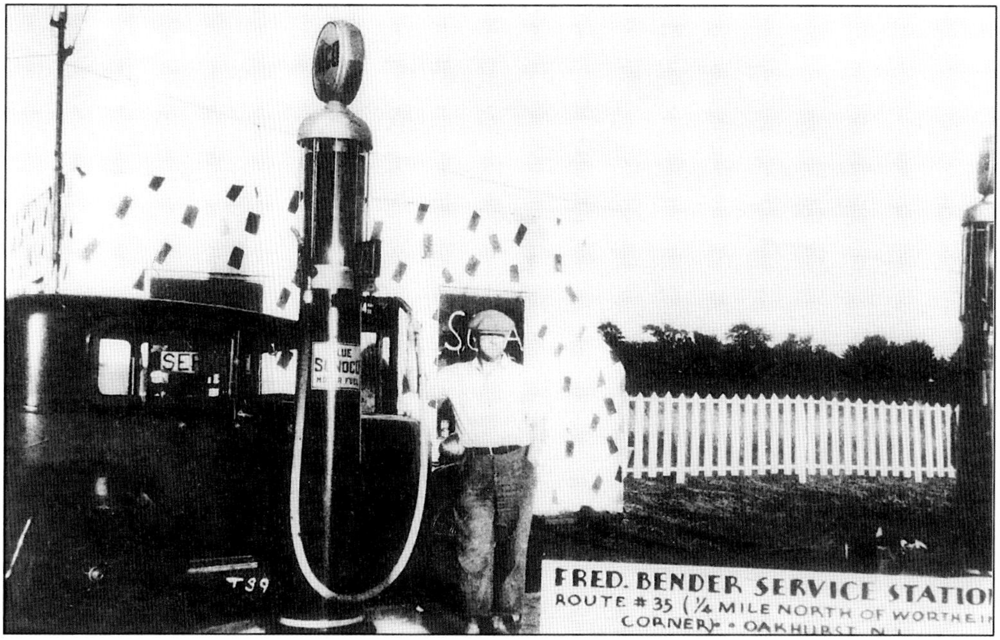

Numerous Sunoco stations were pictured on advertising cards *c.* early 1930s, probably issued as part of the industry's campaign to reflect a cleaner image than the one they garnered in the early days of motoring. They are usually scarcer than scenic cards, as most were likely discarded by their recipients. Note the glass window in the pump, a design to show the motorist the clarity of the product. (Collection of Robert W. Speck.)

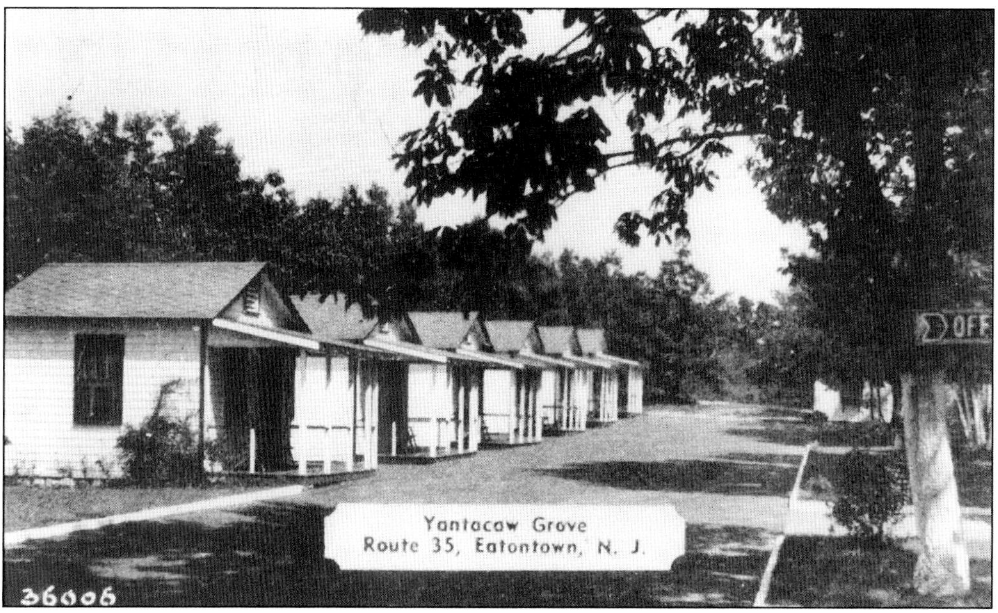

The Yantacaw Grove card claimed it was the Jersey Shore's most modern tourist cabin court, open all year featuring private showers, radios, and hot water. The undated Silvercraft card is likely *c.* 1930s. The precise locale is unknown. (Collection of John Rhody.)

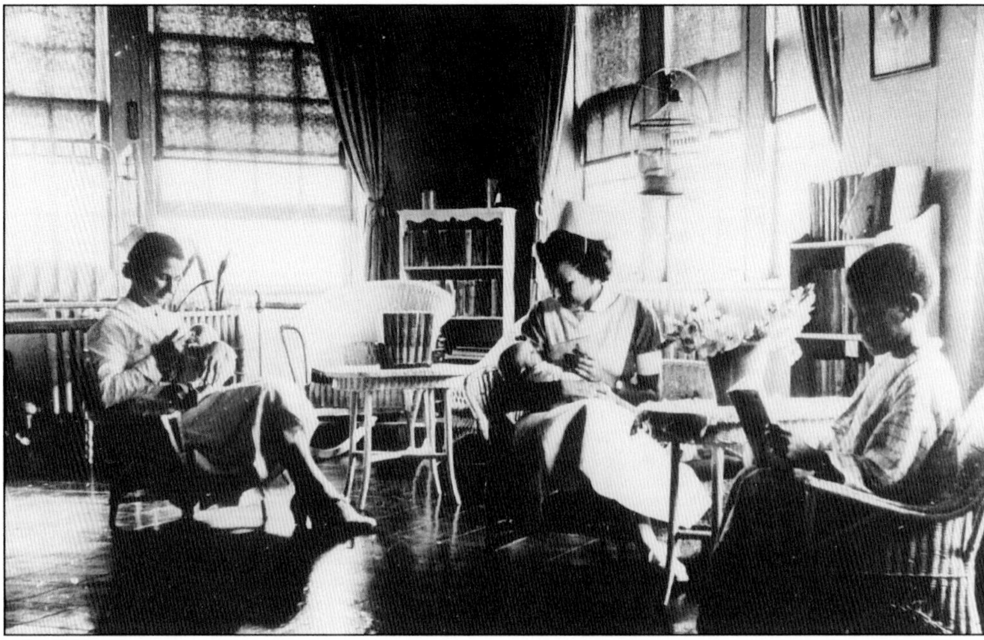

Ann May Hospital in Spring Lake was the antecedent of the Fitkin Memorial Hospital; it relocated to Corlies Avenue, Neptune, following the *c.* 1930 construction of a modern building after a $500,000 gift from A.E. Fitkin, an Allenhurst and New York utilities executive. The memorial was to Fitkin's son Raleigh, who died at Allenhurst *c.* 1915, and Paul Morgan of Interlaken, a former manager at Asbury Park for Jersey Central Power & Light Co. This image is a 1930s photo card. The hospital is now Jersey Shore Medical Center. (Collection of John Rhody.)

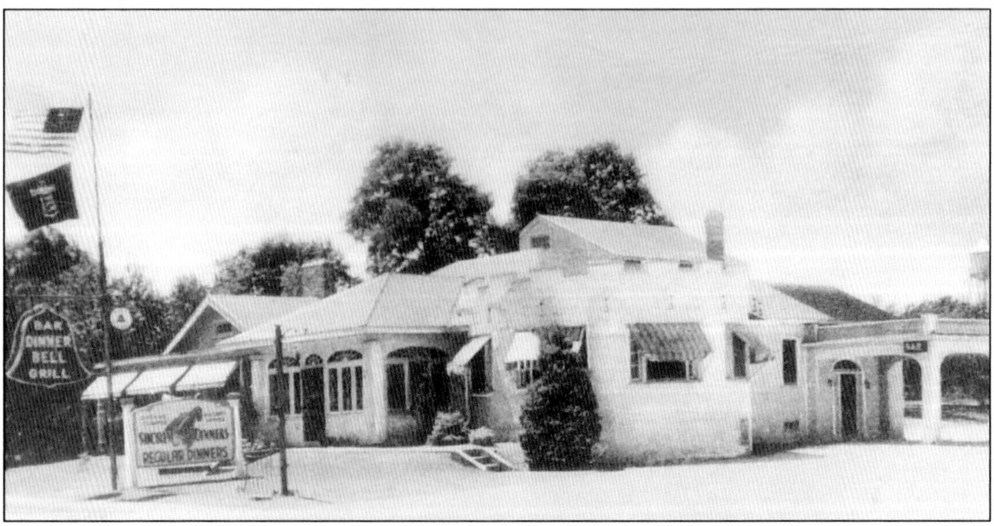

The Dinner Bell was a classic use of a symbol and sign to establish roadside recognition, although their "dinner" bell has more than a passing resemblance to the once-ubiquitous phone company (remember when the term was singular?) coin phone bell sign next to it (from the days when the phone was in a booth). The structure stands on Route 71, near Bradley Avenue, having gone through many name changes. The image is *c.* late 1930s. (Collection of John Rhody.)

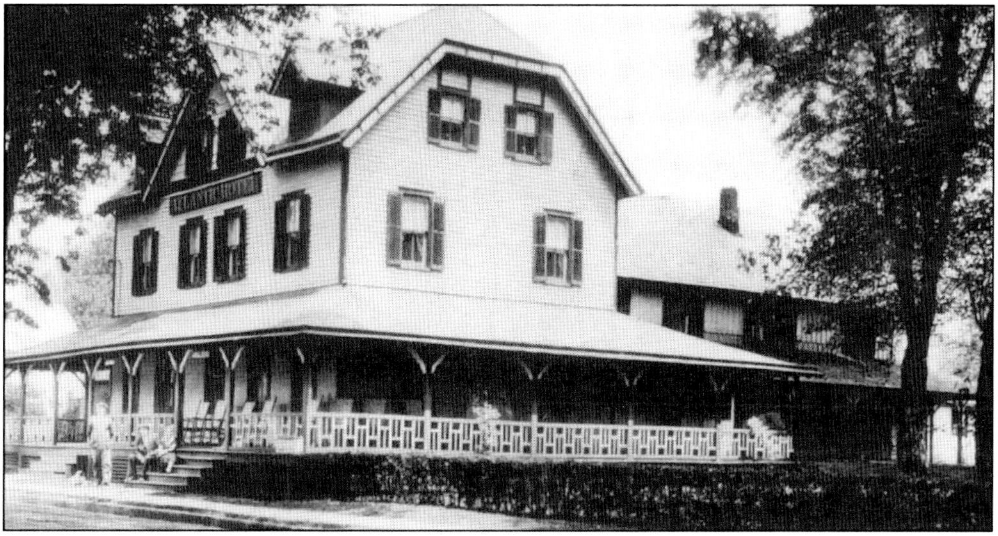

Abe Bennett's Atlantic Hotel, built at 121 Fair Haven Road in 1889, quickly became one of the town's major gathering places; a large theatrical clientele was prominent among its patrons. The building, seen c. 1920s, was little changed over many years; it initially did not have the side porch and the stairs were later relocated along the front. The structure, still standing but with its appearance altered by unsympathetic remodeling and expansions, has been home in the recent past to various restaurants, currently The Varsity Club.

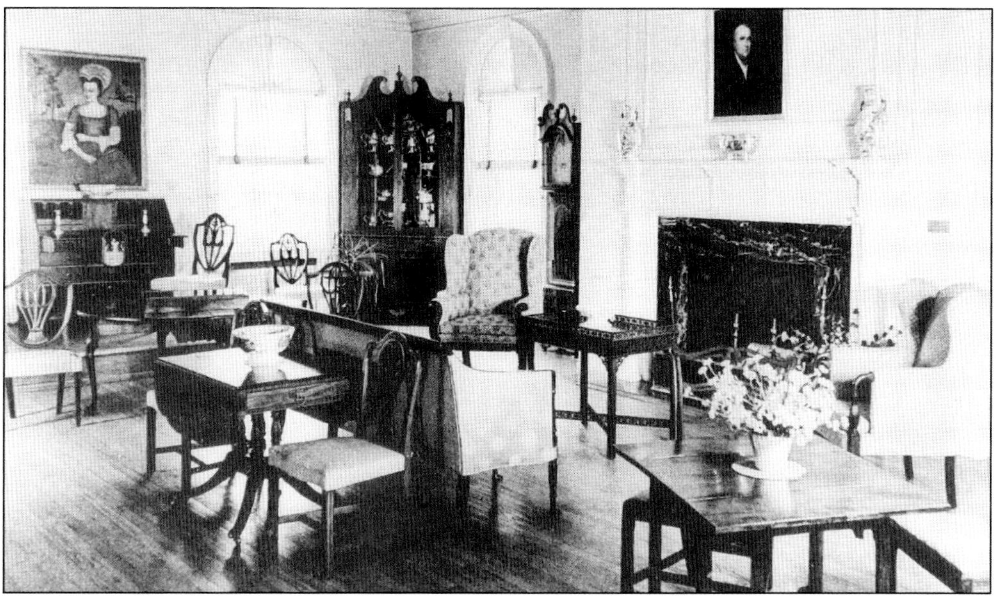

The Washington Room occupies the northern part of the Monmouth County Historical Association's museum, to the right of the hall on entering, at 70 Court Street, Freehold. This c. 1930s Meriden Gravure card shows architect J. Hallam Conover's fine Colonial Revival interior detailing and reflects a no-longer extant exhibition practice. The Association formerly used the room for a permanent display of some of their finest decorative arts objects and paintings; the room is now used for changing exhibitions, the Association drawing on its extensive collections and loans to present varied interpretations of Monmouth County's history.

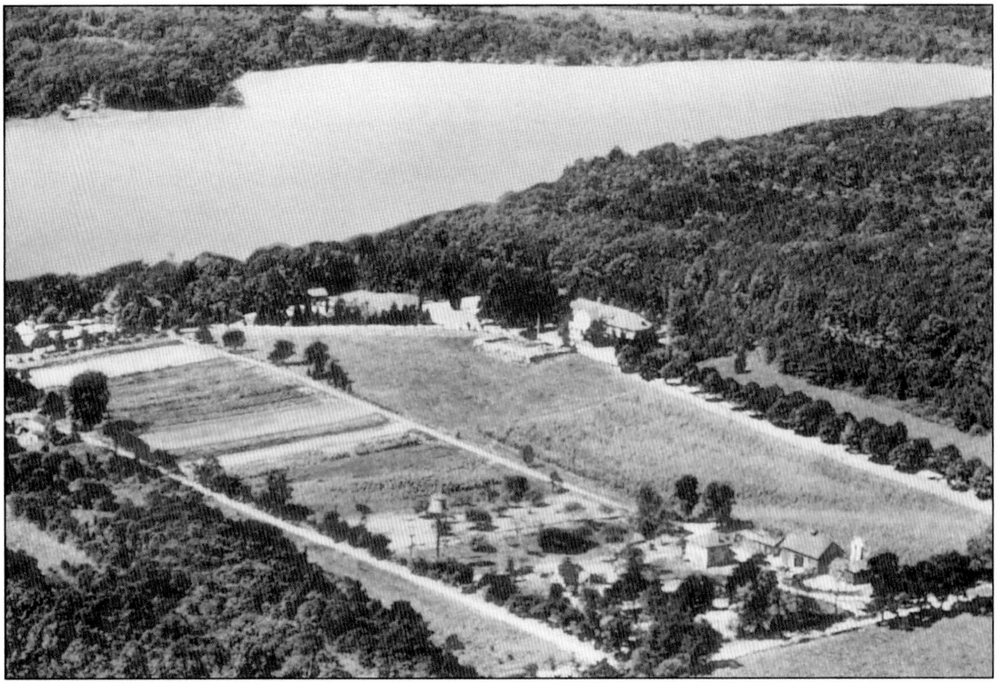

Sunnyside Manor, a nursing home at Ramshorn Drive and Lakewood Road, on the Manasquan River in Wall Township, was earlier Sunnyside Farm, where the Margaret and Sarah Switzer Foundation for Girls established a home for unwed mothers *c.* 1920s. The main house in the center is little changed, but the area in the background, including the farm, has been developed as housing. The Albertype aerial is *c.* 1930.

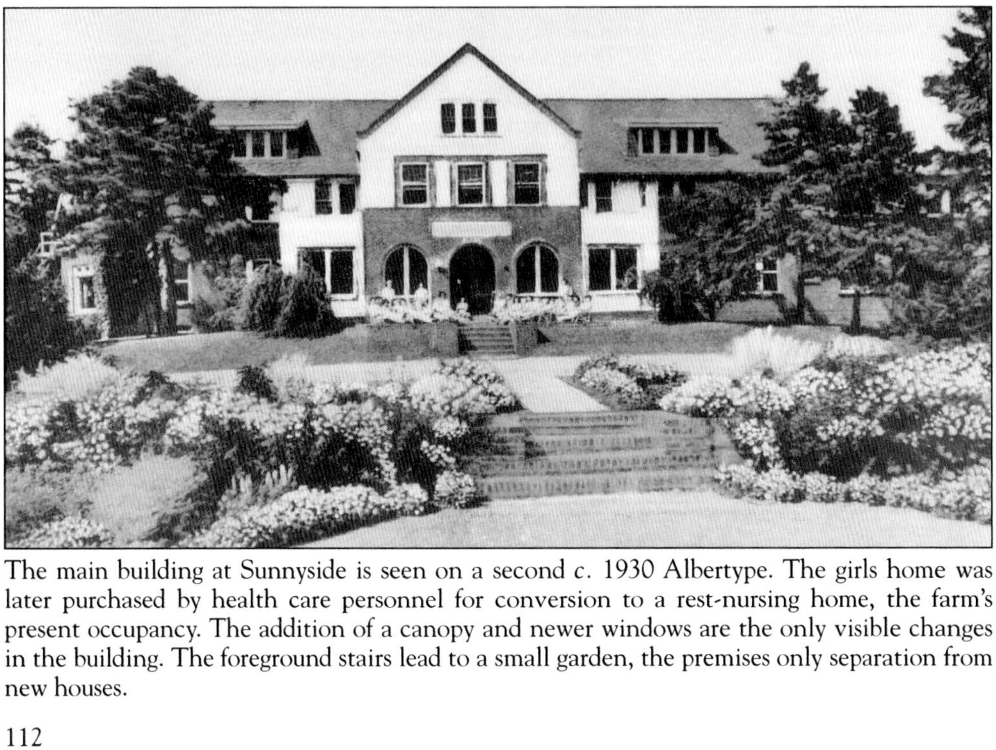

The main building at Sunnyside is seen on a second *c.* 1930 Albertype. The girls home was later purchased by health care personnel for conversion to a rest-nursing home, the farm's present occupancy. The addition of a canopy and newer windows are the only visible changes in the building. The foreground stairs lead to a small garden, the premises only separation from new houses.

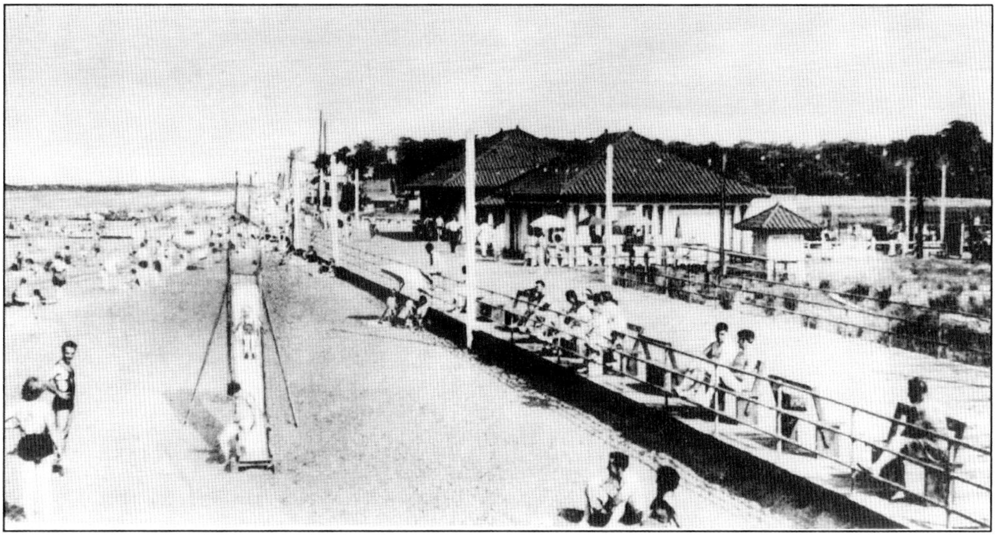

Cliffwood Beach progressed in a typical manner for the bayshore—small cabins built as summer homes became year-round domiciles during the post-World War II suburbanization of Monmouth County. This early-century development of Morrisey & Walker may be best-remembered for its real estate office, the no-longer-standing structure built in the form of a pirate ship. The author's memories of day trips from his youth are anything but nostalgic. The rocks in the sand gave the place the nickname "stony beach," while a stroll on the boardwalk resulted in splintered feet, making the trip a dubious venture. It is an Albertype image, *c.* 1920s. (Collection of John Rhody.)

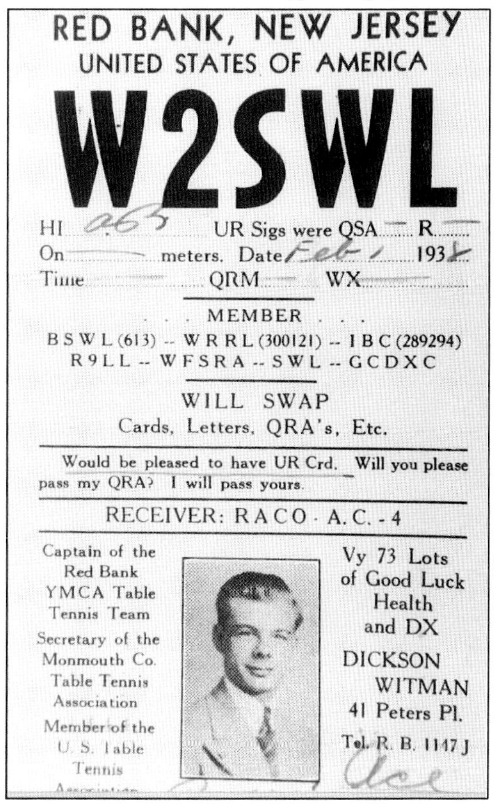

The ham radio operator's QSL card, sent to confirm radio contact, is designed with innumerable variety. However, the cards, dominated by the radio's numbers, are usually of interest only to the radio fraternity. Dickson Witman's has a broader appeal, as we know his appearance and interests. (Collection of John Rhody.)

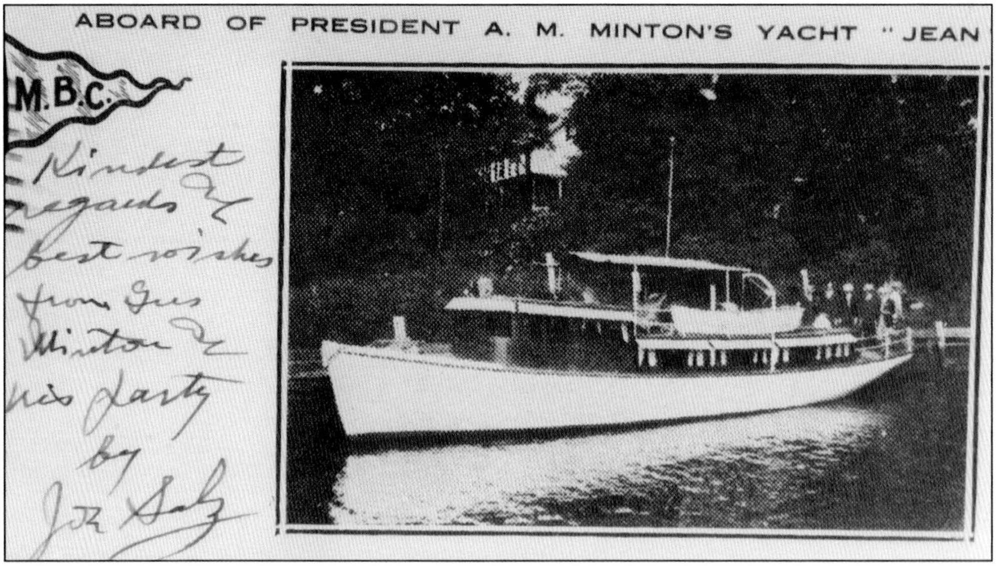

"M.B.C." is the Monmouth Boat Club (Red Bank), which Fair Haven native Augustus M. Minton served as president. He was also mayor of his hometown. Minton was an ardent yachtsman and winter sports participant. This view was printed on a 1¢ government postal card, but postage was paid by a 2¢ Canadian stamp as Red Bank merchant Joseph Salz (see p. 26) mailed this example from St. Jean, P.Q., July 31, 1930.

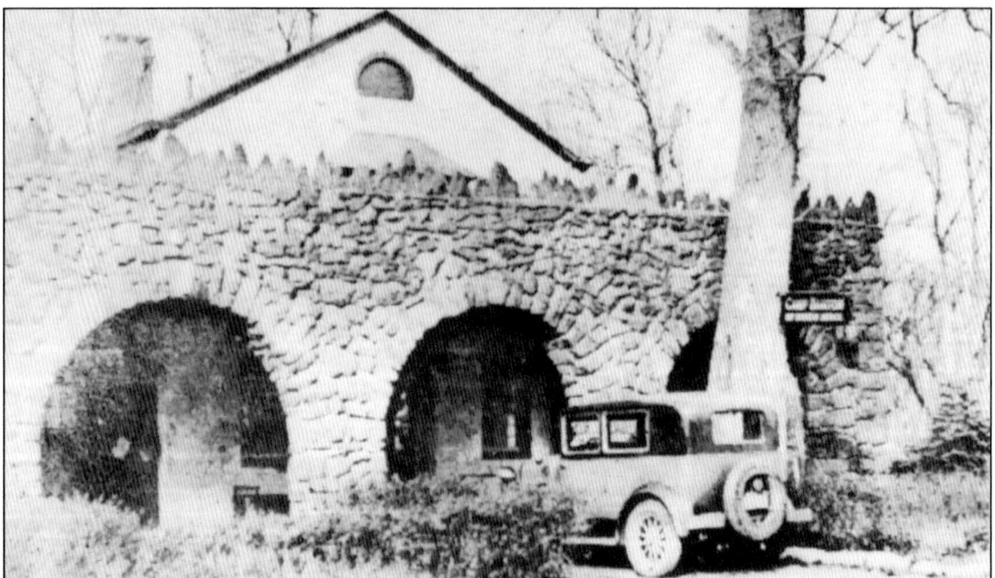

Camp Burton was a Boy Scout facility that met at the Arthur Brisbane estate at Allaire by c. 1929 when an old house was reported being rebuilt for scout use. Brisbane proposed that Allaire become a state park, which much of it is now, at a Camp Burton meeting in 1931. Camp Burton had earlier (by 1924) met for Monmouth scouts on the Metedeconk River, Ocean County, property of Mrs. Frederick Housman, who donated the site in memory of her son, George Burton, who had died in France. The sender of this example wrote in 1932, "I'm archery expert up here."

Six

Chromes and the Modern Era

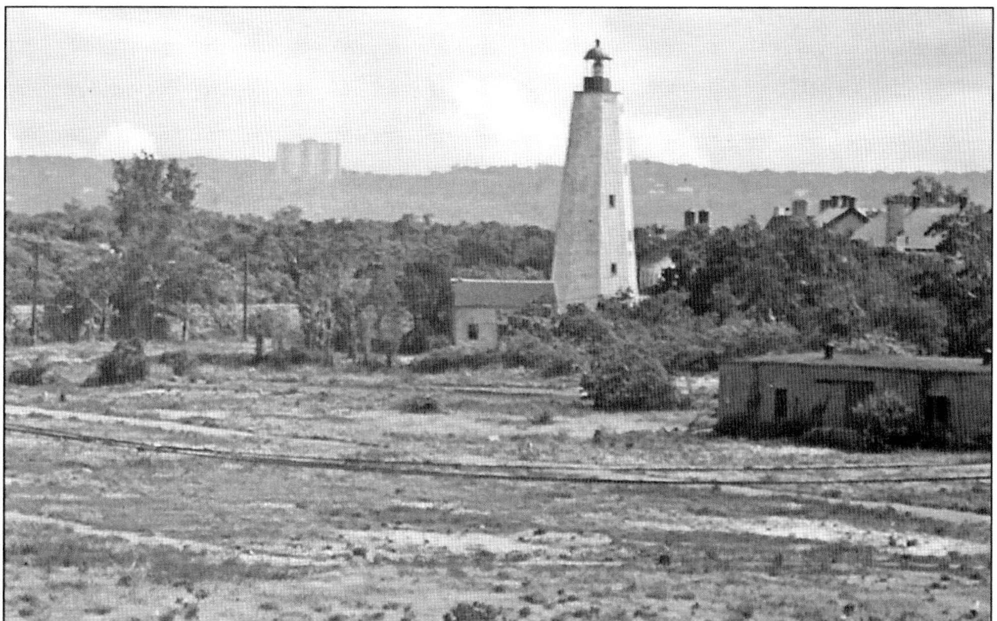

The 103-foot-tall Sandy Hook lighthouse, built in 1764, is the nation's oldest, continuously in-service lighthouse. Its surroundings have changed considerably. The force of the tides have made "new land" at the northern tip of the beach, distancing the lighthouse from its former proximity to the tip of the Hook. The Top of the East apartments, built in the 1970s in the borough of Highlands, is a reminder of the extensive development in the region.

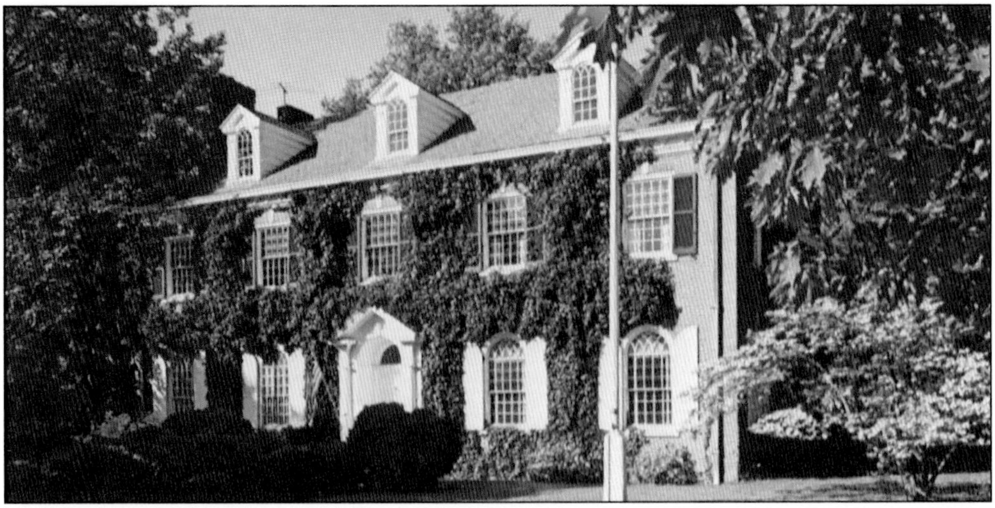

In 1931, the Monmouth County Historical Association, lacking a permanent home in its early decades, opened its museum and library at 70 Court Street, Freehold, following years of planning and an abandoned project to build in Red Bank. Freehold architect J. Hallam Conover's building reflects a high-design Georgian style, rarely executed in brick in Monmouth County during the eighteenth century, but one popular in that material during the Colonial Revival. The building is unchanged since this *c.* 1970 card, except for removal of the ivy and trimming of the bushes.

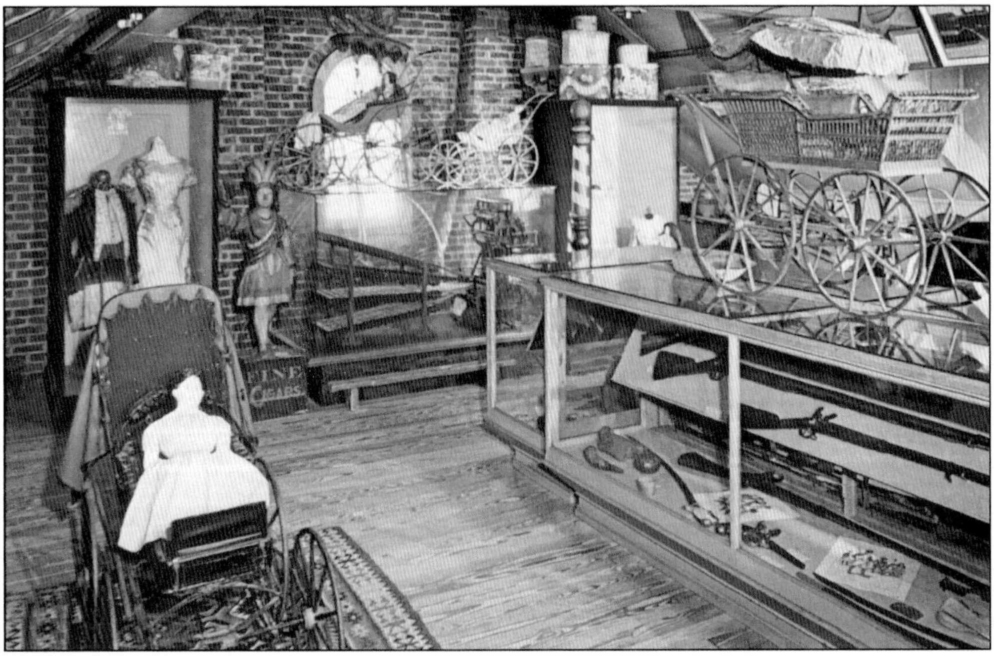

The upper story of the Association's museum long-served figuratively and literally as the county's attic. Eclectic displays of artifacts and art filled the floor, arranged more with the thought of what fit, rather than through an exhibition plan. Any shortcomings were made-up by the display's charm and the appeal of the artifacts. Offices occupy the floor now, while the Association mounts professionally designed and built thematic exhibitions in space better suited to show its fine collections and borrowed items.

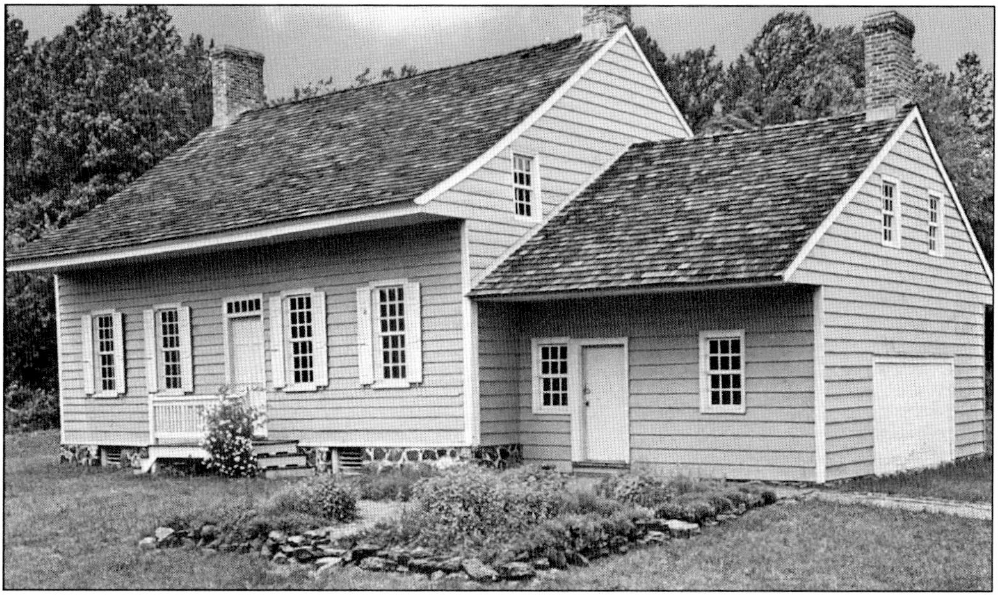

The 1717 Holmes-Hendrickson House was moved from its original location, now part of the property that historians will likely still call for some while, Bell Laboratories, to Longstreet Road. It is one of the county's finest examples of Dutch architecture. Note particularly the sloping roof line of the main block, built as an addition to the original one-story section at right. The finely furnished place is maintained as a house museum and site for history-related activities, by the Monmouth County Historical Association.

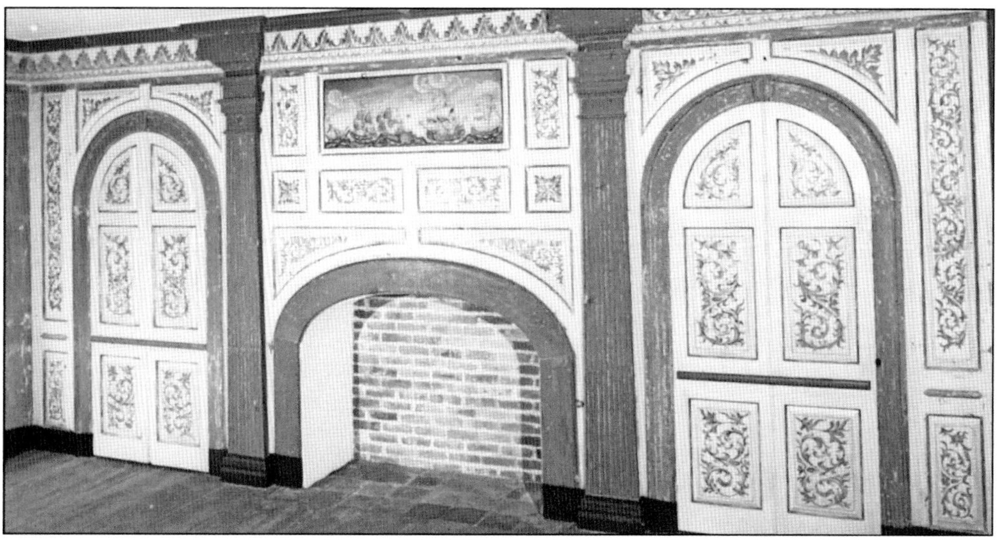

The Covenhoven House at 150 West Main Street, Freehold, was acquired by the Monmouth County Historical Association from the Moreau family in 1966. The second-story master bedroom features rare delicate freehand decoration and an overmantel painting of a naval scene, likely done in the mid-18th-century by an itinerant artist. Most of the panels were covered by later painting and were discovered during restoration. Although the Association designates their property now for the Covenhoven owners, the house was long known as, and is designated on this c. 1970 card as, "General Clinton's Headquarters," as he used the house at the time of the Battle of Monmouth in 1778.

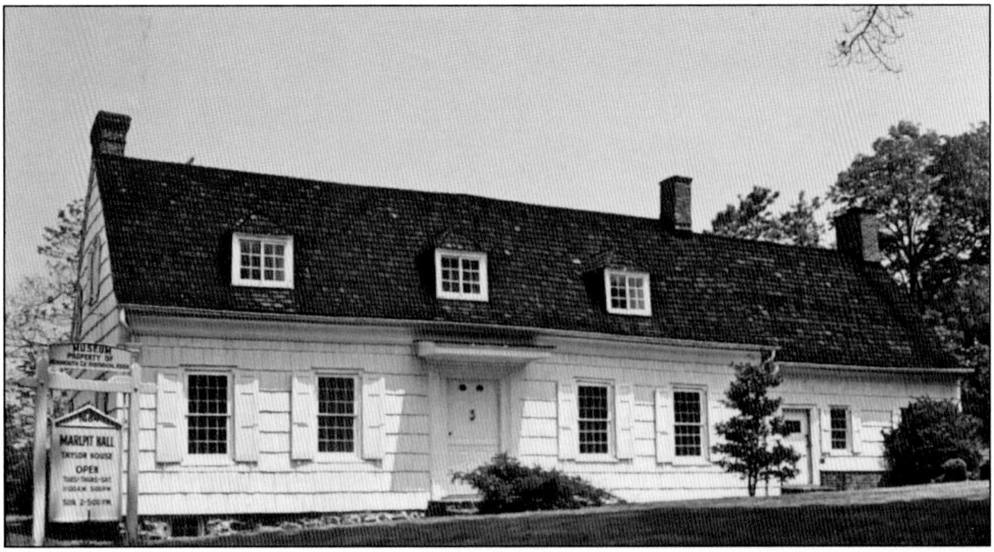

Tradition states that Marlpit Hall had *c.* 1685 origins as a small Dutch house (at right), to which the Taylors built a Georgian addition *c.* 1725. The house had been moved a short distance when Kings Highway was realigned in 1919 and was in a state of neglect when purchased by Mrs. J. Amory Haskell, restored and presented in 1936 to the Monmouth County Historical Association for use as the area's first house museum. Its name dates from that period.

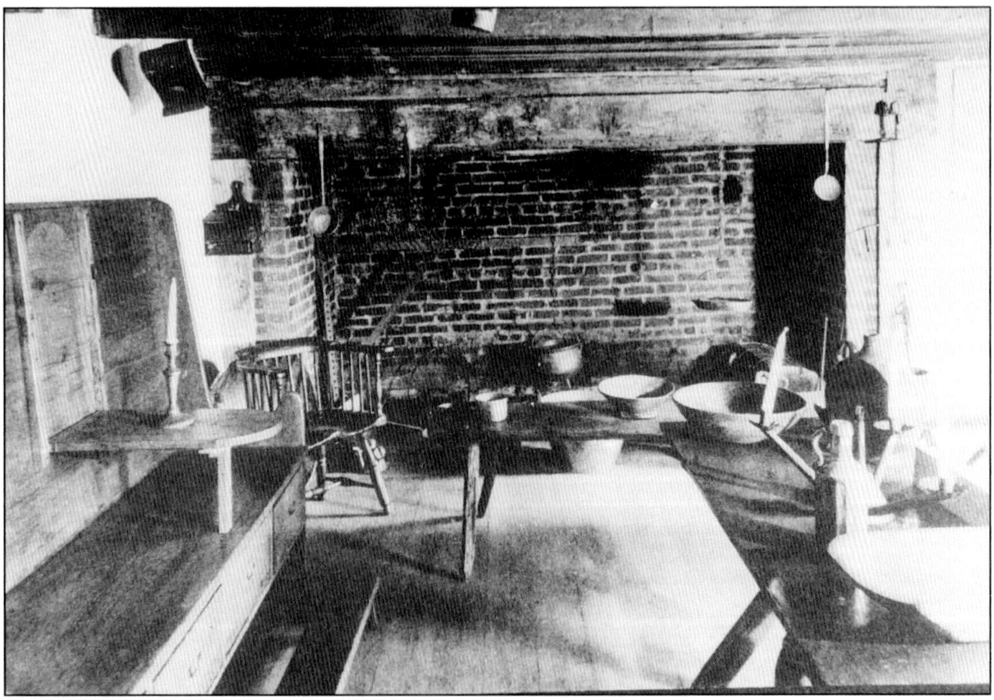

The Marlpit Hall kitchen is seen in an interpretation *c.* 1960s, one abandoned prior to the 1993 closing of the place for a lengthy restoration and research project. Its commonly accepted history is being tested by new research, which may reveal new ownership and construction findings. (Collection of John Rhody.)

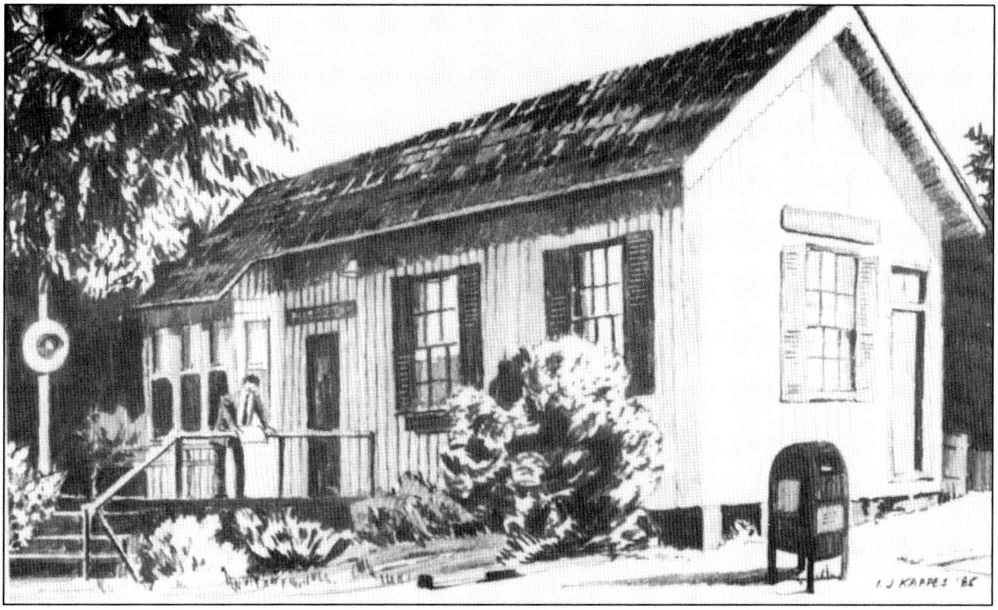

The original Middletown railroad station was built around the June 1875 opening of the New York and Long Branch Railroad line. Railroad stations were a favorite subject of early-20th-century postcard publishers, but Middletown's was shunned. Why? Did its size and style make it appear more like a farm structure? The station endured, despite its long-time inadequacy, while its contemporaries were replaced or destroyed, and served until the 1980s, when the present station was built. The former station houses a not-for-profit organization. The Middletown Township Historical Association published this card in 1986 via offset printing. The design is a pencil drawing by artist and Society member Irwin Kappes.

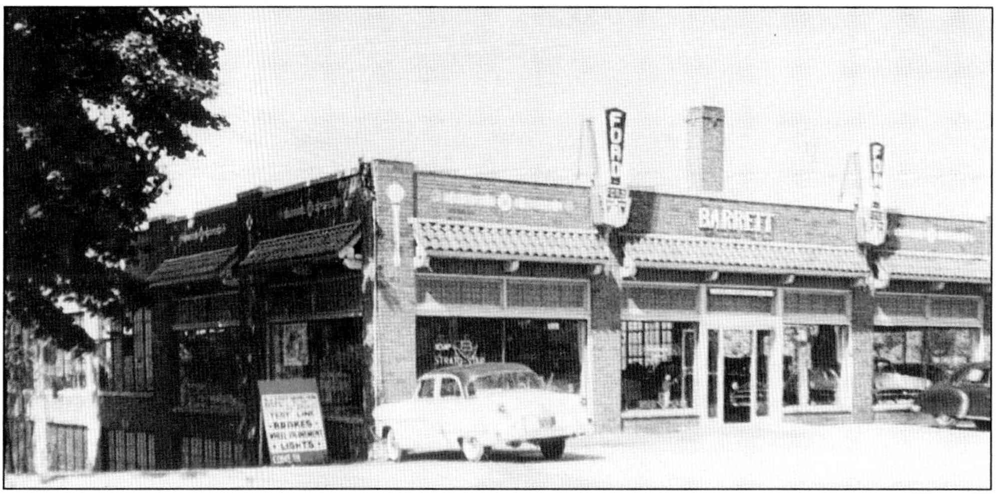

Car dealers have traditionally clustered themselves in stretches of road known as "automobile row." Their locations have changed from in-town business streets to newer, or newly developed, roads on their outskirts. This c. 1950 card shows a Barrett Ford location at 60 Main Street, Matawan. Its building appears to be a state-of-the-art auto showroom of the 1930s. Matawan auto dealers tend to locate on Highway 34 now, while a liquor store now fills the old Ford place. The building is readily recognizable, although the decorative tiles and glass blocks are gone. (Collection of John Rhody.)

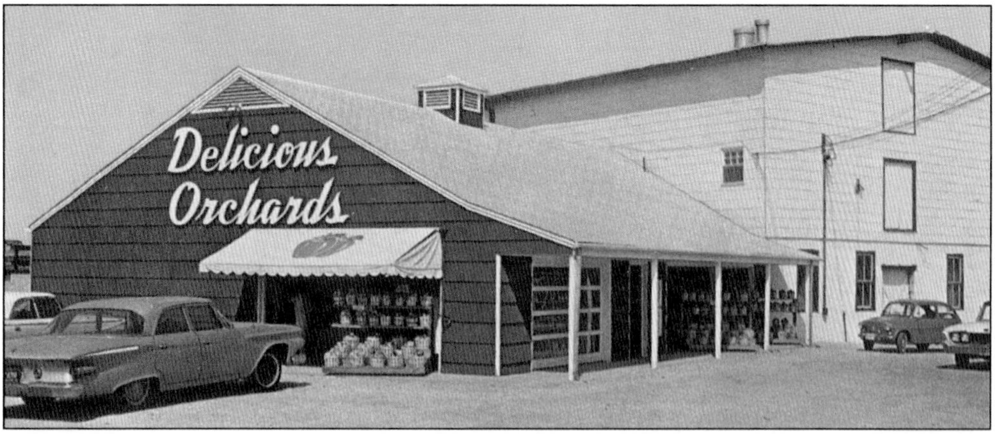

Delicious Orchards grew from a small roadside stand to one of Monmouth County's best-known businesses. This *c.* 1961 view published by Dorn's, Red Bank, shows their early stand adjacent to the firm's warehouse on the north side of County Highway 537. The map on the back indicated its location as Scobeyville, a reminder of the recent past when Colts Neck was known by its neighborhoods. Its printed message announced "200 Acres of Orchards/Apples and Cider the Year'Round/Peaches in Season/Our Own Fruit Pies and Cakes."

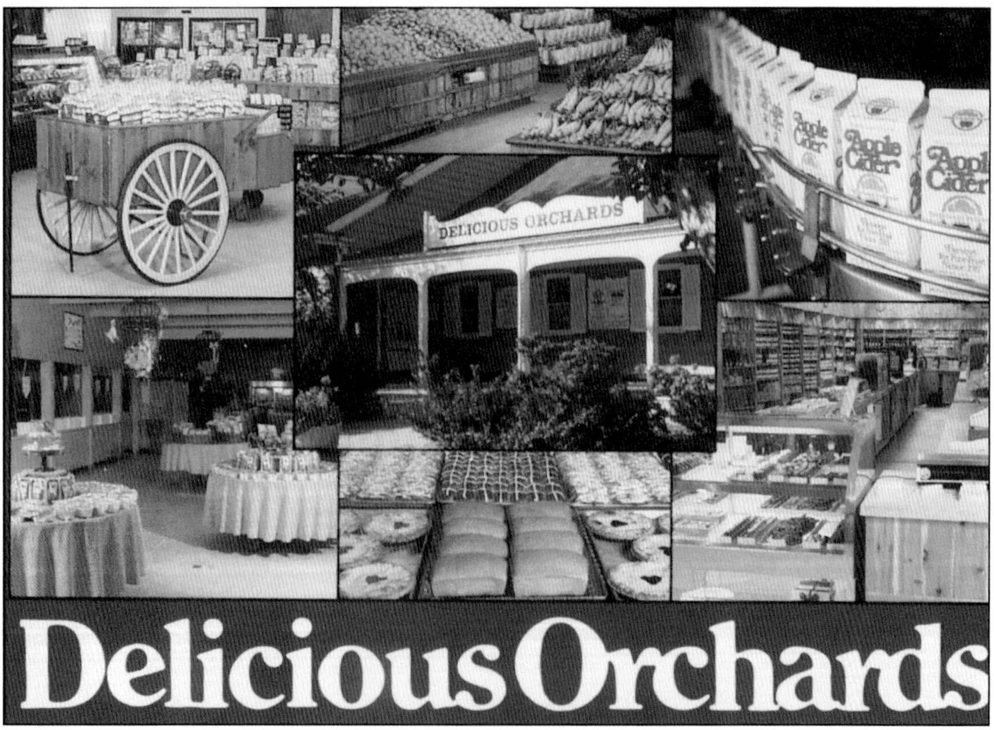

Delicious Orchards has probably distributed more postcards in the past generation than any other Monmouth County site, still believing in their advertising appeal. Early standard-size examples portrayed the growth of the present store-bakery on Highway 34, Colts Neck. The newer Continental size, multi-view depicts their several departments, the printed message announcing: "...one of the largest selections of fresh produce in the northeast...a home style bakery, a wide array of meats and cheeses, fresh-pressed ciders and juices, and gourmet specialty items, coffees, teas and candies."

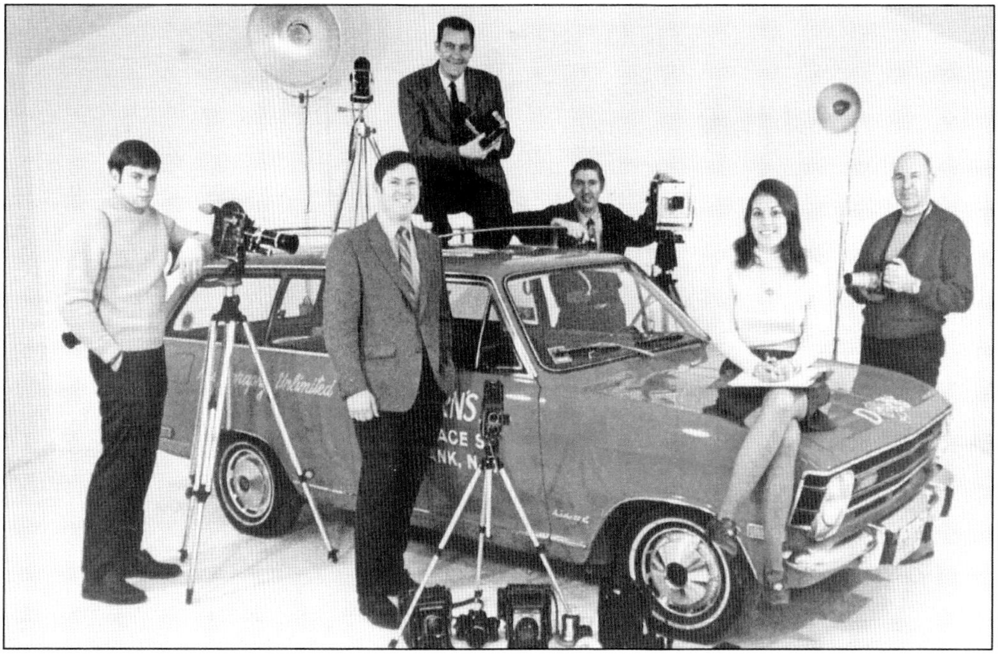

Photography Unlimited by Dorn's, 23A Wallace Street, Red Bank, published this card in the 1960s to demonstrate the size of their studio, which easily accommodated their Opel, staff, and a wide array of equipment. They do less studio work today and the equipment is smaller, but Dorn's is not only still the county's leading photographer, but maintains an extensive collection of available-to-the-public historic photographs. Two of the pictured sextet are still with the firm, owner Daniel W. Dorn Jr., standing by the passenger's door, and Andrew Lustbaum, kneeling on the roof. Also present, from left to right, are Jeff Martin, Peder Gielson, Faye Jamison, and Earl Stout. (Collection of John Rhody.)

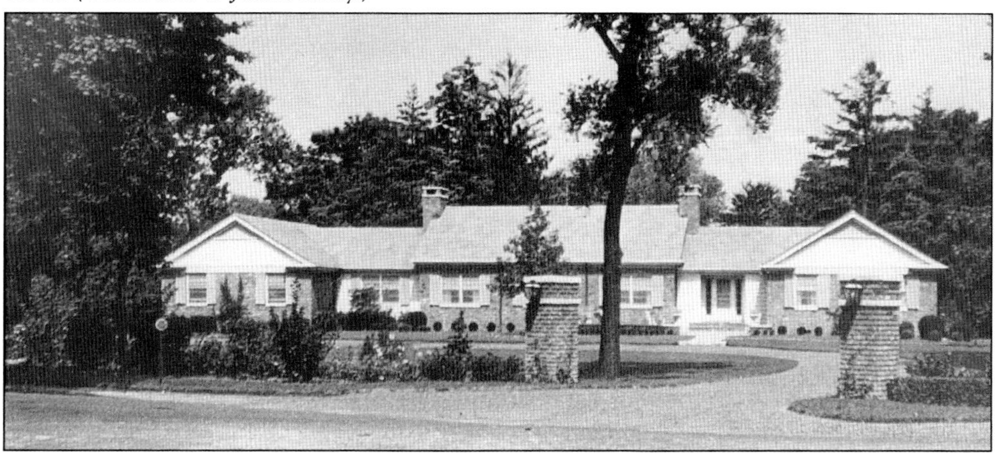

A homeowner publishing a postcard of his personal residence is a rare incidence. The F.A. Seide House, designed by Rumson architect Robert Edwards at the northeast corner of Rumson Road and Navesink, however, is a fine example from a weaker period in Rumson home building. The handsome house has a strong measure of Georgian balance, is well sited for lighting and wind-resistance, and is very well constructed. It won an award when built, although it has not been identified. Thus, one can presume a proud Seide was pleased to use the postcard as a handy communications medium about his new domicile.

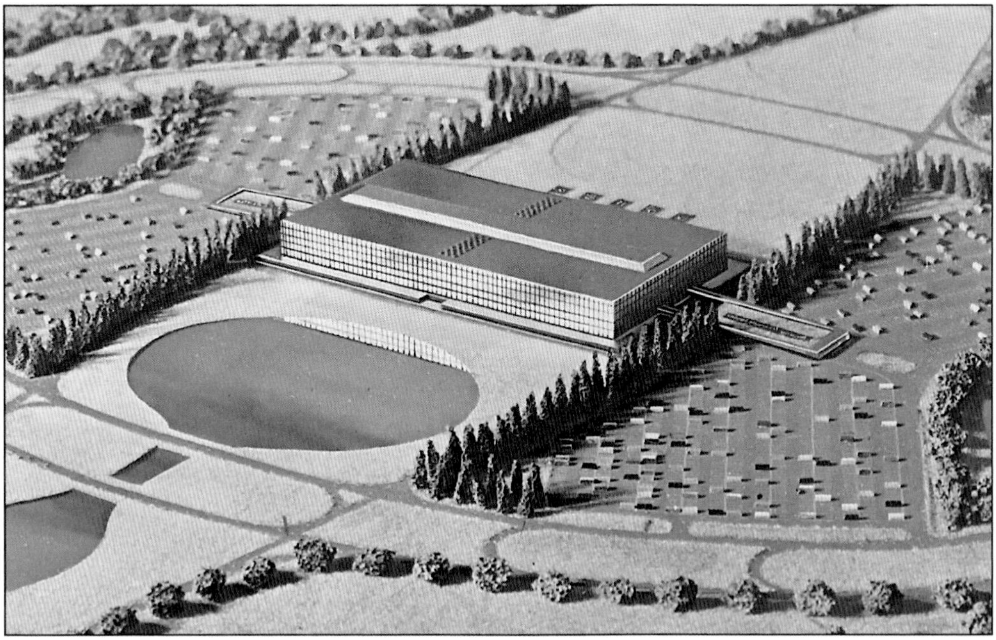

Bell Telephone Laboratories' Development Center, Crawfords Corner Road, Holmdel, is an early and nationally important example of reflective-skin architecture. The four connected buildings were designed by Eero Saarinen and built 1957–62. This card, illustrated by an artist's conception, was printed in 1962 for the sender to notify recipients of their new direct inward dial telephone number, an innovation then.

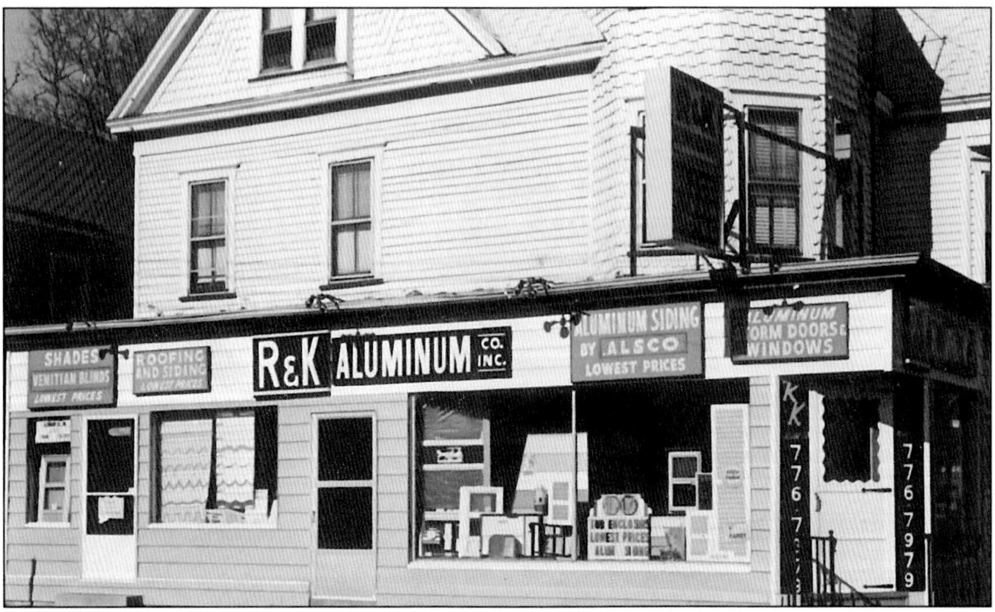

Small business use of the advertising card is a casualty of rising postage and printing costs. Irv Shapiro of R & K Aluminum Co., Bradley Beach, used this one in the early 1960s to inform potential customers of their having completed over 150 siding jobs in Monmouth and Ocean Counties. The store, obviously attached to a residence, at 321–3 Main Street is now divided into a dental lab and a used clothing business.

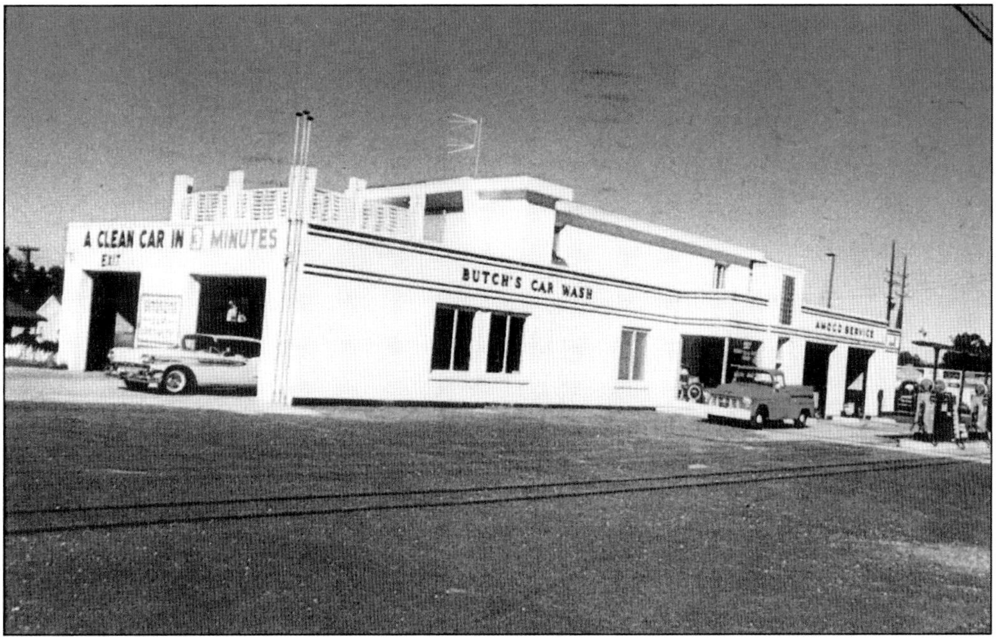

Butch's Car Wash on Newman Springs Road, Red Bank, used a printed message on the back exhorting readers to "Keep Your Car Happy with a Weekly Wash." The card is late 1950s, when a polishing cost $14.95. The business still exists. (Collection of John Rhody.)

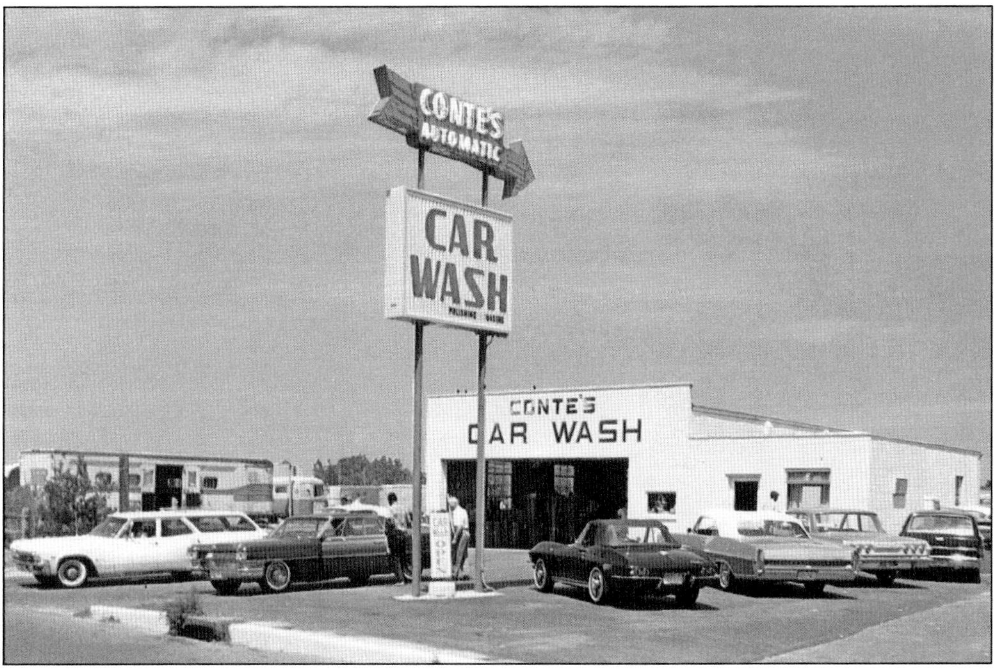

The provenance of Conte's Automatic Car Wash card is known. The donor, Harold Solomon, pointed out that his uncle, David E. Lillthal of Rutherford, solicited and photographed throughout New Jersey for Dexter Press. His Chevrolet is to the right of the attendant in the rear. They are located at 681 Joline Avenue, Long Branch, and still had the cards as this book was completed in March 1998.

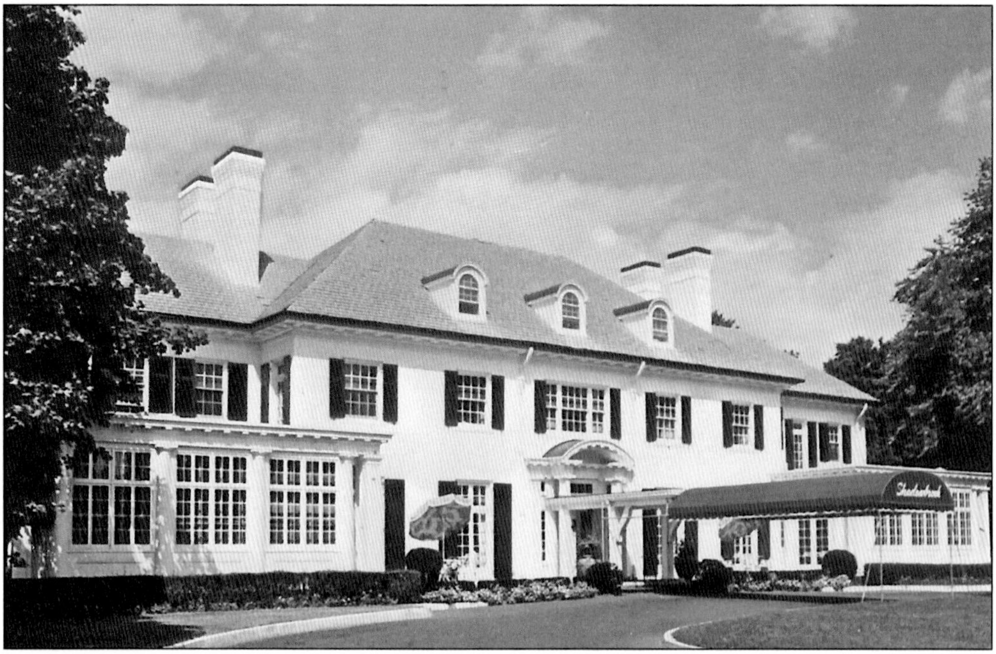

Dr. Ernest Fahnestock built in 1910 a five-bay, hipped-roof Colonial Revival house designed by New York's Albro and Lindeberg on the former George W. Stillwell farm on both sides of Broad Street, Shrewsbury. The house was converted to a restaurant in 1944 by Fred Thorngreen; it is now owned by the Zweben family. In time, the estate name, Shadow Brook, was spelled as one word. Two visible changes have been made after this early 1960s card—a permanent canopy retaining the segmental arch was built and balustrades were added to the enclosed piazza on both sides.

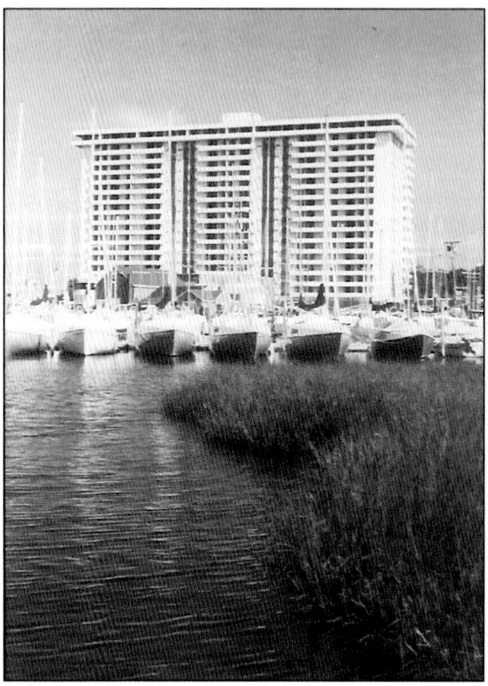

Channel Club Tower on Channel Drive, Monmouth Beach, the tallest and first completed of the three Monmouth Beach high-rises, was begun as a joint venture of Walter Mihm and American Standard, Inc. Condominium construction in general, and particularly the high-rise buildings erected in the 1970s, transformed the Atlantic coast borough with a major expansion of its population and change of life-styles, as the town was founded on the principles of exclusivity and clubishness. Joan Parent, a realtor long-experienced with the Tower and Monmouth Beach, photographed the 17-story, 222-unit building, finished in 1973, and published the card.

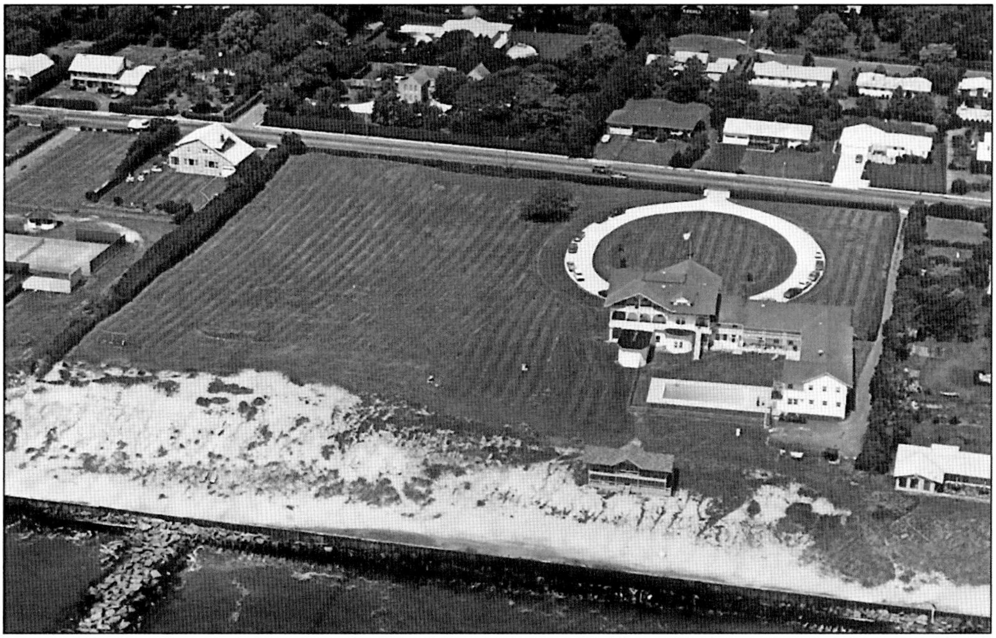

The Stella Maris retreat house, owned by the Sisters of St. Joseph of Peace at 981 Ocean Avenue in Long Branch's Elberon section, is seen *c.* 1970s. The basic structure is the James M. Brown house, Sea Cliff Villa, built 1868 and designed by architect Edward T. Potter. The Sisters bought the property in *c.* 1940, a time when the former home of President Grant stood on the south, or the lot at left. This site has been altered by the 1994 construction of a chapel and meeting rooms attached on the south. The chapel's location facing the sea creates an ambiance of awe and serenity, one better experienced rather than read, such as at the 8:30 daily Mass.

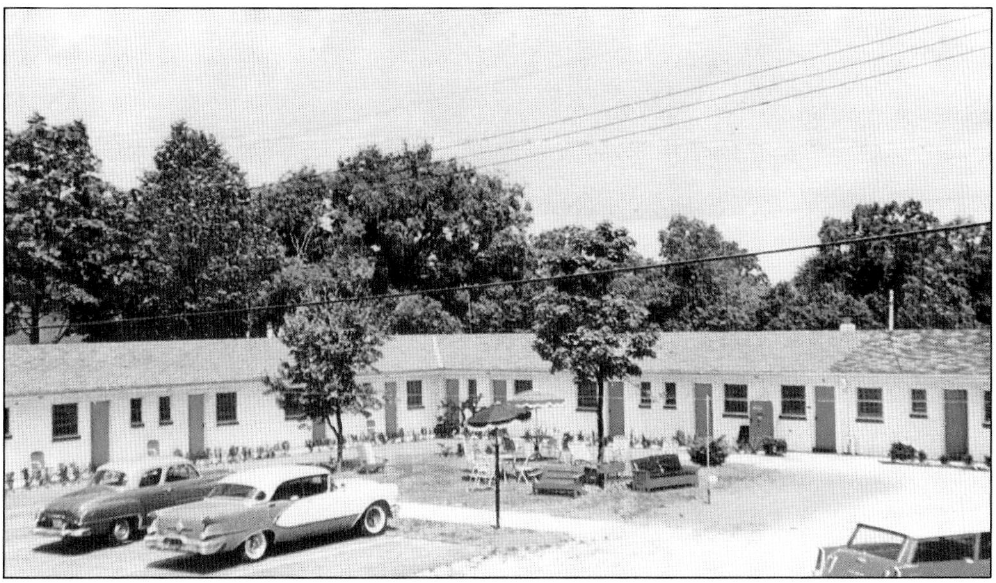

The Circle Motel on Highway #5, south of the Asbury Park circle, is a classic 1950s arrangement of rooms organized in a "U" or "L," reminiscent of a connection of the cabins popular two decades earlier. This example still exists. (Collection of John Rhody.)

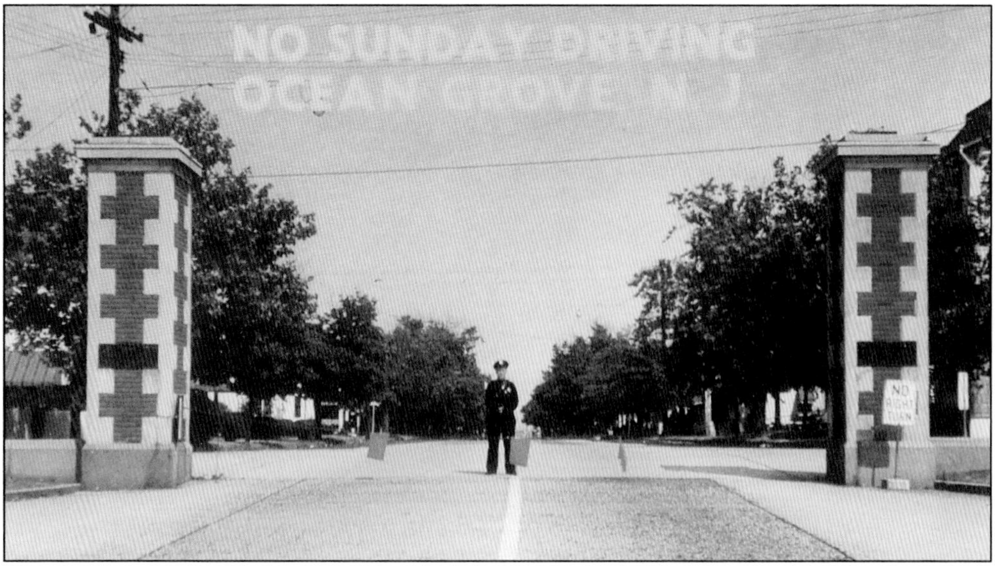

Blue laws enforced by the Ocean Grove Camp Meeting Association dating from their third-quarter of the nineteenth century settlement, strictly regulated Sunday life in that section of Neptune Township. Horse-driven carriages were banned prior to the automotive age. In recent memory, cars were not even permitted to remain parked on the streets on Sundays, necessitating a Saturday night drill to remove them to adjacent spots. The New Jersey Supreme Court overturned certain of the Association's regulatory powers in a separation of church and state decision in 1979, permitting Sunday driving there since. This image is *c.* 1960, but similar views exist for other postcard eras.

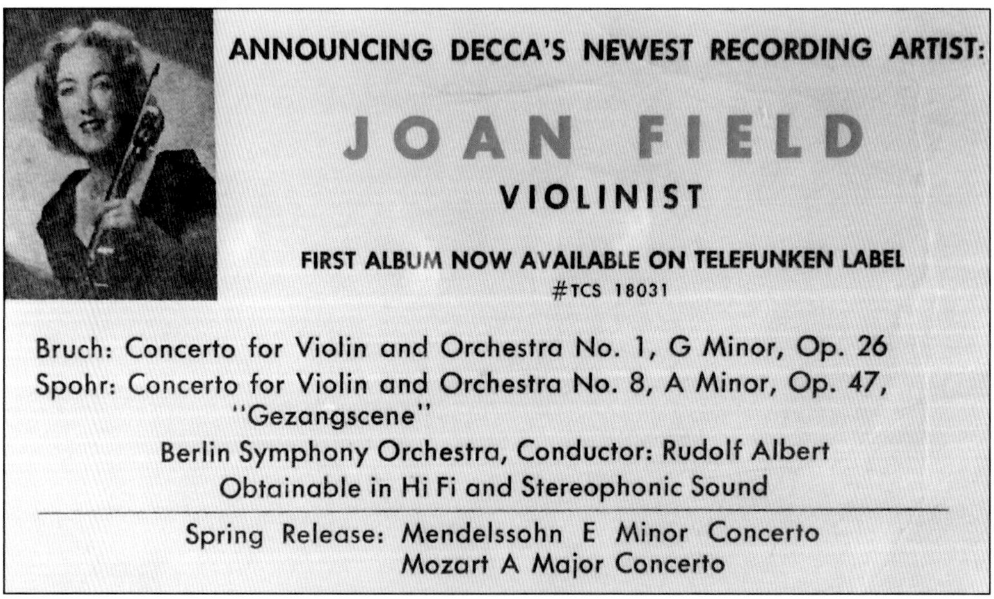

Joan Field, daughter of a Long Branch flower grower, was a child violin prodigy. She was a protégé of Andre Benoist, who discovered and taught Field in her early years. She also studied with Albert Spalding at Julliard. The card is a post-1958 release publicizing new recordings. It is likely that few county collectors realize this is a Monmouth item and it is probably the type of card infrequently saved. Joan Field died in the early 1990s.

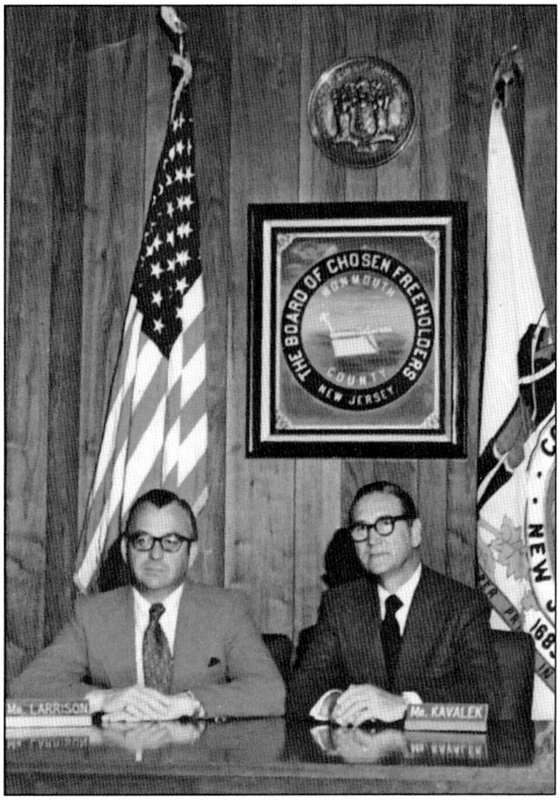

Freeholders Harry Larrison Jr. and Ernest G. Kavalek used this card in their 1972 re-election campaign. Its printed message conveyed the accomplishments of the Republican Board, including a master sewerage plan, a county park and golf course, a vocational educational program, continued development of Brookdale Community College, and a county fire and police academy. Kavalek died in 1985, while Larrison, director of the board, is the longest-serving freeholder in New Jersey, holding office since February of 1966.

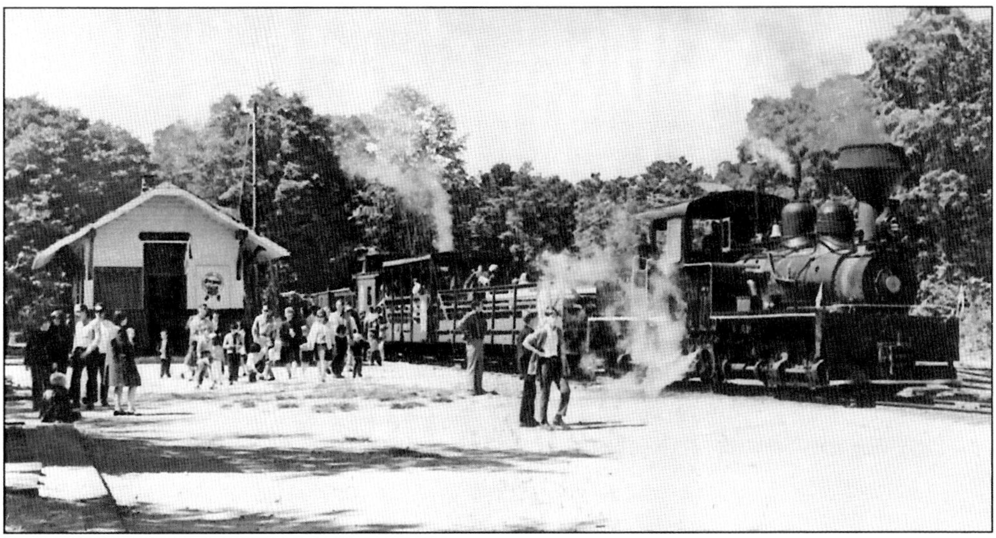

The two-truck Shay-geared locomotive of the Pine Creek Railroad is seen aside the station at Allaire State Park, the former Central Railroad Freneau station from Matawan. The .75-mile loop, previously installed in 1953 on a Highway 9 site which is now the Pine Creek Shopping Center, Manalapan, was moved *c.* 1961; the train was operational by 1964. The 1927 locomotive, built by Lima, was earlier owned by the Ely-Thomas Lumber Company in West Virginia. The railroad, operated by the New Jersey Museum of Transportation, Inc., carries about 7,800 passengers annually now.

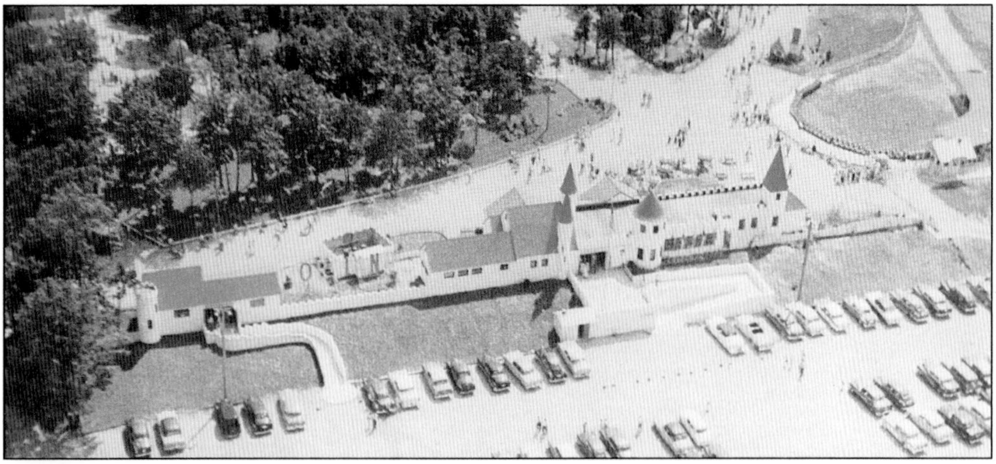

Storyland Village was a child's world where favorite stories came to life. It opened *c.* 1955 and was located in Neptune, on Highway 66 at the Asbury Park circle. King Arthur's Court was at the entrance, as shown in this *c.* 1957 card. Foliage obscured the storied stops, but the Storyland Railroad is visible at right, a miniature of the 20th Century Limited. Features included The Three Little Pigs, Little Bo Peep, Noah's Ark, Mother Goose Land (without Grimm), and Humpty Dumpty. Like Humpty, Storyland Village had a great fall. It lasted about 10 years, prior to being replaced by a Sears store, which has now been replaced by Shop Rite. (Collection of John Rhody.)

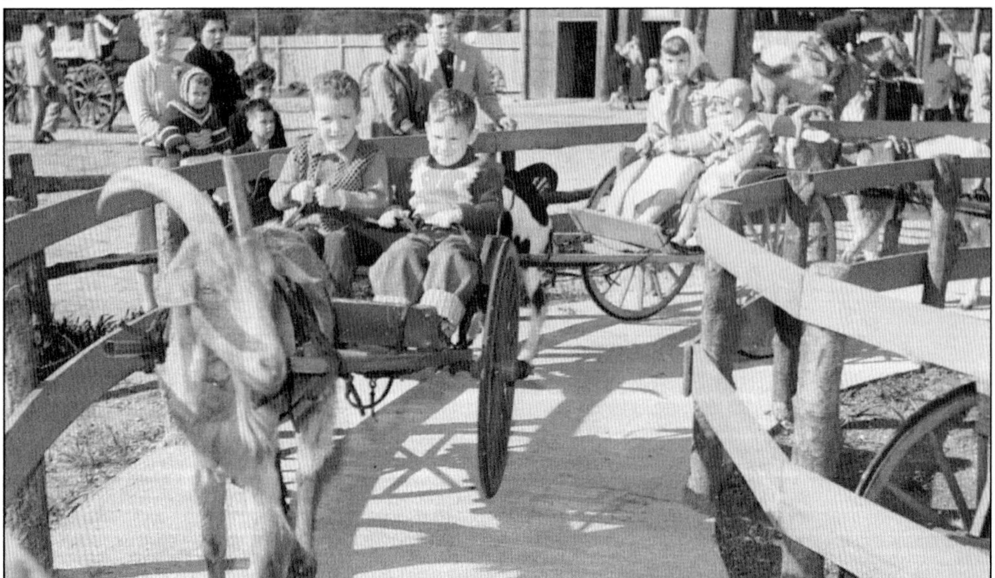

Cowboy City, on Route 33 in Howell Township, their Farmingdale address notwithstanding, was another 1950s Monmouth County child's roadside theme amusement. Several parallels can be drawn with Storyland Village: construction with the expectation local highway traffic would bring prosperity, short life, replacement by a probably higher and better use, in this case, a motel, and lots of postcards. Postage was 2¢, cards could sell 3 for 10¢, and the postal was a cost-effective promotional issue. A shoot-out on Main Street would have been a more representative card, but the author likes goat carts and was pleased to find a contemporary example to close this book. So long, until Volume II. (Collection of John Rhody.)